"When I Can Read My Title Clear"

"When I Can Read My Title Clear"

Literacy, Slavery, and Religion in the Antebellum South

■

Janet Duitsman Cornelius

University of South Carolina Press

Copyright © 1991 University of South Carolina

Published in Columbia, South Carolina, by the
University of South Carolina Press

Manufactured in the United States of America

Library of Congress Cataloging-in-Publication Data

Cornelius, Janet Duitsman.
    "When I can read my title clear" : literacy, slavery, and religion
in the antebellum South / Janet Duitsman Cornelius.
      p.   cm.
    Includes bibliographical references and index.
    ISBN 0-87249-737-2 (alk. paper)
    1. Slavery—United States—History. 2. Literacy—United States—
History. 3. Slaves—Education—United States. 4. Slavery and the
church—United States. 5. Education—Social aspects—United States.
I. Title.
E44.C7 1991
305.5'67'0973—dc20   90-28086

This book is dedicated with gratitude to
my mother and my father,
Mary Ellen Michael Duitsman
and
Heye John Duitsman

When I can read my title clear
    To mansions in the skies,
I'll bid farewell to ev'ry fear,
    And wipe my weeping eyes.

Should earth against my soul engage,
    And hellish darts be hurl'd,
Then I can smile at Satan's rage
    And face a frowning world.

Let cares, like a wild deluge come,
    And storms of sorrow fall;
May I but safely reach my home,
    My God, my heav'n, my all:

There shall I bathe my weary soul,
    In seas of heav'nly rest,
And not a wave of trouble roll
    Across my peaceful breast.

The Psalms, Hymns &
Spiritual Songs of the
Rev. Isaac Watts, D.D.

CONTENTS

Contents

ACKNOWLEDGMENTS

T HIS STUDY HAS SPANNED ALMOST TWO DECADES AND its completion owes a great deal to many people. Robert McColley of the University of Illinois at Urbana-Champaign first suggested the study of slavery as a dissertation topic and supervised my doctoral project, an examination of southern white missionaries to the slaves in the immediate antebellum period. Dissertation research began to uncover for me the rich source materials in black literacy and in the black church. My decision to research literacy in the slave community more thoroughly was facilitated by a National Endowment for the Humanities year-long Seminar for College Teachers in 1980–81, directed by Harold Pfautz at Brown University. Professor Pfautz, his Brown University colleagues, and my fellow seminarians during that wonderful year away from community college teaching responsibilities helped me to develop and focus my research. A National Endowment for the Humanities summer seminar at Princeton in 1984 conducted by Albert Raboteau and David Wills on the topic of African-American religion further stimulated ideas and insights into the African-American slave experience. My research into black and white communities during slavery has long been encouraged by Vernon Burton. He and Edmund Drago provided valuable comments and encouragement in their thorough readings of my work. Vincent P. Franklin gave a very useful and critical reading to an early version of the manuscript. Others who read and commented on parts or versions of this study include the late Herbert Gutman, James Anderson, Brian Gallagher, Susan Westbury, and Richard Pate.

Research over many years has also been made possible by the helpful assistance of the staffs of a number of libraries. Acknowledgements are due to the librarians and directors of the University of Illinois Library and the Illinois Historical Survey at Urbana-Champaign; the John Carter Brown and John Hay libraries, Brown University; the Widener Library, Harvard University; the Library of Congress, Manuscript Division; the Perkins Library, Duke University; the Southern Historical Collection at the University of North Carolina; and the Special Collections Division of the Manuscript Department at Tulane University Library. Gratitude is also due to the cooperation of librarians at the Presbyterian Historical Society and Pennsylvania Historical Society, Philadelphia; the Georgia Historical Society in Savannah; the South Carolina Historical Society, Charleston; the library of the Southern Baptist Theological Seminary, Louisville; Southern Presbyterian Historical Society, Asheville; the Virginia Historical Library; and the Mississippi and South Carolina State Archives. A special word of appreciation goes to Charles Hall, J.D., for assistance in legal research.

Friends, family, and colleagues have made it possible for me to bring the manuscript to completion. Proofing and style were improved from the suggestions by Martha Kay and Roni English and from my mother, Mary Duitsman, and my daughters Valerie Cornelius Viverito and Kristin Cornelius Camp. Assistance in mastering statistical and word processing computer programs came via the Brown University Department of Sociology and from DACC colleagues Dan Winland, Ron Mickelson, and David Kietzmann. John Linville, Jeff Williams, Diane Strong, Nancy Vaglica, and DACC students Ann Miller, Thomas Fourez, and Charles Blakeney also contributed to the manuscript's completion. Family support is essential in a long-term endeavor as demanding as this one and I am grateful to my husband, Eldred, and the rest of my family for support and forbearance. I am also grateful for encouragement and insights into the manuscript's approach from my colleagues Mary Coffman and Gladys Davis, who invited me into their classrooms to present my ideas to critical student audiences. Student support and interest lead me to hope that this book will promote future explorations into the stories of the many African-Americans who learned to read and write during slavery and to the role played by literacy in political consciousness and community formation.

"When I Can Read My Title Clear"

Introduction

> The frequent hearing of my mistress reading the Bible aloud, . . . awakened my curiosity in respect to this *mystery* of reading, and roused in me the desire to learn. Up to this time I had known nothing whatever of this wonderful art, and my ignorance and inexperience of what it could do for me, as well as my confidence in my mistress, emboldened me to ask her to teach me to read. . . . In an incredibly short time, by her kind assistance, I had mastered the alphabet and could spell words of three or four letters. . . . [My master] forbade her to give me any further instruction. . . . [but] the determination which he expressed to keep me in ignorance only rendered me the more resolute to seek intelligence. In learning to read, therefore, I am not sure that I do not owe quite as much to the opposition of my master as to the kindly assistance of my amiable mistress.[1]

Frederick Douglass' moving description of how and why he learned to read while he was a slave is one of the best known and most popular sections of his famous autobiography. The compelling stories of people who were forbidden to learn to read and write and who risked punishment and death to learn forced nineteenth century readers to become aware of the cruelties of enslavement of human beings. Narratives written by escaped slaves in the antebellum United States almost always included "a record of the barriers raised against slave literacy and the overwhelming difficulties encountered in learning to read and write."[2]

What did literacy mean to black people in slavery? Survival, according to Vincent P. Franklin, who points out that "education and literacy were greatly valued among Afro-Americans enslaved in the United States because they saw in their day-to-day experiences—from one generation to the next—that knowledge and information helped one to survive in a hostile environment." Literacy was a mechanism for forming identity, the freedom to become a person, according to James Olney. Olney finds significance in Douglass' conclusion to his narrative, which he ended with the words, "I subscribe myself . . . Frederick Douglass." According to Olney, "in that lettered utterance is assertion of identity and in identity is freedom—freedom from slavery, freedom from ignorance, freedom from non-being, freedom even from time," since writing endures beyond a moment or even beyond a lifetime.[3]

Literacy also reinforced an image of self-worth: Lucius Holsey, who tried desperately to learn to read while an enslaved houseboy, "felt that constitutionally he was created the equal of any person here on earth and that, given a chance, he could rise to the height of any man," and that books were the path to proving himself as a human being. Milly Green's daughter recalled that Milly "was so proud of every scrap of book larnin' she could pick up" that she learned to read and write and that "atter de war was over she got to be a school teacher."[4]

When African-Americans fought to gain literacy, they expressed a desire for freedom and self-determination which had deep roots in modern culture. The movement towards universal literacy and written culture is one of most important democratic developments in the modern world. While scholars of literacy recognize literacy's usefulness as a medium of social control and industrial training, the majority still agree that the basic result of literacy has been and is one of liberation. As Roger Chartier explains in his study of the beginning of universal written culture in the Renaissance, "personal communion with a read or written text liberated the individual from the old mediators, freed him or her from the control of the group, and made it possible to cultivate an inner life." The ability to read and write gave people the power to relate in new ways to one another and to authority. According to Harvey Graff, few in the modern world would question "the value of literacy for achieving fulfilling, productive, expanding, and participating lives of freedom."[5]

For enslaved African-Americans, literacy was more than a path to individual freedom—it was a communal act, a political demonstration of resistance to oppression and of self-determination for the black community. Through literacy the slave could obtain skills valuable in the white world, thereby defeating those whites who withheld the skills, and could use those skills for special privileges or to gain freedom. Scholars of literacy have charted the impact a few literate people can make in a culture of illiterates; they serve as mediators and translators into a wider world for those who do not read.[6] This ability to disperse knowledge from the larger world was a crucial act of resistance during slavery. Word of abolition movements, the writings of escaped slave Frederick Douglass, and John Brown's execution quickly spread through the slave quarters because they were passed on by those enslaved African-Americans who could read.[7]

Literacy was also linked with freedom during slavery because it facilitated the African-American's creation of a liberating religious consciousness within the slave community. To be able to read the Bible was the first ambition of the converted illiterate Christian since, according to evangelical Protestantism, the individual should search the Scriptures in order to be saved. But the African-American used the Bible in an additional way, creating with its imagery a new reality from the slave experience. The ability to read the Bible, therefore, gave the reader the special mastery and control over this "sacred text" essential to leadership in the black church. African-Americans who could read were designated preachers by their own people as well as by whites; they were respected by black people as religious authorities because they held the key to the Bible without having to depend on whites to interpret Scriptures to them.[8]

Traditional "Bible literacy" in the Western world emphasized the reception of the Word from authorities, so religious motives for learning to read are often considered passive, not liberating. For enslaved African-Americans, on the other hand, there was a "close relationship between religion and resistance." The African world view makes no distinction between the secular and the religious; spirituality is at the core of existence. Therefore it was through the black church, "the new religion of oppressed people," that resistance was fashioned. According to Margaret Creel, the religion shaped by enslaved African-Americans "offered a politic for collective consciousness and group conformation within an African-Christian synthesis." The African-American collective religious faith was "a progressive force and shield against white psychological and cultural domination." Their faith provided African-Americans with a will to create and the courage to persevere, helping them to remain spiritually free in spite of physical bondage. Former slaves recalled their determination to learn to read the Bible as an act of rebellion against white oppression.[9]

Though some used their reading and writing skills to escape from slavery, few of the slaves who acquired literacy had illusions that literacy would immediately transform their lives. Their goals were more specific: slaves who learned to read and write could use literacy to gain advantages for themselves and mediate for their fellow slaves. Towards these ends, slaves used ingenuity and patience and risked discovery, death, and dismemberment to learn to read and write.

Slaves also learned to read and write because whites taught them. Slaves maneuvered whites into teaching them, so whites were often casual, even unwitting, instructors, not realizing the impact of the power they were giving slaves. Other whites taught purposefully, for practical reasons; they could use literate slaves for their own needs. Others, influenced by the belief that literacy was an essential component of human progress, taught slaves in the conviction that all people should learn to read. The primary motivation for whites who intentionally taught slaves to read in defiance of law and custom, though, was traditional "Bible literacy," a compelling motive but one with inherent contradictions.[10] Christian belief that all should read the Bible influenced some whites; though the majority of Southerners were indifferent to the withholding of literacy for African-Americans, a handful of white missionaries, evangelists, and lay Christians in the South insisted that slaves should be taught to read the Scriptures. They disregarded or protested any laws to the contrary and contributed to the number of slaves who could read by the end of the Civil War. They not only taught slaves, but stirred the consciences of less missionary-minded Southerners to allow their slaves to learn. They also trained black leaders and, when possible, protected black schools and Sunday schools against mob fears of an enlightened slave population.[11]

These whites were a small percentage of the southern population, but they were missionaries; as Max Warren says, the missionary movement was and has remained a minority movement within the churches in its enthusiasm and unworldliness.[12] This small group devoted time to a largely unpopular cause. Some of them believed in the inferiority (perfectible) of the African, but not in his separate creation. They saw African-Americans as fellow human beings with souls to be saved. While some claimed that they could convert slaves by oral instruction only, in order to make their mission acceptable to the dominant white population, they privately believed that all Christians should read the Bible, and they tacitly or openly violated the law to teach them.

White teachers of slaves clung unrealistically to the concept that they could control the slaves' access to the written word and the uses slaves made of literacy. More of the white teachers taught reading alone than reading and writing both—for obvious practical reasons, since slaves could write passes and run away, but also because writing was a skill which had not been traditionally allowed to the poorer classes.[13] However, their providing slaves with even restricted literacy made these slave-owners, missionaries, and other reformers seem foolishly idealistic to the majority of southern whites, who were reluctant to allow slaves the measure of equality implied by literacy and who feared any skill which could give slaves more autonomy. The first chapter of this book chronicles the reasons for this reluctance, which dates back to the ambivalence with which European colonists refused to accept African laborers as fellow humans and to share with them the full benefits of Christianity, including the right to read the Bible. Fears of slave revolts, the uses literate slaves made of their skills to protest their condition, and the supposition that literacy would remove the slave from total owner control undermined projects for slave education.

Reserving literacy for a privileged class is common in many cultures. In traditional India, for example, those who usurped the knowledge of Holy Writ reserved to Brahmans were punished by having hot oil poured into their mouths and into their ears. In traditional Tibet reading was taught by monks and possession of books was a sign of status. Medieval Europe similarly guarded the word. As late as the sixteenth century Henry VIII barred "all women other than gentle and noble women, together with artificers, journeymen, husbandmen, labourers, and servingmen of and under the degree of yeomen" from reading the Bible in English.[14] However, white Southerners in the late eighteenth and early nineteenth century were in a unique position: they sought to prevent enslaved African-Americans from learning to read just as mass literacy was being vigorously promoted in England and in the northern United States as a positive good, necessary for training the citizens of a republic and for accustoming the population to industrial routine. Their defensiveness at being out of step made white Southerners increasingly adamant against literacy for their own enslaved working population.[15]

Underlying this slaveowner defensiveness was the fear of a literate black population. Despite the protestations of the small group who would teach slaves that "Bible literacy" would uphold the social order, the majority of white Southerners knew better: they knew that knowledge was a two-edged sword which "could defend the social fabric or cut it to shreds."[16] White Southerners were aware of the possibility that slaves who could read the Bible could also read David Walker's *Appeal* or *Freedom's Journal*. In fact, the Bible itself was dangerous, as proven by Walker, Nat Turner, and others who used its messages of liberation to appeal for slave revolution. Opposition to those who would teach slaves never ceased in the antebellum period and advocates of slave literacy were confronted with the contradictions of their position. The second chapter of this book focuses on these contradictions as they were played out in South Carolina, a state in which the tensions of slavery exploded into religious and political conflict in the 1830s.

The major studies of the slave experience in the United States have given little attention to the existence of literacy among slaves. Available sources, however, show the acquisition of literacy skills by African-Americans during slavery and it is my hope that my work will lead further explorations by others. For this study, material from former slaves themselves was used, most of it now available in print, including narratives from escaped slaves in the antebellum and immediate post–Civil War era and interviews with former slaves by journalists and abolitionists. Benjamin Drew, for example, interviewed scores of former slaves living in Canada and published his results, *The Refugee*, in 1856. William Still questioned hundreds of slaves met in Philadelphia who were seeking his help via the Underground Railroad and published some of their stories. Immediately after the war, southern journalist Octavia V. Rogers Albert, northern teacher Laura Haviland, and others gathered slave accounts, often questioning former slaves about whether they had learned to read.[17]

Former slaves also told stories of how they had learned to read in their own biographies and church records. Their accounts include books by single individuals and also compilations of biographies of prominent black people prepared in the decades after slavery. Among the best known of these are William Simmons' *Men of Mark*, published in 1887; Monroe A. Majors' *Noted Negro Women,* published in 1893; and Daniel Culp's *Twentieth Century Negro Literature*, 1902. Religious denominations also published "biographical sketches," for which they gathered brief accounts from their prominent religious leaders. Stories of having overcome obstacles to learn to read and write while they were slaves, or of how their desire to learn was thwarted, were often a prominent part of their narratives.[18]

The Federal Writers Project (FWP) interviews, conducted for the Works Progress Administration (WPA) in the 1930s, provide the greatest number of accounts by former slaves of their lives under slavery. Responses were given by approximately 3,428 former slaves questioned by interviewers. At least 179 African-Americans, about 5 percent of the total, reported that they learned to read or to read and write while they were slaves. The Writers Project interviews show that reading and writing took place in every region of the South and on small farms and large plantations, small towns and cities. While the Writers Project interviews present problems in interpretation, including regional biases, a population that was old and dependent when interviewed, and inexperienced and mostly white interviewers, they are invaluable as a source which provides numbers and information about the slave experience from all regions of the South.[19] The FWP interviews are useful as a guide, but not as an exact measurement of the extent of literacy, however. For example, twice as many men as women interviewed for the Writers Project reported learning to read while they were slaves. While this statistic parallels the process of gaining literacy in traditional societies—males first, females later—it may only reflect the fact that formerly enslaved African-American men talked about literacy to their interviewers while women talked about or were asked about other aspects of slave life. After slavery, when teaching was one of the few recognized occupations for American women, many black women became teachers and some of them had learned to read and write as slaves.[20]

Chapter Three provides the results of combining the FWP interviews and slaves' own narratives and autobiographies to give a picture of slaves who learned to read and sometimes to write: which slaves were most likely to learn, when and where they learned, the methods by which they learned, the relationship of these methods to modern reading theory, and the ways in which their learning was kept quiet.

There can never be exact measurements of the extent of literacy among enslaved African-Americans, just as these are impossible in other cultures of the past. Roger S. Schofield, in his study of historical literacy measurements, admits that there is a certain "vagueness" about literacy in historical discussion, a vagueness which is in part forced by the facts of history. Measures of literacy commonly taken, such as the ability to write one's name on a document, are themselves questionable as an estimate of anything but a certain value placed on writing (illiterates could have been taught only to write their names and nothing else).[21] Even this measure of literacy was not available for slaves.

There is also the problem of defining literacy; no societies define it the same way. Expectations of "literacy" range from the ability to write one's name to "the ability to read a complex text with literary allusions and metaphoric expression and not only to interpret this text but to relate it sensibly to other texts." One scholar offers a definition of a "literate person" as one who "has acquired the knowledge and skills in reading and writing which enable him to engage effectively in all those activities in which literacy is normally assumed in his culture group." [22] For the purposes of reading and writing in the slave community the "ability to read and write" on a basic level meets this definition and the term "literacy" is used in this context throughout the book. As for numbers, W. E. B. DuBois used the figure 5 percent in his 1930s history of Reconstruction, and this figure has been mentioned by other historians of slavery. Carter Woodson, though, who was the first historian to study slave literacy in the Institute of Negro Life and Culture he founded during the early part of this century, used the higher figure of 10 percent.[23] My assessment of the sources supports Woodson's higher estimate for the following reasons.

At least 5 percent of those former slaves interviewed in the Federal Writers Project in the 1930s stated that they had learned to read or to read and write during slavery.[24] Because these former slaves—rural, poor, remaining in a depressed South when other African-Americans had sought better opportunities elsewhere—are not typical of the entire African-American population, they were among the slaves least likely to have learned to read. In order to get an accurate picture, their numbers should be increased with the numbers of urban dwellers and border South slaves taught openly in schools and Sunday schools. Examinations of particular slave populations also support the existence of literacy. Studies of runaway slaves, for example, indicate that a number were literate. A historian of slavery in Kentucky collected advertisements concerning Kentucky runaway slaves and found that of 350 runaways 71, or 20.2 percent, were advertised as being able to read. Thirty-seven of these could write also. Of 625 slaves interviewed by William Still for his publication *The Underground Rail Road*, fifty-five, or 8.8 percent, either mentioned or were described as knowing how to read or write. Others questioned by Still may also have had these skills, but neither Still nor they mentioned them.[25]

Sources from whites also indicate the scope of literacy among enslaved African-Americans. Slaveowner diaries and reminiscences confirm that some whites taught slaves. Records of benevolent institutions which aimed to put a Bible into every household reveal that Bibles and the skills to read them were provided for slaves, even in states where this was illegal. Black and white churches operated Sunday schools where slaves learned to read. The colonization movement inspired activities to make slaves literate before emancipating them for mission work in Liberia. The fourth and fifth chapters of this book explain the motives and activities for benevolent and religious literacy. The sixth shows how the "Bibles for Slaves" campaign became a desperate attempt in the late 1840s and 1850s to reconcile dividing sections of the United States, but was also a source of divisions within the antislavery movement.

Another rich source for assessing the extent of slave literacy has been the number of excellent studies of Reconstruction which have appeared in recent years charting the vigorous, almost astonishing drive of newly freed African-Americans for education. The roots of this drive are traceable to the slave experience; as James Anderson points out in *The Education of Blacks in the South, 1860–1935,* "the postwar campaign for free schooling was rooted firmly in the beliefs and behavior of former slaves."[26] Northern missionaries who came South expecting to enlighten totally ignorant freedmen were surprised to find schools, educational associations, and literate teachers waiting for them. Tales of secret schools and of Sunday schools whose purposes had included teaching slaves to read came to light during Reconstruction. Detailed examinations illuminate in small ways the possible extent of literacy before freedom. For example, Edmund Drago found that of twenty identified black leaders and convention delegates in Georgia from 1867 to 1872, ten were literate former slaves. According to Joe Richardson, by 1863 the American Missionary Association's eighty-three white teachers were being assisted by nineteen "native" assistants or monitors—assumed to be former slaves with some literacy training. In North Carolina, by December 1866, black teachers comprised more than half the instructors in schools for African-Americans. In South Carolina, three out of every four black teachers who participated in South Carolina's state constitutional convention and in the legislatures between 1868 and 1876 were southern-born. The majority had been educated locally and some had been slaves.[27]

The tremendous drive by black people to grasp learning once it was legal for them to do so and the numbers of literate former slaves who appeared from the ranks where literacy was supposedly forbidden show how much enslaved African-Americans valued the liberating qualities of literacy within the slave community. The epilogue to this book explores this drive for learning during and after the Civil War as a vigorous movement by African-Americans for self-determination and links it to the fight for literacy by African-Americans during slavery.

Chapter One

■

Slaves, Religion and Reading in Early North America

THE NINETEENTH CENTURY CONFLICTS WHICH DEVELoped from trying to keep human beings enslaved in an age of mass revolution and education had evolved over centuries of European attempts to justify their enslavement of Africans. This conflict was heightened by the spread of the Protestant doctrine that all individuals should be able to read so that they could seek the scriptures and salvation for themselves. During the English colonization of North America colonizers who obtained slaves were followed by missionaries, who attempted to give the enslaved Africans, as well as the Indians and the white poor, the rudiments of Christianity and literacy. Though Africans eagerly seized opportunities to learn, missionaries always had to fight the reluctance of slaveowners to see slaves as fellow human beings and the owners' fear that the skills of literacy would threaten the slave system. All religious denominations except Quakers accommodated to slaveowner fears, but the enthusiasm generated among African-Americans by the popular churches during the Great Awakening sparked a growth in black churches, black preachers, and black reading.

During the period from 1810 to 1830, the contradictions embedded in modern slavery became more apparent. Benevolent movements focused on campaigns to teach the masses to read the Bible. Black people in urban areas made their own organized efforts to gain literacy. On the other hand, as the slave population increased, emancipation pressures increased white fearfulness and resistance to a recognition of the rights of slaves to learn to read, worship, or assemble. A wave of restrictive legislation passed in southern states from 1829 to 1834 limited the rights of slaves. There was no overall ban on teaching slaves to read, however, because white Southerners afraid of the power of the printed word in the hands of enslaved African-Americans had also been told for decades that all people should have access to the Bible. This message was perpetuated in the 1830s and after by the white southern mission to evangelize slaves, an effort to promote a positive view of slavery but also a reminder of the rights of slaves as human beings who should be allowed to read the Bible for themselves.

In the seventeenth century, as they expanded and rationalized the African slave trade, Europeans refined a definition of themselves as separate from and superior to Africans. Separation and superiority were linked to a knowledge of the printed word, as shown in the spurious "African legend" told by Dutch factor William Bosman in his description of the Guinea coast. In the tale, supposedly told to Bosman by Gold Coast Africans, God created two sorts of men, black and white, and offered them "two sorts of Gifts, viz. Gold, and the Knowledge or Arts of Reading and Writing, giving the Blacks the first Election, who chose Gold, and left the Knowledge of Letters to the White." Incensed at the avarice of the Africans, God further declared that henceforth whites should be masters and Africans slaves.[1] The tale is, of course, a specious effort to justify the slave trade. Also, the implication in this tale that Africans had no knowledge of reading and writing was inaccurate. West Africans lived on the "margins of literacy"; contact with literate Moslem traders and religious leaders and the proximity of Timbuktu, the home of the renowned medieval university of Sankore, permeated West African cultures with an awareness of the written word. This awareness increased Africans' eagerness to learn to read and write when they made contact with Europeans.[2] However, Bosman's fable is significant as an indication of the importance Europeans put on reading and writing skills as a measure of separation between themselves and the Africans they were exploiting and enslaving.

The church's inclusion of African slaves and other non-European peoples under European control as part of the "lowly masses" who should be given religious instructions challenged the use of literacy as a form of racial and cultural separation. In England, seventeenth century religious crusaders who believed the Bible to be the sole source of spiritual authority held that the salvation of a person's soul depended on the ability to read the Bible and to search the Scriptures for oneself. This conviction successfully challenged the tradition that peasants and workers should not be allowed to learn to read. It led to a great effort by working people to acquire the skill of reading and by the wealthy to see that their entire households, including servants, did so as well. It also led (together with the needs of a commercial middle class) to campaigns to teach reading to all, including the laboring poor. Therefore, when in 1660 Charles II ordered his Council for Foreign Plantations to introduce "natives, servants and slaves" to Christianity, this religious instruction was assumed to include instruction in reading whenever feasible or practical.[3] However, during the early years of English colonization the order to teach reading was almost impossible to carry out in the North American wilderness. Distances, the shortage of clergymen, and the dependence of the church on lay vestries who discouraged their efforts left the poor and enslaved, in North America without book learning.

Nevertheless, greater efforts were made by the Church of England to bring Christianity and literacy to the colonies after 1689. James Blair, appointed by the Bishop of London as Commissary for Virginia, proposed a plan "for the encouragement of the Christian Education of our Negro and Indian children" to the House of Burgesses, though with little apparent effect. A new and inspired effort by Thomas Bray, the Bishop's appointee for Maryland, had a much greater impact. Bray served in the colonies for four years and then returned to London to organize missionary and educational efforts to bring the gospel to African-Americans, Native Americans, and the vast number of unchurched whites in the colonies. Bray's creations, the Society for the Propagation of the Gospel (S.P.G.) and the Society for Promoting Christian Knowledge, were born during a time of renewal for the Anglican church, when it could turn its resources and energies away from political conflicts and into humanitarian and social reforms at home and abroad.[4]

From its beginning, education was a focal point of S.P.G. work. Most Anglican clergymen believed literacy to be a prerequisite for baptism. The Society's initial plans included founding

schools, printing and distributing books, and gathering libraries to be sent to America. S.P.G. missionaries held catechism
schools in which they taught slaves and free blacks to read.
They also experimented in training blacks to teach their own
countrymen. Bishop Secker sent a black missionary to Africa
and brought back three African natives to England to train as
missionaries. This plan inspired a similar project in South
Carolina using African-American slaves. In 1740, at the urging
of commissary Alexander Garden, the S.P.G. set aside 1,500
pounds so that Garden could purchase two slave teachers and
begin a school for slaves. He did purchase two blacks, Harry
and Andrew, trained them in Christian principles and basic education, and opened the school in 1743. Spelling books, Psal-
ters, Bibles, and prayer books were sent from England to the
school's sixty scholars. A few influential community leaders, including Pinckneys, Bryans, Pringles, and Wraggs also supported the school. By 1747 forty "scholars" were "graduated"
with some knowledge of Christianity and literacy. By 1755 seventy children were enrolled in the school, which declined after
Garden's departure but remained in existence until 1764.[5]

The S.P.G.'s movement to instruct Africans was thwarted,
though, by the Anglican church's weak colonial structure and
the resistance of slaveowners. Where the church was well supported, as in the Charleston area, the clergy were most active
in carrying out the government's policy of providing religious
services for African-Americans and Native Americans. But extensions of parish boundaries into frontier areas made ade-
quate supervision of the backwaters, where thousands of slaves
were being imported, impossible. Also, the S.P.G. made little
headway in New England; denominational frictions with Congregationalists discouraged cooperation. Leading Puritans,
though, strongly supported the propriety and beneficial effects
of Christianity and argued that Negroes should be taught to
read like other servants and dependents. John Eliot criticized
owners for exposing souls of their slaves to "a destroying Ignorance"; Cotton Mather recommended that masters train their
slaves and furnish them with Bibles and other religious books
for which they should be given the time to read.[6]

The S.P.G. acted cautiously toward slaveholders. Its founders
had intended the missionary organization to act as "a refining
and elevating force, striving to devote itself wholly to spiritual
concerns, rarely meddling with politics as such, and apparently

not desiring to meddle with them." Missionaries were enjoined to take special care not to involve themselves in affairs not related to their calling or function. Their appeals to slaveholders were tinged with respect for the slave labor system and with steady reassurance that missions would not interfere with it. Outspoken criticism was impolitic, and ministers deferred to the sometimes brutal and uncouth land and slave magnates who constituted the dominant element of society in coastal enclaves and inland settlements. Most of these valued monetary profit as almost the exclusive consideration of the slave system and disregarded the humanity of slaves. When the S.P.G. was bequeathed two Barbadian sugar plantations in 1711, the Society became slaveholders, announced that SPG slaves would be "Christianized," but set aside proposals that they be taught to read or encouraged to make Christian marriages. Not until 1795 was the teaching of reading ordered for the Society's slaves.[7]

The Englishman's "exaggerated sense of tribal identity," as characterized by Winthrop Jordan, encouraged this reluctance to see slaves as fellow human beings. African distinctiveness, physical and cultural, made separateness easy to adopt. Missionary Francis Le Jau indignantly reported to his superiors the question by a planter, "Is it possible that any of my slaves could go to Heaven and must I see them there?" and deplored the young man who resolved "never to come to the Holy Table while slaves are received therein." Enlightenment philosophers, including David Hume, reinforced slaveowner beliefs and made them intellectually respectable. Writing in 1753, for example, Hume stated his suspicion that blacks were "naturally inferior to whites," using as his evidence the lack of "ingenious manufacturers," artists and scientists, and "learning" among them.[8]

Latin attitudes were more all-encompassing; perhaps this explains the fact that a number of the most dedicated missionaries to slaves for the colonial Anglican church were Huguenot immigrants from France. One Huguenot representing the Church of England in South Carolina, bemoaning the low number of black converts to Christianity in his region, reminded the Secretary of the S.P.G. that Catholic priests readily christened any Negro who came before them. He suggested that Anglican baptism might be offered on a comparatively broad scale. But he missed the point. A Catholic-style indiscriminate baptism might have resulted in more numbers of baptized slaves, but S.P.G.

ministers would not have carried this out without forfeiting the tenets of Protestantism as they interpreted them. It was the whole process of preparation, including the learning of the English language and the skills of reading and writing it, which made Christianity something socially precious to be offered to the slave and resisted by the slaveowner. Slaveowners feared that literate slaves would acquire new ideas, a sense of their rights and of their power to attain them—a process which would impair their willingness to work and incite their discontent.[9]

The slaveowners were right. Africans who were enslaved quickly recognized the value of reading and writing—not only for their practical uses (from the beginning of slavery, slaves used reading and writing skills to run away) but because literacy, especially the ability to write, signified an establishment of the African's human identity to the European world. Narratives written by former slaves in the eighteenth century show how Africans who had gained knowledge of books established their own "selfhood" by mastering one of the tools of power in the European world. Their recognition of the significance of literacy led them to consider books as having magical qualities. James Gronniosaw, sold to a Dutch trader as a teenager in the 1730s, recalled a revealing reaction to his first exposure to the written word:

> My master used to read prayers in public to the ship's crew every Sabbath day; and when I first saw him read, I was never so surprised in my life, as when I saw the book talk to my master, for I thought it did, as I observed him to look upon it, and move his lips. I wished it would do so with me. As soon as my master had done reading, I followed him to the place where he put the book, being mightily delighted with it, and when nobody saw me, I opened it, and put my ear down close upon it, in great hope that it would say something to me; but I became very sorry, and greatly disappointed, when I found it would not speak.[10]

Of the first five slave narratives published in the eighteenth century, four mentioned this "voice in the text," indicating that it was a common story among Africans in England. Africans, and then African-Americans, quickly perceived the extent to which whites used literacy as a separation between themselves and Africans and used the lack of reading and writing skills as a justification for considering Africans lesser human beings or scarcely human at all. The Africans who published narratives necessarily prized the ability to write, which had allowed them to establish their own identity and history to Europeans. Book learning was also a path to God, as it had been in Islamic Africa. In 1787, the seventy-year-old literate slave Jupiter Hammon urged other slaves to "get those who can read, to learn you" but that "if there was no Bible, it would be no matter whether you could read or not." The Bible was "the word of God, and tells you what you must do to please God; it tells you how you may escape misery, and be happy for ever."[11] A desire to read the Bible was a powerful motive for slaves to gain literacy; in New York and in the Carolinas, Huguenot missionaries described the eagerness with which slaves embraced the few opportunities they had to learn to read Bibles and hymn books. On the other hand, an acute observer of Alexander Garden's school for slaves in Charleston noted that "slaves certainly seemed willing and eager to attend" the school, but "probably for an opportunity at literacy rather than religious instruction."[12]

Literate slaves in the eighteenth century also used literacy as a political act. Slaves protested their condition and used reading and writing skills to gain freedom. Beginning as early as 1661, individual slaves who had learned to write petitioned colonial courts for their liberty. Some used their writing skills to protest the entire slavery institution. One such slave narrative, published in the eighteenth century by Ottobah Cugoano, was a powerful cry against slavery entitled, *Thoughts and Sentiments on the Evil and Wicked Traffic of the Slavery and Commerce of the Human Species*. It combined sound arguments against the institution of slavery with vivid first-person experiences that illustrated the horrors of the slave system. Cugoano was the first former enslaved African to write a lengthy work of protest against slavery; his work was followed two years later by his friend Olaudah Equiano's powerful personal narrative. Equiano, or Gustavus Vassa, also combined his own story of personal and spiritual development with his sufferings under slavery and a cry against the slave system and the slave trade.[13]

The Africans' political use of literacy was exactly what slaveowners had feared, and they moved against literacy and schooling for slaves, even when founded for religious purposes. Citizen outrage after the 1712 New York uprising focused attention and suspicion on Elias Neau's catechism school for slaves. Only support by the colonial governor and other S.P.G. members ensured its survival. Fearful Carolinian planters suspected literacy among slaves after an insurrection in Antigua in 1736 led by literate slaves supposedly taught by Anglican clergy. Planters also curtailed many slave activities in South Carolina after the Stono rebellion in 1739. Among these curbs was a law fining anyone who taught a slave to read and write English.[14] Local support for Alexander Garden's school for blacks in St. Philip's Church in Charleston declined. Although the premise for the school was that enlightened slaves would be less rebellious as they learned the true Christian virtues of submissiveness and obedience, most Charlestonians were not convinced. Masters took away their slave children before they had time to get the benefits of a full education, "being nervous of its results." S.P.G. missionary Joseph Ottolenge produced a similar reaction in Savannah, where he began regular meetings for slaves in 1752. He taught them to read, "that they may be able in Time to comfort themselves in reading the book of God." Some planters objected and few would allow their slave workers to go to classes in Savannah, so his work was terminated after a few years. In 1770 the Georgia colony enacted legislation forbidding the teaching of slaves to read as well as to write.[15]

The Anglican priests and S.P.G. missionaries felt they had no choice but to accommodate planter parishioners who refused them the right to educate their slaves, but Quakers gradually came to a different decision. Quakers had also held slaves in the West Indies and the North American mainland from the mid-seventeenth century. Like Anglicans, Quakers had been concerned with religion for their slaves. Quakers, however, after George Fox's challenge to examine slaveholding in the light of Christian principles in 1676, became increasingly uneasy with the institution of slavery. Their actions began to diverge quite sharply from those of Anglicans. By 1720 Friends in all areas of the colonies and England agreed that buying and selling slaves was "not agreeable to Truth" and essays questioning the ethics of slaveholding appeared in Quaker tracts and journals. Also, by the 1730s Quakers had undertaken the task of teaching slaves in their households, reporting that many could read and write. Through their teaching and in their plans to train blacks as missionaries to Africa, Quakers were the first group to advocate literacy for African-Americans as the first step towards their eventual emancipation.[16]

But Quakers were a small sect in which a declaration of faith was a dedication of one's whole life. Those who renounced the profitability of slavery to remain Quakers gradually found ways of making a living which did not require the holding of slaves. Obviously, Quakers were too exclusive and their communities too removed from the great body of American colonists to serve as a model for the larger society. Instead, it was the Anglicans, the Presbyterians, and members of the "popular" churches who provided slaves with a minimal amount of religious instruction and education while supporting the slave system and who marked the direction for slave evangelization and education during the outburst of religious enthusiasm which converted thousands of the free and unfree during the Great Awakening.

The most powerful and long-lasting result of the Great Awakening in the United States was its impact in extending religious enthusiasm to the lower classes, including free blacks and slaves. The mass appeal of its proselytizers, their zeal for converts, the explosive growth of the "popular" denominations, and the renewal of evangelistic fervor in the regular churches had a profound impact on blacks as well as whites. Slaves responded to the conversion experience as one familiar to them from African religious tradition. They recognized the experience of oppressed peoples stressed by evangelical preachers as their own. For a brief time there was a merging of egalitarianism and spirituality within the emerging evangelical churches. As ministers saw new merit in converting lower class whites, their valuation of African-Americans as potential converts increased also. Jonathan Edwards noted the presence of several African-Americans who appeared to "have been truly born again" in the great Northampton revival of 1735. A black woman was part of the first group of Methodists to meet as an American congregation and black people joined in the mass conversions effected by George Whitefield.[17]

During the Great Awakening, conversion was linked with the ability to read the Bible for oneself. Conversion of the poor led to efforts to teach basic literacy skills to the poor, black or white. Presbyterians were traditional believers in teaching all people to read the Bible and Presbyterian leaders of the Great Awakening, including Samuel Davies, John Todd, and Robert Wright, inspired slave converts, taught those slaves to read and spell, and supplied them with religious books. Davies described the "eagerly attentive" and sincere response of slaves to his message and their enthusiasm and need for psalm and hymn books. Davies was deeply touched by the plight of the "poor unhappy Africans" and responded to their eagerness to learn with sympathy and kindness. In a 1755 letter to the London Society for the Promotion of Religious Knowledge Among the Poor, Davies described "the poor neglected Negroes who are so far from having money to purchase books, that they themselves are the property of others," and asked that they be furnished with Bibles and Watts' psalms and hymns. When the Society obliged, slaves learned to read, though they had little assistance, so that they could use the Bibles sent from London.[18]

After Davies left Virginia to become president of the College of New Jersey, the Presbyterian Awakening in the South was overwhelmed by the wave of new conversions to the popular churches, Methodist and Baptist. New Light or Separate Baptists from New England had begun to filter into North Carolina and Virginia in the 1750s, vigorously transforming the scattered, sedate Baptist congregations already established there. Shubal Stearn's Sandy Creek Baptist Church in Orange County, North Carolina, was the beacon for enthusiastic expansion along the coast and into the almost churchless interior. Baptists gained thousands of southern members each decade during the late eighteenth century, although in the 1770s they were surpassed in some areas of the South by the Methodists.[19]

Baptists and Methodists were aggressive evangelizers and expansionists. While their leaders seldom came from the lowest strata of society, their appeal minimized the traditional assets of birth and education. Committed to the separation of church and state, Baptists challenged authority of all kinds. Rituals such as giving the right hand of fellowship and the kiss of charity contributed to the sense of equality and communion. As a chosen people in sympathy with others cast out from authority, Baptists made special appeals to the outcasts in society, including slaves. Further, a recent historian of Afro-Baptist religion has noted ways in which the white Baptist world view and ritual held affinities with the African "Sacred Cosmos." Baptist revivals, therefore, converted blacks as well as whites in large numbers. The Baptist beliefs in direct action by the individual through conversion, the priesthood of all believers, the dignity and worth of each person, and democracy in governing the church gave blacks more opportunities for participation and religious experience than in any other denomination. By 1795

Baptists estimated that their denomination included over 17,000 black members south and east of Maryland.[20]

Baptists did not require literacy as a prerequisite for preachers or members, but black leaders who seized the opportunities open to them as Baptists showed an interest in learning and teaching fellow slaves to read. David George, a slave owned by planter and Indian agent George Galphin, was converted and taught to read by Connecticut Baptist preacher Wait Palmer, who founded Silver Bluff Church at a Georgia settlement near Galphin's plantation. George took over Palmer's church and removed his slave congregation from Georgia with the invading British, first to Halifax, Nova Scotia, and then to Sierra Leone. George could read and write in a "simple and graceful literary style [with a] strong biblical simplicity," according to historians of the black National Baptists.[21]

David George was greatly influenced and encouraged by George Leile, one of the best known early black Baptist leaders. Leile, also called George Sharp, had been converted and taught to read by Matthew Moore, a white Baptist minister, around 1773. He was reputed to have discovered his religious mission as a preacher by using his ability to read hymns among the other slaves on his plantation. His master, Henry Sharp, freed his slave, who continued to minister to whites and blacks on plantations from his church near Savannah. Leile left with the British for Jamaica after the Revolution, where he established Baptist congregations and a free school taught by one of his deacons. His correspondence with English Baptists indicates his desire to increase the reading ability among Jamaican blacks. He wrote, "I have a few books, some good old authors and sermons, and one large bible that was given to me by a gentleman; a good many of our members can read, and are all desirous to learn . . ."[22]

Just before embarking for Jamaica, Leile baptized Andrew Bryan in Savannah. There Bryan founded the First African Baptist Church, which was to achieve membership in the thousands. Bryan was the eager beneficiary of the religious conversion of his owner Jonathan Bryan, who with his brother Hugh was transformed during the growing religious Awakening by their contacts with Methodist evangelist George Whitefield. The white Bryan family had become concerned with promoting evangelical and slavery reforms in South Carolina. In 1740, under Whitefield's urging, Jonathan Bryan had established a "negro school" and provided it with a teacher. Faced with the South Carolina Assembly's opposition to the school and to Hugh Bryan's suspected antislavery actions, the Bryans tried in 1742 to convince their fellow slaveowners to join together "in the Expence of a Common Teacher for the Negroes belonging to Them." The Assembly objected to this proposal also, but acknowledged that teaching by "Masters and Mistresses in their own private Families, or Missionaries, or School-masters, lawfully thereunto authorized" was acceptable. The Bryans and some of their neighbors then broke away from the Anglican church and formed an Independent Presbyterian congregation which accepted slaves as members, a church headed by the former teacher of the "negro school."

Former slave Andrew Bryan emerged from this ferment determined that his parishioners in the African Church in Savannah should have books and should learn to read. He succeeded in part; a visitor reported to the English Baptist Society in 1792 that "perhaps fifty of Andrew's church can read," though only three could write. Bryan himself wrote to thank the English group for Bibles they had sent in 1800 and reported that he had succeeded in supplying a teacher for his congregation. "A few humane gentlemen" had purchased a slave "to exercise the handsome ministerial gifts he possesses amongst us, and teach our youth to read and write."[23]

Other black Baptist leaders were not as interested in adopting white practices such as reading the Bible as they were in perpetuating African concepts and ritual. In the nineteenth century white Baptists began to scrutinize the African practices which had been incorporated into many black congregations under the independent Baptist structure. But in the initial years of Baptist expansion, both the opportunity to Africanize Baptist practices and to learn English skills such as reading were magnets which attracted thousands of blacks.

Methodists were also effective in drawing large numbers of African-American converts. Methodists were dissenters from the established church, so they developed many practices useful in appealing to the weak and unfortunate as their constituency. Like Baptists, Methodists offered opportunities for responsible and active roles in the church even to the ignorant and lowly. Though most fully licensed ministers were decently educated, exhorters and class leaders were taken directly from congregations, even when the congregations' members were slaves or free blacks. Often these positions were ably filled by leaders of the black community, who found in religious leadership a natural outlet for their talents. To encourage ambitious African-Americans, white Methodist ministers often employed them as attendants, allowing them time to observe, study, and preach. Black exhorters such as Harry Hosier and Jesse Jennet ranked as famous Methodist preachers alongside white leaders Francis Asbury and Freeborn Garrettson. Methodists, like Baptists, reflected the desire of their parishioners to learn to read. The 1790 Methodist conference recommended the establishment of Sunday schools and teachers to teach "all that will attend and have a capacity to learn." The Methodists also recommended that their church publish a textbook so that poor black and white children could read as well as pray.[24]

African-American literacy, even among slaves, was also fostered by the "Great Revival to Christianize the West," or the Second Great Awakening. James McGready's camp meetings in Cumberland County, Tennessee, drew blacks as well as whites. In McGready's Cumberland Presbyterian Church, blacks had permission to exhort, lead singing, hold prayer meetings, and read Scriptures publicly. Black speakers were in demand as religious leaders because most camp meetings of any denomination were segregated. Blacks held their own services, usually in the same building as the whites but at different times, though some blacks also preached to white audiences. Black converts as well as white were encouraged to learn to read.[25]

While popular religious movements encouraged slave literacy in successive awakenings, revolutionary thought and leadership also linked literacy and emancipation. In the northern American colonies, revolutionary slogans which promoted "breaking the bonds of slavery" to England and the equality of mankind were quickly applied by literate slaves to their own situation. Slaves in Massachusetts sent petitions to the legislature in 1773 and 1774 asking that they be freed because of the sinful and evil nature of slavery and because they had "in common with other men a natural right to be free." Connecticut slaves linked freedom and knowledge when they petitioned the state in 1779 to grant them freedom, asking "whether it is consistent with the present Claims, of the united States, to hold so many Thousands, of the Race of Adam, our Common Father, in perpetual Slavery [sic]." Among the evils of slavery they emphasized was the master's deliberate withholding of knowledge from them, "as if the Perpetrators of this horrid Wickedness, were conscious (that we poor Ignorant Africans, upon the least Glimering Sight, derived from a Knowledge of the Sense and Practice of civilized Nations) should Convince them of their Sin. . . ." After independence, slavery was abolished in a few states where the system was neither extensively practiced nor economically advantageous.[26]

Revolutionary leaders believed in the necessity for universal literacy in order for a democracy to survive. Plans for literacy and other schooling for African-Americans accompanied emancipation in many post-Revolutionary state actions. New Jersey's 1788 law, for example, made teaching of slaves compulsory under a penalty of five pounds as a preliminary measure to emancipation. Preparing to abolish slavery, New York's legislature mandated masters to teach all minors born of slaves to read the Scriptures. Northerners, including Jonathan Boucher, Benjamin Rush, and Benjamin Franklin, devised plans to educate slaves for freedom. Southerners who desired gradual emancipation, including George Washington, linked it with schooling. Washington freed his slaves in his will and stipulated that those who were minors without parents be bound out and taught to read, write, and follow a useful trade before being freed.[27]

In the spirit of the Revolution, educators in the early Republic planned to teach reading and writing skills to the whole population, since ignorance was "the parent and stupid nurse of civil slavery." Benjamin Franklin expected that readers would acquire good morals, especially the virtues of "temperance, order, industry, and frugality." The same spirit led the antislavery societies of the late eighteenth century, many of which were led by Quakers, to try to teach African-Americans. The Convention of American Abolition Societies in 1794 urged its branches to have children of free blacks and slaves instructed in "common literature" through tutors or individuals, often indentured servants themselves. In the late eighteenth century abolitionists began black schools in Charleston; Savannah; Washington, D.C.; Philadelphia; Wilmington, Delaware; Georgetown, Maryland; Alexandria, Richmond, and Norfolk, Virginia; as well as in northern states. These schools stressed basic literacy and vocational training. For example, Anthony Benezet's Philadelphia school trained pupils in reading, writing, arithmetic, and plain accounts. All the girls were also taught needlework, according to the stipulations of Benezet's will. The abolitionists' school in Alexandria stressed reading and writing for its African-American students as indicated by the teacher's report in 1797, which concluded that of 108 pupils four could write legibly, "read the Scriptures with tolerable facility," and had commenced arithmetic; others had learned to read but had progressed little in writing; fifteen could spell words of three or four syllables and read easy lessons; and the others were still learning the alphabet and spelling monosyllables.[28]

In the early years of organized abolition, its societies worked not only to free African-Americans but to frame their behavior. In 1796, for example, the American Convention of Abolition Societies wrote instructions for newly freed black people which told them to "acquire reading, writing, and the first principles of arithmetic" as early as possible; to teach their children useful trades; to "refrain from the use of spiritous liquors," avoid "frolicking," and other admonishments. Abolitionists, like other reformers, believed that religious reading would inculcate morality, as in the following advice:

> Some of you can read, such know the advantages of it; you who cannot, strive to acquire that knowledge. Surely this knowledge is an object of great importance, were it only for the opportunity it affords of becoming acquainted with that best of books, the Bible. The holy Scriptures of the old and new testament, contain invaluable treasures of instruction, and of comfort. It would give us much satisfaction, could we oftener see them in the hands of those who are able to read them, and that an increasing anxiety to become possessed of their contents, and to profit by their precepts, might be more and more observable among you.[29]

Free blacks did not need these strictures to encourage them to learn to read and to practice Christianity. Members of black societies such as the African Union Societies in Newport and Providence and the Free African Society in Philadelphia, which were organized to relieve the poor and indigent, also stressed the attaining of literate skills for civic usefulness and moral training. For example, the directors of the African Benevolent Society of Newport, Rhode Island, stipulated that the teacher of the school they established in 1808 should be a "professor of the Christian religion, and a member in regular standing with some church," believe in prayer, and have the Scriptures read in school daily. The Benevolent Society also invited ministers of nearby white churches and speakers from the Friends' societies to hold religious meetings with the school on a regular basis, "as the morals of the scholars are to be particularly attended to."[30]

African-Americans founded their own schools in Newport, Boston, Charleston, and wherever else they had the financial means to do so. As more blacks gained literate skills, they moved to gain control of abolitionist schools also. By the second decade of the nineteenth century, eleven of the sixteen black schools in Philadelphia were taught by black teachers; a decade later blacks operated both the Philadelphia and New York schools begun by abolitionist and manumission societies. In Charleston, the earliest black schools were founded by free mulattos through societies such as the Brown Fellowship Society and the Minor's Moralist Society, established in 1803. Like the abolitionists, the mulattos who founded these schools were concerned for the moral and vocational training and control of indigent children and hoped that literacy would lead to abstinence from "every vicious and demoralizing practice." These subscription schools stressed basic reading and writing. Schools for the mulattos' own children, such as that conducted by Thomas Bonneau, more resembled those proposed by Thomas Jefferson for leadership training. They began with reading, writing, and spelling, but the pupils also read the histories of Greece, Rome, and England and made speeches based on the model of the "Columbian orator."[31]

By the end of the eighteenth century, expanding numbers of black schools and churches and of evangelical churches with literate slave members looked increasingly threatening to white Southerners, whose social and economic system was based more and more firmly on slavery. White Southern evangelicals had to decide whether to continue to accommodate to the slave system. Their decision was forced by violence. American Methodists, who had opposed slavery in 1784 but who had backtracked when reaction was "swift, intense, and hostile," declared in the General Conference of 1800 that slavery was "repugnant to the unalienable rights of mankind, and to the spirit of the Christian religion." However, the Methodist directive was issued shortly after the Gabriel plot in Virginia and fanned familiar fears. When it was printed for distribution in Charleston a mob gathered, burned the leaflets on arrival, tried to drown one

Methodist preacher and threatened another. The South Carolina legislature passed a law forbidding Negroes to meet behind closed doors or at night, an effective bar to religious assembly or to schools. In the next edition of the Methodist *Discipline* in 1804, the entire section condemning slavery did not appear in the copies distributed south of Virginia.[32] North Carolina Baptists responded similarly to an insurrectionary scare in 1802. Whites blamed Baptists for notes they found supposedly attributed to literate slaves organizing revolts in the northeastern part of the state. Baptist revival meetings in the threatened counties had preceded the insurrection threats. In response, white Baptists began to exercise limits on black Baptist preachers and on contact within their churches between blacks and whites.[33]

While it inspired missions to the unfortunate, evangelicalism also justified this accommodation to the slave system. Individual conversion was the catalyst for activism. Therefore, reform was linked to individual action and limited to the sphere over which the individual had some power. While the evangelical fought the evils of society within the realm of his personal influence, he "theoretically fled the world" in matters which he could not control.[34] The universal and equalitarian implications of religious revivalism and religious education, however, continued to produce uneasiness and guilt among many white preachers and church members, particularly those who worshipped alongside African-Americans and were moved by their piety and devotion. Baptist David Barrow spoke out against slavery in Virginia for twenty years before he gave up and left the South in 1798. Francis Asbury and Thomas Coke sought George Washington's support for emancipation in 1785 and Asbury and James O'Kelly encouraged Methodists to emancipate their slaves on a gradual and individual basis. "Father" David Rice, founder of Presbyterianism in Kentucky, campaigned hard for a plan for gradual emancipation in that state's 1792 constitutional convention, though Kentuckians refused to heed his prediction that "a curse has attended [slavery], and a curse will follow it." Rice complained that one of the evils of slavery was that the master could deprive the slaves of all learning. It was put out of the slaves' power to learn to read and their masters kept them from other means of information. Slavery, therefore, must be abolished, "because it infringes upon the natural right of men to be enlightened."[35]

White preachers who remained in the South, however, and who insisted on making antislavery pronouncements were endangering their lives and the lives of their black parishioners, and they risked being barred from the presence of the slaves altogether. As they saw it, white evangelists had to retain the trust of slaveholders if blacks were to have any chance at all for the blessings of the Christian message on earth and eternal life afterward. Asbury rationalized in his journal, "What is the personal liberty of the African which he may abuse, [compared] to the salvation of his soul."[36] Salvation was worth a lot of compromises, evangelicals decided.

Through the following decades, lone voices from all the evangelical denominations called out against the wickedness of slavery and the refusal of others, except Quakers, to root out this evil in their midst. But the majority of white evangelicals walked the tightrope between their desire to convert even the black outcasts in society, their distaste for slavery, and their fear of arousing the wrath of slaveholders.

Their efforts became more difficult as the slave system increased in economic importance and became more regionalized. Slave imports reached their peak in the United States between 1790 and 1810. By 1820 the slave population of the United States was approximately three times greater than it had been in 1776 and had assumed its specific sectional character. Fewer than 20,000 slaves remained in the North in 1820. The slave population was also declining rapidly in the upper Chesapeake. In contrast, five southern states (Kentucky, North and South Carolina, Virginia, and Georgia) gained over 100,000 slaves each from 1790 to 1820. The greatest increase occurred in Georgia, as slaves were needed for more intensive rice and cotton cultivation along the coast and to carve out new plantations in the Piedmont and the interior. South Carolina reopened its slave trade from 1803 to 1808 to import 40,000 slaves; from 1790 to 1820 the state's slave population increased by over 150,000. By 1820 South Carolina blacks again outnumbered whites, as they had in colonial times. Slavery grew in the Southwest also. Emigrants from Virginia and the Carolinas brought their slaves with them to Kentucky and Tennessee by the hundreds of thousands. Newly opened lands in Alabama and Mississippi already held thousands of white settlers and black slaves by 1820.[37]

The black population also increased rapidly in the cities of the South. Freed slaves sought the anonymity and opportunity of the urban frontier, as did mulatto emigrants from the West Indies, who found that in American cities they must form community interests with slaves and free African-Americans. By 1810 free blacks and slaves composed a significant portion of the population of Baltimore, Alexandria, Richmond, Petersburg, Norfolk, and Charleston.[38] As the black population grew, the patterns of membership in the Methodist and Baptist churches established during the Awakenings created giant city churches in southern cities with thousands of black members.[39] Literate black leaders contributed to the establishment of separate churches also, including the African Methodist Episcopal (A.M.E.) Church and the A.M.E. Zion Church. The A.M.E. Church counted thousands of members in the southern cities of Charleston and Baltimore as well as in Philadelphia and other northern cities.

Leadership opportunities in these churches, together with the promotion of learning by the organized evangelical-based reform movements, provided opportunities for urban African-Americans to learn to read and write. The Sunday school movement and the Bible and tract societies, which will be examined in detail in a later chapter, promoted reading for all the masses, black and white. Everyone must learn to read the Bible for salvation, reformers proclaimed; also, reading and writing, when correctly presented, were useful tools for moral training and would encourage obedience to the social order. Added to the impetus for reading in the early nineteenth century was the steam-run printing press, which led to the production of journals for the masses, the "penny newspaper," and the unprecedented expansion of literacy from an educated few to "the most numerous reading public the world has ever known." Black people shared in the demand for reading material and the urgent desire to express themselves in print; when they did so, however, their appeals and warning and calls to end slavery terrified whites and led to suppression of black literacy.[40]

The 1820s threatened and checked African-American efforts to build communities and self-identity. Both the North and the South curtailed the rights of free blacks and slaves to work for themselves, learn to read and write, preach, assemble, emigrate, or hear the word of God. In the North, equalitarian reforms ironically rebounded against black residents. Suffrage expanded to the non-propertied classes and provided direct election of most government officials so that they would be more responsive to the people, but the extensions of political roles to the white masses heightened uneasiness about the propriety of the Negro's subordinate status and created doubts that the growing number of blacks would be content with their status forever. The white working man disliked the thought of having to share his rising place in the world with the African-American and tried to ensure that this would not take place. Therefore, in many states the adoption of white manhood suffrage led directly to the political disfranchisement of the black man. New states admitted to the Union after 1819 restricted suffrage to white males. Most northern states also limited or barred black immigration and qualified black participation in the courts. City codes separated blacks from whites in public transportation, accommodations, entertainment, schools, and churches. Public opinion and direct action by violent crowds enforced these practices. Black schools were particular targets for the mobs.[41]

In the South, nervousness over the growth of emancipation and abolition abroad and rebellion at home made black status more vulnerable. Serious servile insurrections in the Spanish, British, and French West Indies in the 1820s, as well as liberal uprisings in Europe and Latin America, laid the groundwork for southern apprehension.[42] These fears were confirmed in southern eyes by the exposure of Denmark Vesey's organized rebellion in Charleston in 1822. Vesey used both African and Christian beliefs and practices to inspire his followers and showed that literacy could be an inspiration for revolt. One of Vesey's recruits testified that Vesey quoted Bible passages on the deliverance of the Children of Israel from Egypt, invited slaves to challenge white preachers about key Bible verses, and incited violence by reading "from the Bible where God commanded, that all should be cut off, both men, women, and children." Believing that if the cunningly devised scheme had not been exposed, most of Charleston's whites might have been wiped out, the city's leaders cracked down on Charleston blacks. They disbanded the African Methodist Church, where Vesey had occasionally preached and which had served as the center for the conspiracy. They discouraged all debate and discussion over slavery, emancipation, and rebellion, even among whites, and tried to suppress schools for blacks. A few began to agitate for laws banning the teaching of blacks to read.[43]

Another external force in shaping southern defensiveness on this issue was the effect of the British emancipation movement. While American abolitionism had not yet reached a peak in the 1820s, British abolitionism had. Letter and pamphlet campaigns advocating emancipation in the British West Indies intensified after 1824. Many of these appeals had a religious base, and the dissenting or popular churches were particularly active in the campaign. Southerners were quite aware of this movement and of black British seamen who might possibly bring this literature onshore.[44]

British abolitionist literature, however, was mild compared to explosive pamphlets written by African-Americans in the late 1820s. In February of 1829, a pamphlet written by Robert Alexander Young, a New York free black, appeared. Young's *Ethiopian Manifesto, Issued in Defense of the Blackman's Rights, in the Scale of Universal Freedom*, leaned strongly on Old Testament prophecies. Young warned slaveowners of impending destruction and appealed to blacks of all nations to prepare for the revelation of God's judgment. From an "instructive book," he foresaw the appearance of a Black Messiah, a leader who would call slaves to freedom or to race suicide in preference to slavery.[45]

Later in the same year, David Walker's more powerful and more widely distributed *Appeal to the Colored Citizens of the World* appeared. Walker, a North Carolina free Negro, son of a slave father, had moved to Boston, learned to read and write, and became active in abolition circles. His *Appeal*, which he published at his own expense, called for African-Americans, free and slave, to take direct and violent action to change their condition. Like Young, Walker based his *Appeal* on the Old Testament and his use of religious imagery was particularly powerful. God's judgment on white America would be like the destructions which the Lord brought upon Egypt "in consequence of the oppression and consequent groans of the oppressed—of the hundreds and thousands of Egyptians whom God hurled into the Red Sea for afflicting his people in their land." He called on blacks to "prepare the way of the Lord" by throwing off the yoke of slavery.[46]

The power of Walker's words must have disturbed even Bostonians. Walker was found dead near his shop six months after the first printing of his *Appeal*. In the South, his essay was the evidence most often quoted to prove that slaves could not be allowed to read. White Southerners anxiously traced the progress of Walker's pamphlet through their region and rumors of rebellion abounded from 1829 to 1831. A suspected conspiracy in Georgetown, South Carolina, resulted in several hangings and disastrous fires in Augusta and Savannah prompted the Georgia governor to prepare a defense against armed revolt. Two supposed conspiracies were reported in the New Orleans vicinity in 1830 and two companies of infantry were sent to the city in the spring of 1831. The governor sent arms and ammunition to assuage nervous white residents in Virginia counties in 1829. Isolated outbreaks were also reported in 1829 and 1830 in Maryland, North Carolina, and Tennessee.[47]

Fears and rumors were confirmed in August of 1831 in Southampton County, Virginia, when the Nat Turner rebellion left sixty-one white men, women and children dead. Nat Turner seemed to justify centuries of slaveowner suspicions. He could read and write and he used his knowledge of the Bible to inspire his followers to carry out what he believed to be the will of God, quoting the Old Testament as he directed retribution against slaveholding families.[48] Brutal repression of African-Americans following the Turner revolt was at its height when news came from Jamaica that blacks had erupted in a rebellion which was led by Sam Sharpe, a black Sunday school teacher. The revolt was widely blamed on dissenting missionaries and was therefore termed the "Baptist War." The following year, 1833, the English emancipated West Indies slaves. The British example was clear to both slaveholders and abolitionists: first discussion of slavery, then evangelization and literacy for the slaves, followed by slave rebellion and finally emancipation.[49]

The Young and Walker pamphlets, Turner rebellion, Baptist War, and British emancipation pushed white Southerners into enacting a wave of repressive legislation. Georgia in 1829 provided fines, whipping, or imprisonment for anyone teaching slaves or free blacks to read or write. In 1830 a provision of the Louisiana slave code stated "that all persons who shall teach, or permit or cause to be taught, any slave in this State to read or write, shall be imprisoned not less than one or more than 12 months." North Carolina also forbade teaching or giving books to slaves in an 1830 law, since such teaching "has a tendency to excite dissatisfaction in their minds and produce insurrection. . . ." In its 1830–31 legislative session, Virginia provided penalites for whites who assembled with Negroes to teach reading or writing, or who taught any slave for pay. After Nat Turner, Virginians also prohibited preaching by slaves and free Negroes. Alabama also prohibited, under fine, the attempt to teach any slave or free person of color to spell, read, or write.[50] South Carolina's law restricting black literacy, though not passed until several years after the others in 1834, was the most sweeping and will be detailed in the next chapter.

The agitated atmosphere in which these laws were passed can be seen in accounts of the Alabama legislature's session held during the Jamaican "Baptist War." According to legend, the legislature was filled with rumors; it was said that the Jamaican slaves were devastating the country and massacring women and children. The legislature reacted by practically forbidding assembly or preaching by blacks. It also barred the further introduction of slaves into the state, but this was later modified.[51]

Revolts or suspected revolts, fear, resulting summary trials and executions, and harsher slave codes are not of themselves unusual, of course, among slave societies. Every lawmaking body in a slave society has chosen self-preservation over concern for the slave's personal rights when a conflict between the two seemed even remotely possible, and harsher laws tended to be passed as the aftermath of insurrections or suspected conspiracies. The distinctive aspect of the southern reaction from 1829 to 1834 was the stress on religion and literacy as a major cause for the revolts. Denmark Vesey, David Walker, and Nat Turner were all called "preachers" in the fear-filled literature of the South. Even the most idealistic reformer was hard put to make a case for teaching slaves to read in those years. As a South Carolinian put it, there could be no mass literacy in the South "until man can eat of the tree of knowledge and not know evil." He insisted that bans on black literacy would have to continue "until those of our negroes who are taught to read the Bible, shall be unable to read Walker's pamphlet."[52]

The sweeping extent of these laws has been exaggerated, however. Laws banning the teaching of slaves were only in effect in four states for the entire period from the 1830s to 1865: Virginia, North and South Carolina, and Georgia. Virginia's law prohibited assemblies of slaves for learning, but individual Virginia slaveowners could legally teach their own slaves. Two other southern states passed literacy restriction laws in the

1830s but did not maintain them as part of legal codes. Alabama's restriction on teaching slaves, passed in 1832, appeared in its digest of laws in 1848, but not in its legal code in 1852. Similarly, Louisiana's law fining or imprisoning "all persons who shall teach any slave" to read or write, passed in 1830, did not form part of its 1856 revised Black Code, though other provisions of the same act did. In other southern states restrictions on slave movement did not include prohibitions on literacy. Mississippi revised its slave code in 1831 to prohibit blacks from exercising functions of ministers but did not ban reading. Other states, including Maryland and Missouri, barred public assemblages of blacks for religious or education purposes but did not penalize persons teaching individual slaves or free blacks to read or write.[53]

The impact of these state laws is debatable. Judicial comments imply that they were seldom taken seriously by the courts. For example, in 1850 a South Carolina judge explained that the 1740 slave code which was the basis for many of that state's restrictions on slavery "was enacted soon after a violent, barbarous, and somewhat bloody servile outbreak at Stono. Not a few of its provisions took their hue from the exigency of the occasion. . . ." He then implied that "it would seem simply ridiculous" to apply this law to the letter in order to insure the safety of the state.[54]

A search of judicial decisions on slavery issues finds little to support the idea that those illegally teaching slaves to read were prosecuted. Even the single well-known case of such a prosecution indicates that few were ever brought to trial. Mrs. Margaret Douglass, a poor white seamstress in Norfolk, was jailed for one month for teaching slaves in that city. In her defense, Douglass protested that the law against teaching slaves "was violated daily and hourly by those who were regarded as leaders in society, morals and in religion." She called as reluctant witnesses, listed by name, numerous Norfolk citizens who taught blacks in the Christ Church Sunday School. Her defense did her no good and the exposure of these violations probably hurt her case. No prosecutions of upstanding Norfolk citizens resulted from her accusations.[55]

There were indeed reprisals against some who taught slaves to read or allowed them to learn, but these were not restricted to states in which teaching was illegal.[56] The following chapters will show that slave learning and teaching went on in all southern states, regardless of the legal penalties. Restrictions ran counter to the centuries-old tradition that the word of God should be accessible to all people and that Bible literacy would promote order, decorum, and morality. This tradition was reinforced in the nineteenth century by white southern churchmen who, influenced by the spirit of reform but accepting accomodation to the slave system, sought to reconcile both by fashioning a white-dominated mission to slaves. They preached the language of accommodation and stressed the importance of religion as social control. As white leaders of the Baptist and Episcopal churches in Charleston declared after the Vesey affair, African-Americans should still be allowed in Charleston churches because "religion was one the best Securities we have to the domestic Peace & Safety of the State." The best way to avoid danger was not to take away the Bible from the Negroes, but to "take Measures for bringing them to a more full & just acquaintance" with religion through letting them read the Bible.[57]

White southern reformers also joined their appeal to support slave missions with a claim for slavery as a "positive good." Prominent South Carolinian Charles Cotesworth Pinckney, in advocating a southernwide Christian crusade to evangelize slaves in 1829, combined his appeal with an incredibly sanguine view of the American slave system and refused to admit "that slavery, as it exists here, is a greater or more unusual evil than befalls the poor in general." He promised that religious training would make Negroes better servants—less reluctant to work, less likely to feign sickness, better producers, and better contented. Christian slaves would be "more anxious to promote the owner's welfare," so there would be fewer thefts and falsehoods, and a resulting decrease in the necessity for punishment. As proof, Pinckney referred to a Georgia plantation in which the owner combined superior management with a plan for religious instruction for his slaves, with the result that "the crops are invariably the best in the neighborhood."[58]

Not all white southern mission advocates were this pragmatic; some were idealistic reformers. Charles Colcock Jones, for example, embraced reformist concerns from prohibition to women's rights to the rights of the Georgia Cherokees, and had grave doubts about slavery. As a missionary to slaves and as a slaveowner himself, however, he worked within the system. By 1834 his able organizing had created a Presbyterian and Baptist mission to blacks in coastal Georgia. Similar ventures in

South Carolina combined Methodist preachers with Episcopal financial support. Methodists aggressively established plantation and city missions. Jones and others wrote catechisms to be used specifically for slave instruction, and editors of church periodicals popularized the mission campaign with favorable notices.[59]

The slave mission was never as visible as some national benevolent movements since it was never organized on a southern-wide basis. It was conducted mainly within denominations and promoted by a handful of religious leaders. It still had a wide-ranging impact. The statistics at the end of the antebellum era indicating that one in seven southern blacks claimed a church membership is related to the mission movement. Another result was a barrage of publicity, in sermons, tracts, and church magazines, which pressed the message upon white Southerners that religion should not be withheld from the slave.[60] The influence of this message on individuals—who were therefore restrained from banning black churches, or were persuaded to teach their household slaves to read, or to close their eyes to this accomplishment—was pervasive.

While Pinckney and missionaries like Charles Colcock Jones promised that the slaves could be evangelized by "oral instruction" only, this promise was observed in the breach as often as not. Missionaries to the slaves and preachers sympathetic to the mission cause quietly promoted the right of slaves to learn to read the Bible and taught blacks themselves. Even Jones gave books to a literate slave studying the ministry, wrote a catechism which missionaries used to teach reading, and implied his approval for those slaveowners who did want to teach the Bible to their slaves. Also, some slaves on the Jones plantations "somehow" learned to read.[61] If the need for everyone to read the Bible was a masked message within the slave mission appeal, it did still exist, as the following chapters will indicate. The slave mission planted unease in white consciences which could be used by African-Americans as they found ways in which they could learn to read—through teaching each other, through persuading the whites around them to teach them, and through trickery. Often they capitalized on the guilt of whites who knew that withholding literacy from black people was counter to religious morality and also counter to the stated American doctrines of equality and the value of learning.

Chapter Two

■

South Carolina: Repression and Protest

OF ALL THE SOUTHERN STATES WHICH RESTRICTED black literacy, South Carolina passed the harshest law against teaching slaves or even free blacks to read or write. Paradoxically, some white South Carolinians were also the most vocal in opposition to the idea of restricting black access to the printed word. From 1832 to 1835 literacy restriction became intertwined with political factionalism and the nullification fight: nullifiers led the fight to restrict slave literacy, finally successful in 1834, while unionists opposed such legislation. The explosive political issues ignited mob action in 1835 in which abolitionist literature was burned and the Catholic Church's school for blacks was threatened. As a result, black schools were closed in a city which had a long tradition of black education, and Charleston's most promising young black teacher, Daniel Payne, had to go into exile. But the nullifiers and the mobs were not the final arbiters in South Carolina, any more than repressive legislation ended slave learning elsewhere in the South. Prominent South Carolinians spoke out against the state's literacy law, a revived missionary movement subverted it, and a group of upcountry Presbyterians fashioned coherent arguments to the state legislature for its abolishment.

South Carolina's contradictions and its ideological leadership among whites in the South focused unusual attention on events in the state and particularly in Charleston. The city presented in microcosm the contradictions in American slavery and in the question of slave learning. Charleston's early English settlers, including Eliza Pinckney and Alexander Garden, had established a tradition of teaching free blacks and slaves to read the Bible, founding schools for them, and holding black worship services.[1] The Charleston Bible Society had aided religion for slaves for decades, and the city's Episcopal bishops proudly counted black worshippers in their finest churches as proof of their paternalism and catholicity.[2]

Charleston had attracted a group of active, intelligent clergymen who served as spokesmen for white southern religion in the mid-1830s, including many who were particularly interested in religion for African-Americans. William Capers, superintendent of the Methodist mission to the slaves; Baptist Basil Manly; Lutheran John Bachman; and Presbyterian Benjamin Palmer had pioneered in black religious classes, missions and catechisms for slaves. Nathaniel Bowen, Episcopal bishop, had written a ringing defense of religious rights for blacks and was supported in his argument by prominent planters and politicians, including Christopher Gadsden of St. Philip's Church, Charles Cotesworth Pinckney, and Stephen Elliott.[3]

Most Charleston African-Americans conducted their own worship, however. The city's sizeable free black and slave population had supported one of the biggest African Methodist Episcopal churches in the nation until the early 1820s. Even after whites forced it and other independent black churches to close, African-Americans were an important component of Charleston church activity. Thousands of black people belonged to the city's Methodist congregations, and Baptists counted hundreds of black members in the city and neighboring countryside.[4] Charleston's black community was also known for the quantity and quality of its schools in comparison to those of other southern cities. Free mulatto emigrants from the West Indies had established schools for their own children and for the poor. Black church groups and private teachers also conducted day schools and Sunday schools.[5]

Charleston blacks saw the city quite differently from whites, and they sneered that "the Almighty made Charleston on Saturday night, when he was weary, and in a great hurry."[6] With its thousands of slaves and its belligerent proslavery spokesmen, the city presented in microcosm the worst aspects of southern slave society as well as some of its best traditions of patriarchalism. The state's harsh slave code and violent public rhetoric reflected both its Barbadian heritage and a long memory of Santo Domingo, Gabriel, and Denmark Vesey. After the Vesey trials, city authorities had not only disbanded the black churches but also enforced, though only temporarily, city ordinances against teaching African-Americans to read. White Charlestonians had been the quickest and loudest to defend the slave system in the Missouri debates, to see potential dangers in the American Colonization Society, and to predict grave consequences from emancipation and abolition in Latin America and servile insurrections in the West Indies. Depression, economic decline, and the nullification controversy had heightened Charlestonians' sense of isolation from the North by the early 1830s.[7]

Curiously, after the wave of legislation repressing slave literacy which swept through other southern states in the late 1820s and early 1830s, South Carolina did not immediately renew the bans on teaching slaves to read which it had initiated in 1740 and had renewed in 1800 after its own slave revolts. Blocs of South Carolina voters had emerged who supported the rights of blacks to read and worship. In Charleston, with its thousands of slave workers, whites benefitted from blacks who learned basic reading and calculating skills and thus became more valuable properties. Also, since giving Bibles to slaves and free blacks as a form of charity had a long tradition in the state, banning them would remove the mask of kindly paternalism, which many preferred to preserve, from the slave system. When restrictive legislation did pass in 1834, it was in the wake of a political struggle in the state over nullification and secession.

Whitemarsh Seabrook, Edward Laurens, and many other slaveholders and planters who adopted the title of "fire-eaters" in the nullification battle were not hampered by a sentimental vision of paternalistic slavery. Unlike many prominent unionists, who protected and fostered the freedom to read, write, and worship for slaves and free blacks, these skeptical nullifiers vigorously and vociferously supported the move to curtail these rights, supported by white working class Charlestonians angered by competition form the city's thousands of free and slave black workers.[8] Seabrook led this movement, and had campaigned since 1825 to ban black schools and black literacy in South Carolina.

Fussy and somewhat pedantic, Whitemarsh Seabrook had a reputation as an intellectual in the South Carolina Senate. He was a Sea Islander, Princeton-educated, with extensive cotton holdings on Edisto Island. He was born into *noblesse oblige,* a tradition which led other members of the Seabrook family into humanitarian activities. A cousin, in fact, became an Episcopal missionary to slaves. But Seabrook himself had absorbed neither the romanticism nor the commitment to spiritual values which propelled so many young men of his class into service for humanity. He became a leader in the movement to improve southern plantations through rational management. As part of this rational outlook Seabrook postulated that slaves should be considered not as human beings, but as means of production. In his writings, he recognized that the slaveowner had gained so much political and legal power that the plantation had become almost a closed system, where each planter "exercises in his own person, all the high functions of an unlimited monarch." This power brought with it a grave responsibility: since the "safety of the State materially depends on the manner in which his little government is administered," the "entire duty" of the plantation owner was "to keep his people in strict subordination." The principles of rational management decreed that this be done by positive as well as negative incentives. Seabrook recommended that the planter reward as well as punish as an inducement to good work and that he feed, clothe, and house his slaves well and never overwork them nor punish them in anger. However, he also advised that informers be encouraged and rewarded and that entire slave communities be punished for the transgression of one as a further deterrent.[9] These chilling suggestions were hardly surprising, though, from one who simply did not consider slaves as human beings, but as means of production.

If the goal of the plantation owner was complete control, as Seabrook argued, then the slave had to be kept in ignorance of any knowledge except "that to his owner he is bound by the laws of God and man, and that no human authority can sever the link which unites them." There were two threats to this subordination: literacy and religion, most dangerous when combined. Seabrook had no problem finding recent examples to justify his warning. Denmark Vesey, David Walker, Sam Sharpe, and Nat Turner had all proven his point. As for the argument that Christian slaves should have access to the Bible, Seabrook claimed that anyone who wanted to acquaint the slave with the whole Bible was fit for "a room in the Lunatic Asylum." Despite the sanctions of slavery in the Old and New Testaments, the Bible was full of messages of equality which were irreconcilable with the South's social system. The danger to the system was not only from the enlightened slave, but from the awakened conscience of the slaveowner. Seabrook saw clearly that when the slaveowner began to recognize the slave as a fellow human being in need of salvation and with the same thirst for knowledge as himself, the slaveowner would find it difficult to hold such a person in bondage. This, he pointed out, had been the stated and successful purpose of religious instruction in the West Indies.[10]

According to Seabrook, Carolinian safety required that "a portion of the people of the State should be treated in every place and at all times as a subordinate caste." Claims that "God hath made of one blood all the nations of men" or that "God is no respecter of persons," not to mention the Golden Rule, threatened that safety. The latter claims were the "foundation argument on which the emancipationist purposes to erect the superstructure of his schemes." Seabrook remembered that the Vesey conspirators were "catechists" and so were Nat Turner and Toussaint L'Overture.[11]

Supported by these arguments, Seabrook introduced legislation into the South Carolina legislature in 1833 which would have established criminal penalties for teaching slaves or free persons of color to read or write and would have restricted them in other ways also. This legislation failed to pass in 1833, however. Unionists opposed the bill because nullifiers supported it and because many unionists, including Huguenot descendants Joel Poinsett, James Petigru, and Daniel Huger, stressed the value of religious worship for blacks as a civic and a Christian duty.[12] Other Southerners also refused to accept Seabrook's conclusions. They shied away from the naked economic justification of slavery which he so forcefully presented. Some Southerners refused to ignore the spiritual and literary needs of other human beings, even slaves. Others clung to the patriarchal image which was their only justification for commanding unfree labor and could not face Seabrook's exposure of patriarchy as a fantasy.

Still others, who saw social and economic arrangements as clearly as Seabrook, countered his logic with logical arguments of their own. The editor of the Charleston *Courier*, for example, pointed out that if schools and teaching were prohibited in the city, blacks would learn anyway, without white control:

> The march of mind will yet progress under the domestic
> roof, and the effort to arrest it will prove worse than fu-
> tile. Let these schools be rather regulated than prohib-
> ited and good may possibly be done—prohibit them and
> that will be done in secrecy which would not otherwise
> shun the light.[13]

However it was Seabrook's fear-filled message which gradually convinced the legislature. In December of 1834 he succeeded in getting his legislation passed which forbade the
teaching of slaves to read or write, which closed schools for free
blacks in Charleston, and which restricted black worship, movement, and assembly. Penalties included fines and imprisonment
for whites, fines and whippings for blacks, and whippings for
slaves. The bill encouraged informers by allowing them to serve
as competent witnesses and promising them half of any fines
collected. In the same session of the South Carolina legislature
in which his bill was passed, Seabrook also replaced Charles
Cotesworth Pinckney as Lieutenant Governor of the State of
South Carolina.[14]

Seabrook had played well on the very real fears of southern
slaveholders and working class whites and had helped set the
stage for more direct action against blacks in the following year.
The year 1835 became of a year of extraordinary group violence
in many sections of the United States. Popular rioting exposed
major social tensions, including ethnic and religious hatreds,
class conflicts, and economic grievances.[15] The South experienced this tumult in the form of plots and riots against abolitionists and African-Americans, posing the question of whether
black people would be allowed to conduct any religion or preserve any rights to literacy at all.

The southern facet of the mass hysteria of 1835 began in the
summer, when rumors surfaced of a supposed conspiracy organized by the outlaw John A. Murrell to stir up an insurrection
among slaves. Many Southerners kept expecting the Murrell
uprising until Christmas and, in fearful anticipation, lynched
suspected white abolitionists and blacks for "seditious activity."
They also envisioned possible rebellions among mine workers
armed with pickaxes in Virginia and Georgia and among slave
gangs at the Tennessee Iron Works.[16]

White Southerners' greatest apprehension in 1835, though,
was prompted by the increased militance of northern abolitionists that year. After the British Emancipation Act of 1834,

William Lloyd Garrison's American Anti-Slavery Society took on new life and declared that it would organize abolition auxiliaries wherever possible, even in the South. Its members vowed to send agents everywhere, regardless of regional sentiments, to purify the churches from the evils of slavery and to circulate "unsparingly and extensively" antislavery tracts and periodicals.[17] The results of this latter vow were magnified by southern authorities who fearfully traced the movement of a few copies of the *American Anti-Slavery Reporter,* the *Emancipator, Slaves' Friend, Anti-Slavery Record, Human Rights,* and the *Liberator* through the cities of Norfolk, Mobile, Savannah, Nashville, and Enfield, Georgia. Some legislatures tried to further limit "incendiary" distribution of the literature within their states,[18] but white residents of Charleston took more direct action one hot summer night, when southern fears of the consequences of the abolition movement climaxed in mob violence.

The Anti-Slavery Society's dispensing of abolitionist literature in the South touched a particular nerve in Charleston because of the Seabrook group's successful campaign to highlight the dangers of literacy and religion. White Carolinians, warned of the dire consequences should literate blacks come in contact with words of abolition and emancipation, were determined to act. When a steamer docked in Charleston containing copies of the *Anti-Slavery Record,* the *Emancipator,* and the *Slaves' Friend,* hundreds of white Charlestonians, a mob supported by "most respectable men of both parties," met on the hot night of July 29, 1835, stormed the post office, and publicly burned the abolitionist papers.[19]

Studies of this well-known incident have concentrated on its impact on sectionalism, the slavery debate in Congress, and its challenge to federal authority as represented by the United States Postal Service. But the aftermath of the initial event, less well known, is also significant for its impact on black education and religion. After burning the abolitionist papers, the crowd turned to another target of suspicion and fear. Some members headed for the Catholic seminary to lynch Bishop England, destroy the cathedral, and demolish the free school the bishop had just begun.[20]

Bishop John England provoked public irritation for several reasons: he represented "popery" in an anti-Catholic age and had just invited the Ursulines to set up a convent in Charleston, reminding many of the salacious revelations of convent life promoted in the popular press. In addition, England was under suspicion by those who shared Seabrook's way of thinking because he was known for his work in converting, baptizing, and ministering to slaves in his diocese. Even more controversially, England had recently served as papal legate to the black government in Haiti, a service he had found hard to explain in Charleston. Finally, England had begun a school for free blacks which had already attracted eighty students in the two months it had been in operation.[21] Even though England publicly supported slavery, deplored abolitionist interference, and approved the storming of the post office, he was a useful target for violence after the crowd had finished destroying the antislavery pamphlets.

When the crowd first gathered at the Catholic seminary, all England had to protect him were the Irish and French branches of the city militia. But the mob, though unable to burn the buildings and lynch the bishop, refused to disperse. Prominent citizens became concerned. A public assembly replaced regular city government with an emergency committee. "Several of the most respectable citizens of all religions" joined the Catholics protecting England, and members of the Charleston clergy moved in to work out a compromise.[22]

Charleston's Protestant clergymen had had to fight opposition and reluctance to black religion and literacy before. Even though they railed against Catholicism from almost every pulpit, the ministers were just as interested as England in protecting religious institutions from mob violence and in steering popular attention away from the dangerous topic of educated Christian blacks, so they worked out a plan with England. The entire city militia would protect his church and seminary, but England was asked by a "respectable committee" to close his black school. The bishop reluctantly agreed, but only if other churches also closed their schools for blacks. The churchmen acquiesced and closed their schools for a time, making a concession to divert attention from the whole subject of religious and educational rights for blacks. The city remained so tense, however, that extralegal government lasted for two more weeks.[23]

It was clear by 1835 that not only the religious leaders' efforts to teach slaves but all of black education and religion in the South was threatened by demagoguery, restrictive legislation, lack of financial support, subtle threat, and overt violence. Suspicious of religious intentions, aware that the Anti-Slavery Society had pledged to use the pulpit as well as the press as its tool, conscious of those implications in the Christian message which would inspire revolt, white Southerners discouraged schools and religious activities for slaves more vigorously than ever. Presbyterian missionary to the slaves Charles Colcock Jones recalled that in the mid-1830s "it was considered best to disband schools and discontinue meetings, at least for a season; the formation of societies and the action of ecclesiastical bodies, in some degree ceased . . . every movement touching the improvement of the Negroes was watched with jealousy."[24] A Mississippi preacher recalled that "a shade of suspicion, more or less, [lay] on every southern itinerant Methodist preacher, which greatly interfered with our missions to the slaves, and in many instances deprived us entirely of access to them." The number of missionaries who could be supported financially by the Methodist mission dropped.[25]

Charles Colcock Jones left mission work for two years. The South lost other evangelists for good. Not only southern Quakers but Methodists, Baptists, and Presbyterians who could no longer live with slavery had left for the Old Northwest states in the early decades of the nineteenth century. In the 1820s and 1830s southern missionary emigrants, including John Rankin of Tennessee, James Gilliland of South Carolina, and Samuel Crothers of Kentucky made Chillicothe, Ohio, a strong anti-slavery center.[26]

James Birney's career shows the dilemmas and options taken by some uneasy religious leaders. As a slaveowner from an aristocratic Kentucky family, he had tried to make his compromise with slavery as an agent for the American Colonization Society (ACS). But Birney became more and more discouraged about the future of the ACS in the South. In 1833 he wrote a series of essays on colonization which led him to the conclusion that blacks could not be held indefinitely in subjection. If they were oppressed, they revolted; if they were kindly treated and taught to read, they imbibed ideas about liberty and equality. Therefore, slavery could not last in the United States. In the spring of 1834, Birney freed his slaves, gave them back wages for their previous labor, and went to the north to begin a career as an abolitionist.[27]

Most southern evangelists stayed, however, and searched for ways to respond to the hostility surrounding them. A handful of

Protestants in border state Kentucky explored the possibility of a gradual emancipation plan to be effected after slaves had first been prepared for liberation through literacy and religious training.[28] But Deep South ministers did not have this option. They united instead in repudiating the abolitionists. Even those evangelists who were dubious about supporting the slave system, or privately condemned it, saw the abolitionists attacking them as Southerners and threatening their access to the slaves. White southern ministers and slaveowners who were educated in the North, had many northern friends and relatives, and admired much of northern life, took on a newly defensive tone about the virtues of the South in the 1830s. White Catholics, Episcopalians, Lutherans, Methodists, Presbyterians, and Baptists raged officially and privately against the "mad and fanatical spirit of abolition" which threatened "the liberty and peace of our Southern country." At the same time ministers tried to link their attack to protection of blacks; they pleaded with legislatures "not to curtail or restrict the religious privileges of [blacks] nor to adopt any measures with respect to the colored people, which may seem to have been dictated, either by retaliation on the innocent, or by suspicion and dread." These mainstream church leaders also responded with appeasement. Calls for support for black religion by prominent religious spokesmen after 1835 contained fewer calls for heroic exertions on the part of the slaveholders and more emphasis on the benefits of Christianity as the "surest safeguard of every interest they could desire to protect," and assurances that the master would find the properly instructed Christian slave "the most industrious, honest, submissive, and well ordered of his charge."[29]

White ministers in the Deep South did not openly oppose the ban on teaching blacks to read the Bible and insisted that they could be catechized effectively through oral instruction, though many surreptitiously taught them or winked at the practice within their churches. For example, Virginia Episcopal bishop William Meade, who had insisted in earlier years that slaveowners should teach their slaves to read, now suggested *either* teaching to read *or* oral instruction. He still recommended, however, that slaves be supplied reading material: "catechisms, tracts, explanations of select Scriptures, and sermons adapted to the condition and character of servants." Catechisms written by missionaries for the instruction of slaves were adaptable to use in the teaching of reading and were used in that way, despite the claim that they were written for oral instruction. Most were prepared in simple, clear, short questions and answers, a method also used in primers. Robert Ryland's *Scripture Catechism for the Instruction of Children and Servants,* for example, was recommended by its publishers as "equally well adapted to the instruction of children in families, sabbath schools, and bible classes." Charles Colcock Jones' catechism for slaves, the most popular, was not limited to oral use. A Memphis lawyer gave the book as a reading tool to "one of our Negroes who is studying to be a minister." Missionary John B. Adger translated Jones' catechism into Armenian and used it along with the Bible to teach Armenians how to read. Another missionary translated it into Chinese. After slavery a new edition of A. C. Chambliss' *Catechetical Instructor* was reprinted for use in teaching reading in Sunday schools—with the section on the duties of masters and slaves deleted, of course.[30]

The content of the catechisms emphasized salvation, not subordination, though most did include lengthy sections on duties of slaves to masters—after all, they had to be approved by masters in order to reach the slaves. One of the most widely known catechisms, William Capers' *Catechism for Little Children and for Use on the Missions to the Slaves in South Carolina,* stressed fragility and mortality, humility, obedience, and the afterworld. Bible verses to be memorized emphasized obedience and servitude and forbade the sins of drunkenness, sexual immorality, lying, stealing, and Sabbath-breaking. Capers omitted statements about the equality of master and servant under God, but he was an exception; most catechisms did include some word about the equality of human beings on judgment day.[31]

White missionaries thus accommodated their teaching to the slave system and the mission to slaves revived and expanded after 1835. Increases in numbers of black converts to white churches; black churches and church members; missions to slaves; churches and chapels for slaves; full-time missionaries, white and black; preachers and priests who spent time ministering to the special needs of blacks; and whites who were willing to protect blacks' right to worship indicate the scope of the mission effort.

Some scholars have interpreted this expansion of missions to slaves, when they have recognized it, as the charting of an accommodational course for bringing limited religion to enslaved African-Americans. As Eugene Genovese explains in *Roll, Jor-*

dan, Roll: The World the Slaves Made, "step by step, the several churches embraced the proslavery argument . . . won the trust of the masters and freed themselves to preach the gospel to the slaves."[32] But it was never this clear-cut. First, ministers did not win the trust of the masters: slaveowner suspicion was never far from the surface and periodically exploded into hostility against evangelists and slaves. Furthermore, evangelists never embraced all of the proslavery argument. They did use more of the language of appeasement in addressing slaveholders after 1835. Events of the 1830s had made it clear that if they did not, they would not be allowed to reach the slaves. The southern clergy had no real power, as shown by their helplessness to protect black schools and religion in the mid-1830s. Their response was to try to maintain limited power by adopting a special role in the militant South—a role which has been described as that of a "strategic elite," providing moral standards which reinforced social solidarity.[33] By serving as the conscience of the South, evangelists hoped they could insure their own positions and also maintain their access to slaves and protect the spiritual rights of African-Americans.

The neglected slave filled some white Southerners with guilt; the converted slave was so compelling a goal that missionaries became determined that no one should bar their way to the slaves, even if the church had to compromise with slaveholders to a greater extent than the missionaries themselves would ever have desired. As a Methodist later recalled, "we believed that African slavery would terminate some day and somehow, but we did not believe that opinion any reason why we should let the current generations of negro slaves go down to death and hell without the enlightened and persistent offers of salvation from sin and its eternal consequences through the gospel of the Son of God."[34] Another Methodist defined the missionary's responsibility as to "look upon the blacks *just as we find them,* and ask, 'What shall we do to accomplish for them the greatest possible benefit?' " The answer, of course, was "not to civilize them—not to change their social condition—not to exalt them into citizens or freemen—but to save them. . . . Sweeten their toil—sanctify their lives—hallow their deaths."[35] Convinced that slaves would be lost without salvation, touched by the response of the slaves they did reach, most white evangelists tried to make their peace with the proslavery argument for the sake of the slaves and suffered the crises of conscience and compromise.

Sometimes, however, the limits of their position were brought home to southern white Christians in an almost unbearably personal way. The story of Daniel Payne is a case in point. Payne was a Charleston native of African, English, and Indian ancestry, born into the free colored community of the city. Small, intense, candid, and possessed of "uncommon moral fiber" even as a young man, Payne was guided all his life by a deep devotion to education and religion. His parents were members of the Cumberland Methodist Church, and Payne was converted at eighteen. Orphaned at an early age, with only a few years' formal schooling in a school for free blacks, Payne applied uncommon energies to his goal of self-education. As a teenager he worked as a carpenter's apprentice during the day, then read and studied until midnight and began reading again at 4:00 AM. In this way he taught himself some basic English grammar, geography, Greek, Latin, French, and natural science. He opened his own school when he was nineteen. By 1835 Daniel Payne was offering his black students training in English, botany, and biology.[36]

Payne's scientific curiosity led him to Lutheran minister John Bachman, who showed the young man his own naturalist collection and introduced him to the Bachman family, where, as the impressionable Payne remembered later, they conversed "as freely as though all were of the same color and equal rank."[37] The Bachmans and other members of the Charleston clergy undoubtedly accepted Payne for his own personable and quiet manner, but also for other reasons. A self-taught colored man who learned biology by catching and processing his own specimens was more than a curiosity. As Christians, the white clergy were committed to a belief in the brotherhood of man and descent of all human beings from Adam, and they were defending these beliefs against the challenge of rational and skeptical thought. Bachman, in fact, became deeply involved in refuting Josiah Nott's theories of the separate creation of races.[38]

To Bachman and other white Charleston members of the clergy, Daniel Payne was a "brother" who embodied all the virtues of the Western world with which evangelists and reformers wished to imbue the African and others of the nation's poor: devout belief in Christ, sobriety, eagerness and capacity for hard work, capability for organization, and a reverence for Western learning. Payne personified the potential capabilities of his race in their eyes and provided justification for their cru-

sade to instruct blacks in religion and Western learning. Payne
was invited into homes of other Charleston ministers. He became particularly close to Mary and Jane Palmer and their father Benjamin, a Presbyterian minister who had written a
catechism for slaves. According to Payne, the discussions in the
Palmer home even included, "in whispers," speculations about
the abolition movement in the north.[39]

As a black man, though, albeit free, Payne held no illusions
about southern society—not when he lived in a city whose authorities refused an Episcopal priest's innocent plea for permission to preach at night to free blacks and whose patrollers
whipped black missionaries who had not only preached to plantation slaves, but who had had the temerity to organize a mission to evangelize poor white farmers![40] Payne saw clearly how
slavery damaged the cause of Christianity by exposing slaves to
the hypocrisy of masters who went to church on Sunday and
abused them on Monday or who listened to sermons on adultery
and went home to exercise their sexual dominance over their
female slaves.[41] But Payne was not a racist; he acknowledged
goodness and morality whenever he found it in whites as well
as blacks. While his closest mentors and confidantes were black,
he valued his association with Charleston whites without accepting the reconciliation they had made with slave society.

Inevitably, the ways of power and race relations in antebellum Charleston could not allow Daniel Payne to survive. He believed that the literacy law which Seabrook and other fire-
eaters finally pushed through the legislature in 1834 was
directed specifically against his school, particularly those provisions which levied fines and whippings against free colored persons who continued to teach blacks. Most of the schools in the
Charleston black community continued untouched by the law
until the summer riots of 1835 and resumed operations after.[42]
They were, after all, useful to the city because they trained
black workers in basic skills and provided an orderly outlet for
the talented and ambitious who might otherwise have been
dangerously frustrated. But Payne's school was too much in the
public eye. He had already excited suspicion because of the comparatively rigorous and systematic training he was giving his
pupils. He consulted on possible plans of action with his white
friends and acquaintances, including Palmer, Bachman, William
Capers, Christopher Gadsden, and Theodore Dehon, as well as
his own pastor and his black friend and Methodist class leader,

Samuel Weston. They all agreed with his decision to close his school in the spring of 1835 and "seek a field of usefulness in the free regions of the north."[43]

Closing his school brought bitter grief to Payne and must have forced his white counselors to face harsh truths also. In advising Payne to leave, they were forced to admit that the finest product of their plan for Christian evangelization—the converted, intelligent, civilized black man—had no place in their society, or at least had much more opportunity outside the South. They all tried to smooth his path: Bachman, who expected Payne to become a Lutheran clergyman, gave him letters to Lutherans in New York and Philadelphia. Capers provided him with a general letter of introduction to northern Christians. Palmer furnished introductions to Congregationalists and Gadsden to Episcopal clergymen in New York.[44]

The ministers and their families also tried to help Payne deal with his bitterness in leaving his "hospitable, beautiful, romantic city" and to find reasons which would satisfy him and themselves. Bachman lamented that "a mysterious providence has so ordered it that your usefulness in the profession you have chosen is at an end in your native city," and advised him to "submit to the laws of the land." Palmer was more optimistic that "your door of interesting usefulness in your native State is closed by a providence that orders all things well, only that a wider field elsewhere may afford scope for the exercise of your talents and the influences of your piety." Palmer envisioned Payne as the instrument for black advancement. He advised Payne that as he planned for the future, he should remember his "colored brethren on whom the light of hope begins auspiciously to dawn."[45]

It is easy to scorn the white ministers' use of a "mysterious providence" to explain Payne's tragedy as their refusal to face the enormity of the crimes of their society. From a secular point of view they might better have sought the explanation in the Charleston authorities' need to cater to popular fears and prejudices, the belief that a caste system must be maintained by ignorance, the political ambitions of the Whitemarsh Seabrook group, or in the ministers' own refusal to speak out in defense of Payne or his school. But reactions to an easily identifiable—and no longer present—evil cannot be judged accurately without comparing them to reactions to other social evils, whether they be war, poverty, inequality, injustice, or all the other manifestations of sin. Religious believers have always used their faith to come to some terms with the sinful society of which they are a part, and these terms do not always lead to the direction of confrontation.

According to Clifford Geertz, one of the functions of religion is to explain the world in meaningful terms and to guide the individual in ways of coping with it. But religion's "moral vitality is conceived to lie in the fidelity with which it expresses the fundamental nature of reality." Part of reality is the existence of evil, which cannot be assuaged through consolation alone. One function of religion is to force the believer to recognize evil. No wonder, then, that "over its career religion has probably disturbed men as much as it has cheered them; forced them into a head-on, unblinking confrontation of the fact that they are born to trouble as often as it has enabled them to avoid such a confrontation." The reality of evil is "accepted and characterized positively," and an attitude toward it—"resignation, active opposition, hedonistic escape, self-recrimination and repentance, or a humble plea for mercy—is enjoined as reasonable and proper."[46] The southern white Christian's faith explained—often in terms of a "mysterious providence"—why there were such evils as slavery and directed responses to it: confrontation for some, pragmatic compromise for most, covert resistance or avoidance for others—but faith did not delude the believer into insisting that slavery was not evil. While the proslavery ideology was being fashioned around the doctrine that slavery was a blessing to both the slaveowner and the slave, no serious white religious spokesman who worked closely with slaves ever presented slavery as anything but a sin—a sin because it was a human institution, and like all human institutions, rooted in the dark side of natural law, "one of the natural effects of the primeval curse," as were poverty, sickness, disease, and death.[47] As part of the complexity of the situation, though, even those southern white ministers who taught slaves to read and scolded whites for withholding literacy from them sometimes presented slavery as a blessing in their sermons to slaves. Their zeal to appease slaveowners and their own cultural biases allowed them to ignore the consequences of their recognition of slavery as a sin, in a typically human failure.

There was a distinction in the antebellum South between the proslavery ideology and evangelical religion. The proslavery ideology was linked to religion for African-Americans by the use of Biblical example and metaphor by those who fashioned it, but evangelists to the slaves were not its advocates. If southern churchmen promised that Christian slaves would bring material benefits to the slaveowner, they also warned in no uncertain terms that if the slave "is denied the knowledge of God according to the Scriptures," his condition "is spiritually worse than that even of the savage freedom from which he has been rescued." As a South Carolina Episcopal bishop warned his slaveholder parishioners, "Deny your slaves the privilege of access to the means of Christian knowledge, and you characterize their condition by a moral hopelessness, to which not even the roamer of the wilderness, and the tenant of the forest, are consigned."[48] This was not the language of appeasement.

The gap between an oppressive society and Christian morality was hardest to bridge for the most thoughtful and devout. The more deeply and pervasively the white Southerner—urban slaveowner, planter's wife, missionary, or churchman—believed the Christian message to be "really real," in Geertz' term, the more trouble he or she had with the proslavery ideology. "Real" white Christians lived within the slave society, and learned to deal with it, and were sometimes broken by the compromises and contradictions inherent in its conflicts, but the fact that they did not oppose their society openly nor flee from it does not mean that they wholeheartedly accepted all its precepts.[49]

Daniel Payne understood this. When he closed his school and his "heart seemed ready to bust with grief," and when he was ready to deny God "or to blaspheme his holy name for permitting one race to grind another to powder," he saw his white friends as "God's angels," sent to strengthen him in his time of trial. He particularly treasured Mary and Jane Palmer's letters of consolation and clung to Mary's assurances that "when you leave the land of your nativity you will carry with you the respect and esteem of the *wise* and the *good*," and he was heartened by her prayer that God "might open before you an extensive field of usefulness, so that you may have reason to bless his holy name for causing light to spring out of present darkness. . . ." In his memoirs, written more than fifty years later, Payne judged many whites harshly, but he still remembered his old friends from the white Charleston churches with gratitude and love.[50]

In the years after Daniel Payne's exile from Charleston, black schools resumed in Charleston, tacitly ignored by the law. In addition to allowing the schools to operate, a few white South

Carolinians continued to show their discontent with the law banning black literacy in other ways. Some insisted that the law was not and could not be obeyed. Others protested openly against the laws themselves. John B. Adger, Presbyterian missionary to slaves in Charleston, called the law "useless," since it was so often violated, and "hurtful," since it threw an obstacle in the way of religious instruction.[51] Judge John Belton O'Neall, South Carolina Baptist, moderate unionist and advocate of slave missions, proclaimed in his recommended radical restructuring of the entire southern slave code that the law barring slave literacy which "grew out of a feverish state of excitement," should be repealed:

> When we reflect, as Christians, how can we justify it, that a slave is not to be permitted to read the Bible? It is in vain to say there is danger in it. The best slaves in the state are those who can and do read the Scriptures. Again, who is it that teach your slaves to read? It generally is done by the children of the owners. Who would tolerate an indictment against his son or daughter for teaching a favorite slave to read? Such laws look to me as rather cowardly. It seems as if we were afraid of our slaves. Such a feeling is unworthy of a Carolina master.[52]

The strongest and broadest southern white protest against South Carolina's restrictive literacy law, however, came from outside Charleston. In November of 1838, thirty-six "citizens of Chester" petitioned the South Carolina legislature to repeal that part of the 1834 law which prohibited the teaching of slaves to read. Their petition was followed four years later, November 1842, by a similar petition from forty-one "sundry citizens of Sumter." Sixty-two Abbeville petitioners joined their protest against the 1834 law. The Abbeville signers declared that they delayed presenting their petition "until that excitement, which was the ostensible ground for enacting the law forbidding servants to be taught to read, should have somewhat subsided." They concluded that "this excitement has in a good degree abated, and we now come forward with our petition."[53]

The strong protests by the upcountry petitioners suggest that many whites disobeyed the restrictive literacy law out of passionate religious conviction. Their well-reasoned arguments for repeal of the law indicate some of the other reasons why whites violated literacy laws and custom to teach slaves.

The history of the communities which the petitioners represented helps explain the vigor of their protests. The upcountry Piedmont and central areas where Abbeville, Chester, and Sumter districts were located had been settled by Ulster Scots and French Huguenots. The Scotch-Irish influence was predominant in the names of the petitioners and all three districts were strongly Presbyterian.[54] Therefore, residents of all three districts came from a tradition which maintained a high regard for literacy and for religious freedom. Ministers in the Piedmont churches had included serious questioners of the morality of slavery.

The economy of the upcountry was more diversified than that of the lowcountry districts around Charleston: production of cotton was important but so was livestock, corn, lumber, flour, wagons and boots. However, cotton production was overtaking other agriculture by the 1830s. The volume of cotton produced surpassed that of most lowcountry districts. Slaveholding was correspondingly increasing and blacks outnumbered whites in all three districts.[55] Although slaveholding increased in importance, upcountry plantations had a different character from those of the lowcountry; because the area was healthier, more upcountry slaveholders were year-round residents and slaves were healthier and more prolific.

Residents in Abbeville, Chester, and Sumter had been divided on the unionist-nullifier question in the early 1830s. Some were apprehensive about possible slave uprisings. Slaves had supposedly been hung in Abbeville after Nat Turner's revolt. Residents of Abbeville asked a minister to leave in 1838 because they suspected from some of his statements that he disapproved of slavery.[56] Still, upcountry legislators had rejected the bill to ban literacy for blacks the first time Seabrook brought it to a vote in 1833, and the petitioners from Abbeville, Chester, and Sumter undoubtedly had some community support when they made a public protest against the restrictiveness of the literacy law after it was passed.[57]

The petitioners all focused their protest on the part of the 1834 law which prohibited slaves from being taught to read. Their petitions centered around what they saw as the four major defects in the law. First. Abbeville petitioners argued strongly that the law was unconstitutional and an infringement of the right of conscience., since it was the duty of Christians to teach all under their control, slaves as well as others, to read the word of God. The law violated the eighth article of the South Carolina constitution, which guaranteed "the free exercise of religious profession and worship . . . to all mankind." Slaves were "a part of mankind: they [had] immortal souls, and surely to them the constitution [allowed] the free exercise of the enjoyment of religious profession and worship":

> We hold it to be one of the chief privileges and enjoyments of our religious profession and worship, to be permitted to search the Scriptures for ourselves, and we consider that law which robs our servants of this enjoyment to be a violation of the Constitution.[58]

Therefore, the law forbidding slaves to read was "an unwarrantable interference of the State in church affairs." It was the duty of the church to see that all church members read and obeyed the word of God, and many slaves were church members. However, according to the law, the Christian who would presume to teach a black church member to read the Bible would be heavily fined and imprisoned. "This we consider persecution for conscience sake; and in this matter we hold that the State is intruding on the rights and principles of the church."[59]

Second, the law was unchristian. Sumter petitioners, like the others, assumed that reading the Bible was intrinsic to Christian life and salvation and asked "if it be not an inconsistency in a government professing to be Christian, to suffer any portion of her citizens to say, with impunity, that the truths of the Bible shall not be told to those for whom Christ died." Abbeville citizens explained that "oral instruction once in seven days, or once a month . . . is not sufficient to prepare servants to meet their God." If the master, with learning and opportunities, is often poorly prepared to meet his Maker, "how . . . can an ignorant man, such as our servants are, be prepared for the Eternal state by hearing a sermon or a lecture once a week, much of which they do not understand?" They asked the right "to teach our servants to read, with so much fluency and correctness, that they will be able to peruse the word of God and other religious books with pleasure and profit to their souls." Petitioners also called attention to the inconsistency between advocating missions to distant lands "to enlighten and save the benighted Heathen," but at the same time enacting laws "excluding that glorious light from a portion of our own households—from our servants, many of them dear to us from other than mercenary considerations." Sumter petitioners asked simply but tellingly "that the Heathen in your own borders should be placed upon an equal footing with the Heathen in that land whence they originally came." They further demanded "that men, under the protection of your laws, shall not have the power of forbidding the word of God to be proclaimed to any portion of our people."[60]

The petitioners' third argument was that the law was unwise. They attacked its supposed purpose of self-defense against slave uprising as impracticable, since hundreds of slaves could already read and it was impossible for masters to prevent them. Also, literacy itself could be a useful instrument of control. Chester petitioners doubted the assumption "that intelligence is more productive of dangerous insurrections than ignorance" and affirmed "that the State has less to fear, even from general intelligence among the slaves (for which we are not pleading) than that ignorance which seems to be contemplated by the law in question, which would make our servants the fit dupes of every Nat Turner who might chance to pass along." Abbeville citizens argued that religion promoted stability:

> Experience fully proves that those servants who live in religious families and have been taught to read and understand their duty from the word of God, are, as in a general thing, much more trusty in every respect, than those servants who souls have been entirely neglected. Wherever men are destitute of moral principles they are dangerous members of Society. But where are those moral principles to be obtained, calculated to render a man safe and trusty, either as a servant or a citizen, unless it be from the work of God?[61]

Sumter petitioners recognized "the morbid sensibility which has possession of the public mind on the subject of slavery in consequence of the mad and unfortunate measures adopted by our northern neighbours, in their 'zeal without knowledge' " but argued that "the effectual mode of sustaining your system [of slavery] is not by shutting your eyes to existing evils: but rather by removing those evils, whenever they can, with safety be applied." Chester petitioners scornfully asked, "does chivalrous South Carolina quail before gangs of cowardly Africans with a Bible in their hands? Let it not be said."[62]

The last argument made by the petitioners was that the law was ineffectual. Chester petitioners argued that the law "could not be enforced—a Jury could not be made to see how the teaching a slave to read the Bible, or any book strictly religious in the Christian's sense, could jeopardize any interest human or divine." Since "multitudes of citizens . . . believe the law in question to invade the rights of conscience, and as such to be unconstitutional . . . it is by no means unusual to hear good citizens say 'I am prepared to disrespect such a law.' "[63] Abbeville petitioners concluded that "many of the best citizens in the state felt themselves under strong obligations to teach their servants to read the Bible before the law as enacted against it: and there may be many yet, who feel these obligations unimpaired."[64]

In these petitions, scores of upcountry white Carolinians had declared their allegiance to a "higher law" than that of their state. Their petitions were a courageous and unpopular act in a time of political agitation and fear. Their objections to the literacy law were echoed publicly by a few prominent South Carolinians and were to be followed in 1854 by a passionate public protest by a young Abbeville lawyer, to be treated in detail below.

There was a strong implication in their petitions that these upcountry protesters intended to violate the law and teach slaves to read. Evidence suggests that some of them did: in an examination of religious instruction for slaves conducted in 1845, a Presbyterian minister in Chester reported that of the 213 slaves belonging to members of his congregation, twenty-three were members of his church and almost all of them could read. Also, when they were interviewed after slavery some former South Carolina upcountry slaves recalled being taught to read by their owners. Literacy was valued by former slaves in the upcountry region of South Carolina; just after the war, blacks in that area were among the first to establish their own schools, a further evidence that the esteem for literacy and learning which led to white protests was at least equally shared by upcountry African-Americans.[65]

Chapter Three

■

Slave Testimony: "We Slipped and Learned to Read"

THOMAS JOHNSON, AN ENSLAVED AFRICAN-AMERICAN hired out to work in a Richmond tobacco factory, was intelligent, diligent, and resourceful. At twenty-one he had become a Christian convert as a result of the Great Revival of 1857. He joined a Richmond Baptist church with his mother and the two of them "went down into the water hand-in-hand," were baptized and "went on [their] way rejoicing." Soon after his conversion, Johnson felt a deep desire to preach the Gospel, but he was faced with two difficulties: he was a slave, and he could not read the Bible, a skill which a preacher was expected to have. His mother had taught him all she knew—the alphabet and numbers to 100—and had paid a free black man fifty cents to tutor him, but the lessons had lasted only a month, and Johnson's owners opposed further learning. He therefore decided it was up to him to gain the skill he needed "by taking advantage of every opportunity to learn all [he] could."[1]

In later years, as a missionary speaker in England, Johnson often told how he accomplished his goal. He secreted an old Bible in his room and pored over it in his spare time, beginning with Genesis and calling out the letters of each word he could not understand: "In the b-e-ginning God c-r-e-a-t-e-d the heaven and the earth." His young master read aloud a chapter from the New Testament every night and Johnson tried to get him to read the same one over and over. When Johnson knew this chapter practically by heart, he recognized the words in the chapter. Then he found identical words elsewhere in the Bible and traced identical syllables of other words. "In this way," he related, "I got to understand a little about the Bible, and at the same time I was learning to spell."[2]

In addition to his desire to preach, Johnson had another motive for wanting to learn to read and write. As soon as he was old enough to understand, his mother had explained to him what it meant to be a slave and the difference between the condition of black people and white people, but told him that if he would learn to read and write then some day he might be able to get his freedom. His ambition was further encouraged when fugitive slave Anthony Burns was returned to jail in Richmond, and Johnson's owner pointed out to him that Burns was in trouble because he had written himself a pass and escaped. Johnson determined to write his own pass to freedom. He stole copies of "nice-looking" block letters from a box in a church and practiced printing them, but found "that the white people did not use the large letters of the Alphabet as I did when writing." So he sent out to learn cursive writing. He saw that his master's youngest son had a copy book, so he bought one for himself and practiced writing the letters over and over.[3]

In his later years as a missionary, Johnson also enjoyed telling groups how he took advantage of his young master in his efforts to learn more. Johnson bought a spelling book but could not understand all of it. At night, while the young master was studying, Johnson would choose some word from his spelling book which he didn't know and challenge the boy to spell it. He would do so and Johnson would exclaim, "Lor's over me, you can spell nice." Then Johnson would go out and spell the word over and over again. He also encouraged the boy to read part of his lesson out loud for Johnson's benefit and Johnson would compliment him and ask, "lor's o'er me, read that again," which the boy often did. Johnson concluded that, by fooling the child, "each week I added a little to my small store of knowledge about the great world in which I lived."[4]

By the time war came to his hometown of Richmond, Johnson could read well enough to understand the newspapers and he was teaching his own class of pupils to read. He also met secretly for Bible study with other Richmond black people who could read. As he recalled later, the chapter they studied most was Daniel 11, whose prophecies they interpreted to predict an ultimate triumph for the northern army over the South.[5]

Thomas Johnson's story, one of hundreds of accounts by African-Americans of their experiences in slavery, makes clear how and why reading and writing were so important to some slaves that they would risk death or mutilation to achieve them. Slave testimony supports Paul Escott's conclusion from his analysis of the 1930s Federal Writers Project interviews with former slaves that the antebellum South "encompassed two worlds, one white and one black, one the master's and one the slave's." Learning to read and write could empower slaves in their battle against the white world. Enslaved African-Americans "saw in their day-to-day experiences—from one generation to the next—that knowledge and information helped one to survive in a hostile environment." Thomas Johnson's story further demonstrates that learning to read and write gave a slave the satisfaction of tricking the white man out of something which was supposed to be withheld from the slave.[6]

Reading and writing, above all, pointed the way to freedom—first of all in the mind and spirit, and often in the body. Slave testimony, therefore, illustrates how acquiring reading and writing skills was an act of resistance against the slave system and an assertion of identity by the literate slave.[7]

Slave recollections also provide insights into the laborious process of learning to read and write under oppressive conditions. Their accounts show that most slaves who learned to read began to read as children, though many adults also learned; that their motives and opportunities for learning were intermittent and that it often took years to gain even rudimentary skills; and that only the occasional slave had a chance to be in a classroom or meet with a trained teacher—though, surprisingly, some did. Most slaves taught themselves by sound and pronunciation, most often with Webster's "blue-back" speller. Writing was harder to learn than reading, and presented the challenge of finding or making writing materials in a mostly rural society which had little use for these tools.

Most slaves who learned to read and write had some relationship with whites which made this possible: they were house slaves or city workers or children who went to school with their playmates. However, some field slaves did learn and many had black teachers. Some learned in Sunday schools run by either blacks or whites. The practice of acquiring reading and writing skills was not limited to the border South or to the cities, as has often been assumed, but went on in the Deep South and in rural areas as well.[8]

Slave accounts also indicate the reasons it will always be hard to measure the extent of literacy among black people in the slave South. A typically ambiguous recollection comes from African Methodist Episcopal Bishop William Heard, who recounted his attendance at a white-controlled Methodist Sunday school in Elberton, Georgia as a ten-year-old slave. Heard admitted that some slaves were literate, but remembered best the prohibitions:

> We did not learn to read nor to write, as it was against the law for any person to teach any slave to read; and any slave caught writing suffered the penalty of having his forefinger cut from his right hand; *yet there were some who could read and write* [italics mine].[9]

Whites were reluctant to teach openly and seldom bragged in print about teaching slaves; where laws were not a discouragement, custom was, and slave narratives include stories of whites who were punished for going against the community's wishes. More common in slave accounts was the knowledge of grim punishments meted out to literate slaves. These deterred some slaves from learning or at least taught them to keep their learning to themselves.

Even former slaves who wrote their own narratives tended to denigrate the possible extent of literacy among blacks. During slavery, their narratives were written in collaboration with abolitionists or for abolition purposes, so they necessarily exaggerated the prohibitions against learning. Frederick Douglass, for example, refused to admit that many slaves could read or that owners would permit them to have Bibles.[10] Those who were prevented from learning while slaves expressed their bitterness openly and volubly for a sympathetic northern audience prepared to value literacy for its spiritual, intrinsic, and practical worth and to be shocked by its prohibition among slaves. Other accounts by former slaves written after freedom focused on the gains made by themselves and other blacks since slavery. They were therefore prone to ignore achievements made before slavery ended.

Another reason the extent of slave literacy has been underestimated is the impact of what Carter Woodson termed the "Reaction" when after 1825 the South fashioned a proslavery argument, stifled antislavery sentiment, and passed restrictive laws against slaves assembling or learning to read. Woodson estimated that black literacy rates declined by half after the 1820s.[11] However, the Federal Writers Project interviews with former slaves, added to the scores of narratives written by former slaves during and after slavery, indicate that more slaves learned to read after 1825 than Woodson could have known about and that the acquisition of literacy skills by southern black people did continue in large numbers after 1825. For example, George Perry, who was born a slave in North Carolina in the 1830s, related that he learned to read in 1842. Perry recollected that by the 1840s the effect of the restrictive literacy laws passed in the 1830s had subsided and that "anxiety to learn and the ability to read rapidly increased among the colored people" after that date.[12] Accounts by former slaves, protests against the laws by southern whites, statements by whites that blacks were being taught to read, and recollections by former slaveowners corroborate this. For example, more than two-thirds of those former slaves who told interviewers for the 1930s Federal Writers Project that they had learned to read and write did so in the decade between 1856 and 1865. Autobiographies and narratives by former slaves also confirm literacy activity in the decades immediately before the Civil War; at least seventy slaves who wrote their own accounts learned to read after 1836.[13]

According to former slaves who wrote their own narratives and autobiographies or who were interviewed by abolitionists or for the Federal Writers Project in the 1930s, some reading and writing took place in every region and every state in the South. Former slaves related that they learned to read, or knew others who did, in border state cities or in the Deep South centers of Savannah and Charleston; in small towns in Virginia, the Carolinas, Kentucky, and Tennessee; on small farms in Maryland, Alabama, and Missouri; big plantations in South Carolina, Mississippi, Florida, and Georgia; and the frontiers of Arkansas and Texas. The slave accounts also show how the passage of restrictive laws influenced but did not halt slave literacy. Slaves and masters were aware of the existence of these laws and even exaggerated their extent. The laws, and extralegal actions where laws were not enforced, convinced whites and blacks to keep quiet about most literacy for slaves. Fear also made some slaves reject learning. Lucinda Washington, a field worker in

Sumter County, Alabama, in the 1850s, for example, refused the opportunity to learn to read. She recalled that "we was taught to read an' write, but mos' of de slaves didn't want to learn. [We] would hide our books under de steps to keep f'um having to study."[14]

Even though laws banning the teaching of slaves were seldom enforced, and were only in effect in four states for the entire period from 1830 to 1865, slaves recognized their symbolic power. Former slaves accurately recalled the existence of such laws in Virginia, North and South Carolina, and Georgia; interestingly, they inaccurately reported similar laws in other states where these laws did not exist. Tab Gross, for example, paid his owner's son to teach him to read in Maryland in 1842. According to Gross, his owner stopped the lessons after three months, not because the owner objected to them, but because it was "an offense against the law of the state to teach a slave to read, for which his son would have been put in prison if found out." This was not actually true in Maryland. Other slaves were convinced that the laws allowed reading but not writing, as reported by Elijah Marrs in Kentucky, where neither reading nor writing were prohibited. On the other hand, Benjamin Russell in South Carolina, insisted that while "we were taught to read, . . . it was against the law to teach a slave to write. The legislature passed an act to that effect." Reading may indeed have been taught in violation of the law in the Chester community where Russell was a slave, but that was not the letter of the law in South Carolina, where both reading and writing were prohibited.[15] The Chester community may have permitted teaching slaves where the law prevented it, but other communities banned the teaching of slaves even when the laws did not forbid it. Some "officious men" visited Moncure Conway's Virginia home upon the rumor that his mother was teaching slaves to read. Owners were in fact allowed to teach their own slaves by law in that state, but Conway's father was a magistrate and wanted to avoid appearance of offense, so the family stopped even Bible lessons for slaves. Charlie Hudson's owner was more stubborn; he aroused community opposition in Georgia in the early 1860s when he agreed to let a white man, Bill Rowsey, come to the plantation and teach his slaves in the ginhouse. For three Sundays school was held; on the fourth Sunday, night riders set a coffin-shaped box in front of the ginhouse with a warning. Whatever the owner's original sentiment had been about slave learning—he had made no effort to teach them himself—the night riders "made Marse David so mad he jus' cussed and cussed. He 'lowed dat nobody warn't gwine tell him what to do." But eventually he had to give in to the justified fears of his slaves. He had a brush arbor built for a classroom but when the night riders destroyed it also, schooling ended.[16]

Both Elisha Green and Henry Bibb remembered Kentucky patrollers, appointed by slaveowners, who broke up slave Sunday schools and whipped all the grown pupils. Patrollers invaded plantations, searching for books and papers in slave cabins, and forcing owners to protect their slaves. Doc Daniel Dowdy, quite a storyteller, was born in 1856 in Madison County, Georgia, on a plantation where his mother was the cook. He recalled an owner who came to the defense of two slaves who were Baptist preachers and could read:

> One old master had two slaves, brothers, on his place. They was both preachers. Mitchell was a hardshell Baptist and Andrew was a Missionary Baptist. One day the patroller chief was rambling throo the place and found some letters writ to Mitchell and Andrew. He went to the master and said, "Did you know you had some niggers that could read and write?" Master said, "No, but I might have . . ." Mitchell was called first and asked could he read and write. He was scared stiff. He said, "Naw-sir." Andrew was called and asked. He said, "Yessir." He was asked iffen Mitchell could. He said. "Sho'. Better 'n me." The master told John Arnold, the patroller chief, not to bother 'em. He gloried in they spunk.[17]

Knowing of community opposition, sympathetic owners tried to keep slave learning quiet. As Elijah Hopkins recalled from his experiences in the Deep South in the late 1850s, "Those white people [who] thought so much of their slaves that they would teach them how to write and read . . . would teach them secretly and they would teach them not to read or write out where anybody would notice them." On a large plantation near Buckhead, Georgia, in the 1830s, Henry Wright's father learned to read with the help of his master's son, but the master told him to keep it to himself, because if the men of the community found out that he could write they would cut the fingers of his hand off.[18]

Slaves who could read did risk grim punishments. In his autobiography, written after he escaped from slavery, Leonard

Black declared that when he first bought a book, his master found the book and burnt it, warning him, "If I ever know you to have a book again, I will whip you half to death." Black bought another, however, and suffered the punishment: he related that his master "made me sick of books by beating me like a dog . . . He whipped me so very severely that he overcame my thirst for knowledge, and I relinquished its pursuit until after I absconded." In Ashley County, Arkansas, in 1862, Joseph Booker's father, Albert, was charged with "spoiling the good niggers" by teaching them to read and was whipped to death when Joseph was three years old. James Lucas' owner "hung the best slave he had" for trying to teach the others how to spell.[19] However, the most common widely known penalty for learning to read and write was amputation. African-Americans who were slaves as children in South Carolina, Georgia, Texas, and Mississippi told similar stories about this punishment. Doc Daniel Dowdy recited the lesson well: "The first time you was caught trying to read or write you was whipped with a cow-hide the next time with a cat-o-nine tails and the third time they cut the first jint offen your forefinger." Former slaves were sure that amputation was in the law: George Washington Albright, born in 1846, told how he learned to read by trickery, because "there was a law on the Mississippi statue books, that if any slave learned to read or write, he was to be punished with 500 lashes on the naked back, and to have the thumb cut off above the second joint." Samuel Hall claimed that amputation was also the law in North Carolina: "If the Negro ever learned to write and it was made known, the law was that he or she must suffer the loss of a finger to keep him from writing." While it was not true that amputation was a legal penalty, the belief in its use was widespread. None of the blacks who told these stories had actually suffered amputation for having learned to read or write, but some had personal knowledge that such atrocities had been committed for the purpose of deterrence. For example, Henry Nix, who was a slave in Upson County, Georgia, in the 1850s, recalled that his uncle stole a book and was trying to learn to read and write with it, so "Marse Jasper had the white doctor take off my Uncle's fo' finger right down to de fust jint" as a "sign for de res uv 'em."[20]

To what extent did fear keep slaves quiet about their achievement of learning to read? The fact that former slaves remembered the atrocity stories so well from their childhood suggests that their parents and elders—and sometimes their owners—had drilled this lesson into them: don't read, or if you do, do it with stealth. It also might give rise to speculation that the children themselves did not know how many people in a single plantation community might actually know how to read and write, since the knowledge of this possession led to so much danger. As Sarah Fitzpatrick observed from her experience as a house servant in Alabama in the 1850s, many slaves could read but "de kep' dat up deir sleeve, dey played dumb lack dey couldn't read a bit till after surrender."[21]

In addition to illuminating the possible extent of literacy, narratives and interviews with former slaves also shed light on the processes by which slaves learned to read and write, who were their teachers, and how they managed the difficult circumstances under which they had to learn. An understanding of the obstacles to slave learning can be aided by a comparison with European working people who learned to read and write. Studies of sixteenth and seventeenth century English workers who tried to acquire reading and writing skills (because of religious conversion) where these skills were seldom in demand for the working class and, in fact, were discouraged (though seldom violently, as in slavery) provide parallels and contrasts to the struggles of North American slaves.[22] Like English workers, slaves experienced family breakup and had to struggle to find time to learn because of long working hours. The age at which a person began to read was similar: most of the English workers who did learn to read in the sixteenth and seventeenth centuries began to read at seven or eight. Slaves recalled that the most common age when they began to read was also between six and eight.[23] On farms and plantations, children were usually assigned jobs in or around the house until they were eight or ten and physically able to work in the field. Those who spent most of their time around the house sometimes learned as the white children learned.

The slave experience was different from beginning readers in other societies in the slaves' lack of classroom exposure. The premodern English workers had some acquaintance with the classroom but slaves, with a few exceptions, did not. English workers were usually able to stay in school long enough to learn to read, which usually took them from four to six months. It is much harder to compare the length of time it took for a slave to learn to read without any time in the classroom. Slave accounts give a picture of sporadic but intensive learning. Thomas Johnson was taught for only a month at the age of seven but learned two-letter syllables during that month. It took Elijah Marrs a year of night school in Kentucky to learn how to write his name and to read cursive writing, but he could only attend school a few hours a week. Other former slaves described efforts which spanned years before they could read, let alone write.[24]

Today's reading theories illuminate the complex process of reading and explain why it can take so long. Reading is considered to be a two-pronged effort, involving both decoding and comprehension. Switching from decoding to comprehension is time consuming—the best parallel is that of reading in a foreign language, in which first the words are translated (decoding) and then meaning is derived (comprehension).[25] With fragmented time, few teacher guides, and limited vocabulary, no wonder it could take even a determined slave years to read. Add the physical threats to other obstacles and the process becomes heroic.

Lucius Holsey's account of his attempts at reading illustrates the ordeal. When he decided to learn, Holsey, a house slave, collected and sold enough rags to buy five books: two Webster's "blue-back" spellers, a school dictionary, Milton's *Paradise Lost,* and a Bible. White children and an old black man taught him the alphabet, and the rest he did on his own. As he recounted:

> Day by day, I took a leaf from one of the spelling books, and so folded it that one or two of the lessons were on the outside as if printed on a card. This I put in the pocket of my vest or coat, and when I was sitting in the carriage, walking the streets, or working in the yard or using hoe or spade, or in the dining room I would take out my spelling leaf, catch a word and commit it to memory. When one side of the spelling leaf was finished by this process, I would refold it . . . with a new lesson on the outside. . . . Besides, I could catch words from the white people and retain them in memory until I could get to my dictionary. Then I would spell and define the words, until they became perfectly impressed upon my memory.[26]

Holsey used decoding and then comprehension to learn. He memorized individual words and spelled new ones—decoding—and then defined them—comprehension, which impressed them on his memory. He learned from the printed page by carrying it with him, a method recommended to beginning adult readers today, and also from listening to the words, which is another path to reading. Thomas G. Sticht and James H. James, for example, propose that "in learning to read, people *close the gap* between auding and reading skills, that is, they become capable of recognizing in printed form words and syntactic constructions they could previously recognize only in spoken form."[27] An excellent demonstration of learning to read by sound comes from John Sella Martin's account of his childhood as a slave. Separated from his mother, he was forced to work as an errand boy in a Columbus, Georgia, hotel where he listened to his white co-workers holding betting matches over spelling. In this way, he recalled, "I learned to spell by sound before I knew by sight a single letter in the alphabet." Then he tried to spell the signs he saw along the streets. Street and store signs were common decoding manuals for urban slaves. Benjamin Holmes, for example, was an apprentice tailor in Charleston. As he carried bundles of clothing around town, he studied all the signs and all the names on the doors and asked people to tell him a word or two at a time. By the time he was twelve, he found he could read newspapers.[28]

Most slaves who learned to read, though, like other American children of that era, did so from a speller, and most often the "blue-back" speller—the book which, next to the Bible, was most common in the average home. Noah Webster's *Elementary Spelling Book,* which sold over twenty million copies in the nineteenth century, would be a challenge to the beginning reader in today's schools. Its words were printed about the size of those in a modern fifth-grade reader, it had few pictures, and its lessons were crowded on a few pages, beginning with the alphabet on one page and on to syllables and consonant combinations on the next.[29] Its step-by-step method, which heavily emphasized pronunciation, may have been tedious in the classroom but was a useful decoding tool for the resourceful person who had to teach himself, including those slaves who took on this challenge.

The speller's wide usage was shown by the number of former slaves who could quote those first vowel and consonant combinations decades after they had learned them. These combinations were part of a common body of reference. Everyone knew how much learning was signified by having gone through the "ab, eb, ib, ob, ubs." Several former slaves proudly remembered having mastered the speller as far as "baker" and "shady," the first two-syllable words in the speller.[30] To "spell to baker," the beginning reader had already confronted nine pages of syllables, words, and consonant combinations, with from 80 to 200 new combinations introduced on each page, and had read one-syllable sentences like these:

> Fire will burn wood and coal.
> When you eat, hold the fork in your left hand.
> Good boys and girls will act well.[31]

An illustration of how sound a foundation these first few pages provided is seen in the narrative of Thomas Jones, who escaped from slavery and wrote his own story, published in Canada in 1853. Jones worked in his master's store in Wilmington, North Carolina, bought a speller, and eventually found a white boy who taught him every day during lunchtime for six cents a week until he learned words of two syllables. After the teaching was stopped, however, Jones continued to work through the speller by himself until he got into words of five syllables.[32] To do this in Webster's speller meant that he had gone through over sixty pages of new words and sentences and would have been reading sentences like these:

> An extemporary discourse is one spoken without notes or premeditation.
> Intemperate people are exposed to inflammatory diseases.
> A love of trifling amusements is derogatory to the christian character.

These former slaves who claimed to have gone all the way through the "blue-back" and on to other books were reading at what would now be considered at least twelfth grade level.[33]

Former slaves recalled a reverence for the speller which was surpassed only by their regard for the Bible. Some former slaves, however, also recalled their sudden realization that they could read. Mastering the speller only provided the decoding; reading also involves comprehension, which requires that the reader bring a memory store to reading: knowledge of grammar, word associations, and general knowledge of the world. As S. Jay Samuels and Michael L. Kamil describe it, there is a "click of comprehension" when the textual information coming in from outside the head matches with the concepts stored inside the

head.[34] When she was ninety years old, Belle Myers still recalled her childhood experience with this "click of comprehension," her sudden realization that she could read. She had
learned her letters while caring for the owner's baby who was
playing with alphabet blocks. Despite brutal discouragement
(her master, seeing what she was doing, kicked her with his
muddy boots), Myers had slipped around and practiced her letters and studied the blue-back speller. One day, she recalled, "I
found a Hymn book . . . and spelled out, 'When I Can Read My
Title Clear.' I was so happy when I saw that I could really read,
that I ran around telling all the other slaves."[35]

Sella Martin also remembered vividly his "click of comprehension" the day he first discovered he could actually understand
the ideas represented by words on a printed page. Trying to
learn to read so that he could run away from slavery and be
reunited with his mother, he had persuaded a fellow hotel boy to
give him a few lessons from the boy's book and had also gotten
into the habit of spelling signs and trying to read advertisements on buildings. Slaves who saw him spelling out words assumed he could read, so one Sunday three older black men
dragged him out into the woods, shoved a newspaper at him,
and said, "Dare read dat ar, and tell us whut him say 'bout de
bobblishunis." Martin, afraid, decided to bluff his way through,
but found to his surprise that he actually could understand
enough to make out the headline: "Henry Clay an Abolitionist."
He was able to read enough words in the article to perceive that
the editor was trying to show abolitionist tendencies in one of
Clay's speeches. Martin recalled, "Of course I did not make out
fully all the long words . . . but I made a new discovery about
my being able to read at all, and that, too, in a newspaper."
Reading comprehension is "the process of bringing meaning to a
text." Martin's great desire for his own freedom and his fellow
slaves' hunger for knowledge about the climate of antislavery in
their world brought meaning to a newspaper story about abolition and led to his discovery that he could read. That night,
when he returned to the city, word had spread. Martin's hotel
kitchen was unusually full of neighboring slaves, each of whom
had taken a book or newspaper from their owners for Martin to
read, acknowledging the value and importance of his skill for
the Columbus, Georgia, slave community.[36]

To the enslaved African-American, writing was an even more
important skill to acquire than reading. However, studies of be-

ginning working class readers in sixteenth century England have shown that reading was more easily achieved than writing. This was also true for nineteenth century American black people in slavery. Writing involved the making and mastery of special equipment; it was much easier to recite the alphabet than to cope with the acquisition of ink, paper, penknives, and so forth.[37] This lack of equipment was particularly acute in the rural South, where pens and paper were not common household articles. To solve this problem, one ingenious slave cut out blocks from pine bark and smoothed them for tablets, cut sticks from white oak or hickory for pens, and soaked knots from oak trees overnight to make ink. Others simply practiced by writing with their fingers on the ground or in the sand. Frederick Douglass related that "my copy-book was the board fence, brick wall, and pavement; my pen and ink was a lump of chalk." Louis Hughes learned off a wall; his friend Tom wrote figures on the side of a barn for Louis to copy.[38]

There were other reasons slaves found it harder to learn to write than to read. Owners and other whites were more reluctant to teach this potentially dangerous skill. Also, the two skills of reading and writing were entirely separated in traditional teaching. Unlike today's learning, in which the child begins to trace letters on paper at the same time he or she is learning to pronounce them, the nineteenth century child was expected to master reading completely before going on to writing. Slave children might be taught to read while they were working in the house, but by the time they were ready to learn to write, they had to go to the fields with the adults.[39] Also, while spellers and primers presented a methodology in successive steps for the teaching of reading, there were no "how-to" books on writing, presenting problems to the slave who wanted to teach herself or himself.

When language is set down on paper it takes on a separate identity from its spoken counterpart. Self-taught writing by slaves shows characteristics similar to those by other members of societies who communicate primarily in spoken language: for example, a lack of capitalization and punctuation and grouping of thoughts in phrases rather than complete sentences.[40] As for writing form, some aspiring learners copied the letters out of the blue-back speller but found to their chagrin that they were expected to use cursive style, not the letters printed in alphabet books. In towns slaves could at least see cursive writing, though they could ferret it out only with ingenuity: Noah Davis, bound out to a shoemaker, watched his employer write customers' names on the lining of the boots and shoes he made and tried to imitate the writing. Frederick Douglass watched ships' carpenters and copied their letters for shipping lumber. Slaves seldom saw any handwriting on farms, so in rural Mississippi John Warren bought a copy of the letters in cursive writing from a white boy for the considerable sum of half a dollar. He had never seen anyone write, so he didn't know how to hold the pen correctly. However, as he related after he had escaped from slavery, "I kept that copy of the letters three years, and learned to write from it." Warren used his skill to write three passes for himself and, with the passes, ran away to Canada.[41]

Warren's story shows the most obvious and immediate reward for learning to write. Despite the difficulties, writing was a path to freedom. Other slaves gained temporary freedom, including Stephen Jordan, who wrote passes for himself so he could see his wife on another Louisiana plantation. Mobility could result from writing ability; slaves who could read and write could be chosen to travel with the master so that if anything happened to him they could write back home. The ability to read also assured some privacy. Sarah Fitzpatrick, a house slave in Alabama in the 1850s, pointed out that if a slave wanted to court a girl and couldn't write, his master had to write his love letter for him, so "anytime you writ a note white folks had ta know whut it said." Reading and writing could even tap white financial resources: one slave forged his master's name on a check and was able to cash it.[42]

There were other reasons in addition to the immediately practical, however, for some slaves' "insatiable craving for some knowledge of books," as one former slave put it. More former slaves mentioned a desire to read the Bible as a motive than any other. To most enslaved African-Americans the Bible and the black church gave central identity to their communities and their lives. Slaves were also aware of the promise of literacy as a path to mobility and increased self-worth. Messages about literacy's intrinsic and practical value, espoused by educational reformers in England and the northern United States, had an impact even in the South. An interesting interpretation of this message came from a poor white boy who assured a slave that "a man who had learning would always find friends, and get along very well in the world without having to work hard, while those who had no learning would have no friends and be compelled to work very hard for a poor living all their days."[43] Lucius Holsey, who identified in many ways with the white world, "felt that constitutionally he was created the equal of any person here on earth and that, given a chance, he could rise to the height of any man," and that books were the path to proving his worth as a human being.[44] Another important reason was that so many owners tried to prevent slaves from gaining literacy skills. Perception by slaves that reading and writing must be extremely valuable simply because they were withheld from the slaves, and that these skills could greatly expand their world, underlay much of their desire to learn. Overcoming the barrier to learning was a small triumph over the world that kept them in bondage. As Jenny Proctor said,

> De say we git smarter den dey was if we learn anything, but we slips around and gits hold of dat Webster's old blue back speller and we hides it til way in de night and den we ights a little pine torch and studies dat spellin' book. We learn it too.[45]

Slaves challenged circumstances in many ways in order to learn reading and writing skills. Slaves "borrowed" books from their owners or bought them with treasured small savings. Lucius Holsey gathered rags and sold them for money to buy books. Richard Parker picked up nails and sold them until he had enough money to buy a primer.[46]

Former slaves told how they used the little spare time available to them to study reading and writing. Dan Lockhart, overseer on a Virginia plantation, would carry his gun to a hollow, ostensibly to go hunting, then get out his secreted divinity book and study it. John Irvine was a slave on a farm near Clarkesville, Virginia, in the 1850s and early 1860s. While holding the horse for his owners during church, he used his slate, pencil, and his young master's books, and made up for lost time. Edmund Kelly, hired to a schoolmaster in Tennessee in the 1830s, slipped candy to the school children in exchange for a speller and a few lessons, then tried to find the time to study: "Early each night he retired with a prayer that God would guide and direct him and wake him at eleven P.M. . . ."[47]

According to former slaves, who usually had to learn at night, one of the great difficulties was getting enough light to read by. Some Tennessee ex-slaves told Fisk University student interviewers that they had to slip old planks into the house in summer, where they would light them and sit down and read from the light of the fire. The trouble with light was most serious when studying had to be kept secret. His Colbert County, Alabama, master had told Wilson Northcross that if he was caught with a book he would be hung by the white men of the community, so Northcross got some old boards and carried them to his house to make a light by which to read secretly. This was a hazardous undertaking, as he recalled:

> I would shut the doors, put one end of a board into the fire, and proceed to study; but whenever I heard the dogs barking I would throw my book under the bed and peep and listen to see what was up. If no one was near I would crawl under the bed, get my book, come out, lie flat on my stomach, and proceed to study until the dogs would again disturb me.[48]

The most obvious way for slaves to learn was to get the knowledge from whites. His granddaughter recalled that Beverly Nash, a barber in Columbia, "learned to read and write before 1865, because he was in favor with both white and black folks practically all his life. . . ." Paul Jenkins recalled that in Walterboro, South Carolina, his father "learned to read, write, and cipher while he was a slave. The Jenkins family help him, he say, 'cause he always keep the peace and work as he was told to do." The arrangement continued to be an advantage after slavery; when Jenkins was set free, the white family helped him get settled and loaned him books.

Not all white teachers were slaveowners. Some slaves paid whites to teach them or persuaded them in other ways. Sella Martin beat the white boys at marble games and exchanged reading lessons for their marbles. Frederick Douglass made friends with the white boys he met in the street and converted as many as he could into teachers. Some poor whites were glad to get paid for teaching a slave the alphabet or give some reading lessons. At least one Greene County, Alabama, white teacher, William Freeman, must have taught slaves for the company, or for the satisfaction of irritating the community. As a neighbor complained:

> We have known of [Freeman] being drunk . . . but we never intended to medle with it until other things come

to light he give Negrows passes goes in the old fields
and woods on Sundays and is teaching them to write
and cipher I do hope you will take him from this
neighborhood.[49]

White children taught their slave playmates secretly or were
unaware of violation of law or custom. As a girl growing up in
Charleston, Sarah Grimkē was aware of the law against teaching slaves, but deliberately violated it, as she recounted:.

> I took an almost malicious satisfaction in teaching my
> little waiting-maid at night, when she was supposed to
> be occupied in combing and brushing my long locks. The
> light was put out, the keyhole screened, and flat on our
> stomachs, we defied the laws of South Carolina.[50]

Sometimes the children were tacitly or openly encouraged by
white adults, who may have allowed their children to dare to do
what they could not. One former slave in Arkansas, Eva Stray-
horn, told about the relationship between Solomon, her black
overseer, and his little mistress Liza: "She was his special
charge and he would a died for her." He took her to school, and
she taught him to read every day. "As she growed up she kept
learning more and Solomon had married and Miss Liza would
go down to his cabin every night and teach him [and his wife]
some more." When his master, an Arkansas legislator, caught
him with a Bible in his lap and found out Liza had taught him,
he was pleased and amused and even had Solomon show off by
reading the Bible to some of his friends, able to parade Solomon's accomplishment since he had not been personally responsible for it.[51]

Former slaves also recalled that it was customary for young
whites, especially young white women, to serve as Sunday
school teachers for their slaves. When she was about sixteen, for
example, in the late 1850s, Squire Dowd's mistress taught him
to read in a Sunday school class on his plantation of 50 slaves in
Moore, North Carolina.[52]

Other times white children were unwitting teachers of their
slave playmates. Milly Green, her son recalled, kept a school
book hidden in her dress, and when the children came home
from school she would ask them questions about what they had
learned that day. They taught her because she was so proud of
every little scrap of learning she picked up. William Head lis-

tened to the spelling matches at school when he and his sister carried lunch to his young master. He tried to memorize the speeches he heard and went to the library with the white children to study at night.[53]

Moses Slaughter's mother used her position in the household to learn from the children through trickery; as the housekeeper, she would say to the owner's daughter, "Come here, Emily, Mamma will keep you place for you," and while little Emily read, "Mamma" followed each line until she too was a fluent reader and could teach her own children.[54]

A slave's standing as an owner's child sometimes, but not always, gave him or her an opportunity for learning. Louisiana slave Stephen Jordan, son of his master, went to school with his white half-brothers and sisters shortly before the war. Some slaveowners even sent their children by slave women North to be educated. The school established at the Ohio resort of Tawawa Springs, later Wilberforce University, housed and taught over 200 children of slaveowners in the 1850s. This preferential treatment for owners' children was not always the rule, however. Lucius Holsey, also the son of his master, was orphaned when he was six and had to ferret out opportunities to learn on his own.[55]

Next to learning from white children, working with the women of the households offered slaves the most opportunities for reading. While some women owners of slaves were cruel and harsh, many others established bonds with the enslaved black women with whom they spent most of their time and taught them to read as part of general education and instruction. Charity Jones' mistress, for example, taught her to read and write as part of her instruction in house management. The rest of her education included learning how to card bats and spin, weave cloth, sew, and sweep. Betty Ivery, house servant on a large plantation in Arkansas, recalled that her mistress taught her to read after the housework was done, "long after dark."[56]

Literacy was a skill and a power which was shared with the slave community by those who learned. Enslaved African-Americans often used the knowledge they had gained to teach fellow slaves. Anderson Whitted's father lived fourteen miles away from him, but was allowed to visit him every two weeks and taught Anderson to read on his visits. The children in Henry Bruce's family on a small farm in Missouri learned from their white playmates and then taught each other: "The older one would teach the younger, and while mother had no education at all, she used to make the younger study the lessons given by the older sister or brother, and in that way they all learned to read" and some to write. A man on Levi Branham's master's Tennessee farm would make figures and letters on a wooden pad to teach the boys how to read and write. Teaching was, however, not only a hazard for the black teacher, but also a terrific responsibility. Enoch Golden, known to the slaves as a "double-headed nigger" because he could read and write and "knowed so much," was said to have confessed on his deathbed that he "been de death o' many nigger 'cause he taught so many to read and write."[57]

Free African-Americans in the South also played a key role in spreading literacy among slaves. In the cities and small towns, slaves and free blacks intermingled; they worked together, belonged to the same churches, and intermarried. Even in the country, free blacks were teachers of slaves. The existence of a few literate people in a community also creates a climate where the importance and power of literacy is recognized.[58] This was particularly true when it came to the spread of information about freedom throughout the slave South. As whites had suspected when they tried to keep literate black seamen from stopping in southern ports in the 1820s, the existence of a free, literate black population in the South was a never-ending source of information to the slaves. Also, the increase in mass literacy meant that writings by northern abolitionists and calls for freedom and literacy by northern black leaders spread into the South.

In southern cities, free African-Americans led educational efforts. They taught and financed those few schools and classes for black people which did operate in the antebellum South. While the schools operated primarily for other free blacks, slaves sometimes did attend them. Also, free and slave African Americans cooperated in founding and conducting southern black churches, including the Sunday schools where many free blacks and slaves learned to read.

Despite restrictions and difficulties, free black people had opportunities to gain literate skills which were seldom available to slaves. In some southern states, free blacks were taught to read and write because they were apprentices. Eighteenth century statutes in Virginia and North Carolina stipulated that apprentices, including black apprentices, be taught to read as part of their training. Even after these were amended to exclude blacks in the early nineteenth century as a reaction to rebellions by literates Gabriel Prosser and Nat Turner, free black apprentices were actually still taught to read. John Hope Franklin noted that most free Negro apprentices in Craven County, North Carolina, were still under indentures in the 1850s which specified that they were to be taught to read and write. Apprentice contracts in other states, including Louisiana, also stipulated that employers teach their charges a trade and also give them the fundamentals of reading and writing.[59]

Free African-Americans got their education by taking advantage of their mobility within the South, or traveled North. Carrie Pollard's grandmother, a free servant in Tuscaloosa, Alabama, sent her two daughters to school in Mobile by boat. William Pettiford's parents sold their little farm and moved to a county in North Carolina where Pettiford could get a private education. Inman Page's father moved his family to Washington, D.C., where Page went to George Cook's well-respected school.[60]

Other southern free blacks who could afford to do so took advantage of the educational opportunities in the North for their children. Among those who did so were the parents of James Rapier of Florence, Alabama, who had their son taught by private tutors and then sent him to Canada. Henry Alexander, storekeeper and grain merchant in Mayslick, Kentucky, sent two of his daughters to Philadelphia to school in 1846 and three younger daughters to Oberlin in the 1850s. One of the older daughters, Maria Ann, educated in Philadelphia, then came back to teach in Covington, Kentucky. Edward Brawley's parents sent him from Charleston to Philadelphia when he was ten; Mary Ann Shadd spent six years in school in West Chester, Pennsylvania, before she returned as a teenager to open a school for black children in Wilmington, Delaware. The Harris family left Fayetteville, North Carolina, for Cleveland so that the youngest son, Cicero, could obtain a high school education.[61]

Free African-Americans established private schools—paid schools, church schools, or tuition-free schools—throughout the South. The number and accessibility of their black schools varied considerably from city to city. Washington, D.C., was the southern city with the most private schools for African-Americans; from oral recollections and records, its District Commissioner for Education described at least seventy-two teachers for black people in the city in the antebellum nineteenth century. As an historian of urban black life recently observed, "Washington free blacks appear to have been determined to secure the advantages of education for their children at whatever cost." Nashville and Savannah also had numbers of schools, and a historian who delved into his own and other black family records and gathered oral histories in Charleston named at least fifteen different schools and teachers for blacks in that city in the period from 1820 to 1860. In Richmond, on the other hand, laws against learning were strict, as Thomas Johnson found out when he sought opportunities for literacy. According to a northern missionary, Richmond free and slave blacks still learned to read, but were taught "by the poor whites secretly and at exorbitant rates."[62]

Free blacks in Mobile had special permission to operate public schools in the city because of political privileges granted to Creoles by the Louisiana Purchase before Alabama became a state. Even where schools were not legal, free blacks operated them, often through the churches—in fact, Ira Berlin has labeled the schools operated by black churches as the chief instruments of literacy for the black community. Charleston exemplifies Berlin's claim. All but one of Charleston's schools for blacks were supported through the churches. One of these schools was established by black Methodists in Charleston. After Daniel Payne's school closed in 1835 and he was forced to leave the city, his good friends William and Samuel Weston gathered a group of fellow black Methodists, organized a Board of Trustees, rented a house, opened a school and persuaded a white Methodist college student to become its teacher. The school quickly became so large that two more teachers were added.[63]

Slaves did attend the schools established and operated by free blacks. Their best opportunities came in Sunday schools, but other schools were also sometimes open to them. An example is William H. Gibson's school in Louisville. Gibson grew up in Baltimore and studied under Daniel Payne and other black educators. In 1847 he moved to Louisville with the Rev. James Harper and began both a day and a night school in the basement of a Methodist church. Many of his pupils, who numbered from fifty to one hundred, were slaves whose masters gave them written permits to attend school. In Savannah, according to Susie King Taylor, a free black woman kept a school in which she and her daughter taught twenty-five to thirty free and slave children every day. In North Carolina Robert Harris, a plasterer by trade, also held a secret school for slaves.[64]

A key group responsible for schools for African-Americans in the antebellum South were the French West Indies immigrants and their descendants. Mulattoes, or *gens de couleur,* fled French and Spanish slave colonies in successive emigrations after the first slave revolts in 1790 and settled in southern coastal cities, including New Orleans, Mobile, Savannah, Charleston, Washington, and Baltimore. They organized brotherhoods and schools designed to perpetuate the separate colored caste and Creole culture to which they belonged in the West Indies colonies, but which was not recognized as a separate culture in Anglo-America. The *gens de couleur* were also noted for their efforts to teach blacks in the spirit of *noblesse oblige.* A good example of their work is Charleston's Brown Fellowship Society, established by emigrants from the French West Indies in the 1790s. Many of the members of the Brown Fellowship Society were slaveowners themselves who emphasized racial divisions by admitting to membership only "colored" students of mixed blood. But the Society also helped two kinds of schools: it gave its support to Thomas Bonneau's school for its own children but also established the Minor's Moralist Society to maintain and educate free colored and black orphans.[65]

Education was a particular responsibility of the Catholic orders for black and colored women. The Oblate sisters, whose order was founded in Baltimore in 1829, and the Congregation of the Sisters of the Holy Family in New Orleans, founded in 1842, taught schools for black children in Nashville, Baltimore, and Washington, D.C. The first school for mulatto children in New Orleans was administered by the Ursulines and then by the Carmelites. Ursulines also trained young black and Creole women to instruct black children. Sulpicians carried out the same function in Baltimore. The Sisters of St. Joseph of Carondelet opened a school for the education of Negro girls in St. Louis in 1845; two other schools were opened there by Catholic orders in the 1850s.[66]

"Colored" Catholic efforts to educate blacks and mulattos contributed to the fact that the three cities which offered most schools for blacks—Baltimore, New Orleans, and Washington, D.C.—were also the cities with the highest number of West Indies Creole emigrants. Creoles would have preferred to remain separate from blacks, but since the white power structure refused to recognize a separate mulatto class, many of the *gens de couleur* became leaders of the black community with whom they were forced to associate. Ironically, also, Catholic orders and their schools had another effect on black education: Protestants began mission churches and schools for blacks in New Orleans, Baltimore, and Mobile in order to combat the effects of "Romanism."[67]

African-Americans in the North expanded their educational opportunities in the antebellum years. It is difficult to measure black education, largely private, in the days before accreditation and certification, but numbers of black children attending schools, according to census figures, declined in slave states and increased markedly in northern states from 1850 to 1860.[68] Little public education was available for African-Americans in the North. They were barred from public education in border cities, including Cincinnati, and in other northern cities their admission to public schools was limited and segregated. Still, the number of private schools, largely financed by blacks themselves, increased. Schools established in Quaker settlements and in colonies of former slaves throughout the Old Northwest educated increasing numbers. Sunday schools operated by black churches and schools and tutors supported by black relief societies maintained instruction in the rudiments of education. New York City's public schools for black children were far from equal to those for white, but improved as a result of petitions and publicity from a committee of black people. Philadelphia counted fifty-six private black schools in 1860, only twelve of them conducted by whites. In addition, some public elementary education was available for black people in Philadelphia. Public support of black or integrated schools made some gains in Pennsylvania, New Jersey, Rhode Island, Connecticut, Massachusetts, and Ohio. Nevertheless, hostility and indifference from whites prevented an all-out effort to educate black children and adults. Thousands of African-Americans left the United States for Canada in the antebellum decades, explaining that better educational opportunities for their children in Canada was a major factor attracting them.[69]

Increasingly important to southern black literacy in the two decades before the Civil War were northern black educators and political leaders. While their achievements and challenges can only be briefly touched upon in this book, northern black leaders as promoters of education and of protest held out opportunities and goals to slaves who had access to the printed word and inspired others to gain that access.[70] Northern African-American religious, political and educational leaders promoted the urgency and necessity of literacy for their people. Conventions of African-Americans passed resolutions encouraging the pursuit of learning and literacy, and benevolent societies such as New York's Phoenix Society ran schools and urged parents to send their children to learn. Frederick Douglass and Samuel Cornish were among the journalists who praised the benefits of education in their journals. As editor of *Freedom's Journal,* Cornish deplored the low state of education for black people and recommended steps toward improvement, including a thorough grounding in fundamental skills. The tone of these black leaders was militant. The *Anglo-African Magazine's* editor typically declared:

> Instruction is the great want of the colored race; it needs the light, ideas, facts, principles of action, for its development and progress. In this armor alone can it fight its battles, and secure its rights, and protect its interests amid the forces of civilization.[71]

Another strong spokesman for an educated black people was Daniel Payne. With a sound educational background from his Charleston days and then as an A.M.E. preacher and bishop, he fought for an educated ministry and congregation—a fight which he characterized as "that struggle between darkness and light, between ignorance and knowledge, between baptized superstition and Christianity." He led in the development of Sunday schools, a church newspaper, and in the founding of Wilberforce College. Since the A.M.E. church was a strong force in the border states, Payne's influence for literacy was felt by black people in his home region as well as in the North.[72]

Northern black leaders recognized the potency of literacy in protest. When Henry Highland Garnet gave his famous "Address to the Slaves" at the National Negro Convention in Buffalo, New York, in 1843, he told slaves that it was their Christian duty to rebel. It was, according to Garnet, "sinful . . . to make voluntary submission" to oppression. Among the oppressions Garnet described was a prohibition on learning.

> Nearly three millions of your fellow-citizens are prohibited by law and public opinion (which in this country is stronger than law) from reading the Book of Life![73]

The way in which Garnet phrased this sentence implies that Garnet was addressing *literate* slaves. The Convention which Garnet addressed refused to publish his explosive speech, but Garnet had it printed anyway. According to his recent biographer, Garnet may have actually wanted and expected the slaves to have a copy of his speech.[74] Therefore, he must have assumed that some would be able to read it.

Garnet may have had reasons to believe his message would reach literate slaves. He had interviewed fugitive slaves and knew that those he spoke with were well acquainted with developments in nonslave areas. Former slaves who spoke with Federal Writers Project interviewers or wrote their own reminiscences related that news about significant events, such as the war, travelled fast. Vincent Harding, in *There Is a River: The Black Struggle for Freedom in America,* described how "the fugitive, exciting word from white political sources, telling of arguments and debates over the operation of the institution of slavery, continued to seep into the life of the southern black community, hinting, suggesting, revealing the basic tensions which lurked deep in the larger white society." This word was often spread by literate slaves, as evidenced in the FWP narratives. In Georgia Minnie Davis' mother stole newspapers during the war and kept the other slaves posted as to the war's progress. Cora Gillam's uncle "had a newspaper with the latest war news and gathered a crowd of fellow Mississippi slaves to read them when peace was coming."[75]

J. B. Roudanez, a free mulatto Creole from New Orleans employed as an engineer and mechanic on sugar plantations, estimated that "generally upon every plantation there was at least one man who had somehow learned to read a little, and in secret learned to read to the others," and he gave a specific example of how quickly news traveled. On the day after New Orleans learned of a dramatic piece of news, a slave seventy-five miles upriver told Roudanez all about it. His master had given one of the slaves a newspaper for wiping machinery in the sugar house. The slave had kept the newspaper and had later secretly read it to the whole slave community. It contained an account of John Brown's execution.[76]

Chapter Four

■

"The Onliest One Who Could Read the Bible":
Southern Black Leadership in Literacy and Religion

R HINER GARDNER, A FORMER SLAVE INTERVIEWED IN the 1930s by Fisk University students, recalled that dur- ing slavery "if there chanced to be among the slaves a man of their own race who could read and write, he generally preached and would at times and places unknown to the master, call his fellow slaves together and hold religious services with them." Enslaved African-Americans developed their own com- munities and culture and centered them around religion. "Cre- ative community-building," as it is termed by Margaret Creel, was a form of resistance to oppression through the religion developed in antebellum black communities, a religion which served as a positive force enabling slaves to remain spiritually free.[1]

The leaders of black religion under slavery were the key to the resistance through community building which Creel describes. Literacy was one of the tools the preacher used; he or she was expected to learn to read and write in order to guide fellow slaves as they formed their religious community. Knowledge was a necessary part of resistance against the slave system and the leader was expected to provide this knowledge. The most ambi- tious African-Americans sought to become preachers, since the church was practically the only leadership role open to them in the South and in slavery. Religious leadership was inevitably linked with literacy; for centuries in Christian societies, even where the majority of people were illiterate, religious leaders were expected to be able to read the Scriptures and interpret them for the rest of the people. Black religion became the focus for resistance to white oppression, so most African-Americans responded to religion only when it was preached by one of their own. Recognizing that black leaders were the only way to get black acceptance for Christianity, white religious leaders gave in and recognized black religious leaders among slaves, in many cases allowing them to learn to read or teaching them.

Anthony Dawson, a field hand on a large North Carolina plantation, recalled that during slavery, "mostly we had white preachers ... but when we had a black preacher that was Heaven." Former slaves remembered many church services conducted by whites, but scorned the themes of the sermons— obedience to masters, strictures against stealing the master's property, and acceptance of suffering. Even a good sermon by a well-meaning white preacher was unacceptable because it was given within a slaveholding context; as William Humbert recalled, African-Americans saw that "the ministers preach to please the [white] people, and not in the fear of God."[2]

By the last decades of slavery, with only a few exceptions, black people had fashioned a religious faith which embraced Christianity as a system of morals, a promise for a future life, and a "spiritual release from anxieties, frustrations, and animosities," but they rejected Christianity as practiced by white slaveholders. The black church leaders preached the gospel of freedom and God's support and justice for oppressed peoples. Scholars of black religion and Black Theology have found a "close and explicit relationship between religion and resistance." Black Christians believed that the Bible spoke to them in a special way, and they resented the slaveholders' abuse of God's word. Therefore, it was crucial that some people in the slave community gain reading skills, to "take the Bible back," to read what it really said. In some instances, the white sermon was followed by a later, secret meeting to "set the record straight." On Douglas Dorsey's plantation in Florida, after the white sermon, "the driver's wife who could read and write a little would tell them that what the minister said 'was all lies.'" Inevitably, the ability to read became linked with religious leadership in the slave community, and even in the black community after slavery.[3]

Knowledge of the Bible, the sacred text, was a tool for attaining salvation and for living in a personal relationship with God, but the ability to read the Bible gave practical as well as spiritual benefits to a slave preacher. Religion was practically the only leadership role available for southern black people in slavery. Slaves often chose their own religious leaders and chose those who could read. Literate slaves could be employed by slaveowners to preach on plantations. Out of necessity and acknowledgment of their effectiveness, white religious leaders and missionaries trained black preachers and Sunday school leaders and even encouraged or allowed them to teach others to read. African-American preachers could use the skills of literacy to gain advantages for themselves in the white community and at the same time mediate for their fellow slaves. In order to do this, black leaders who obtained skills in reading and writing monopolized by whites learned the acceptable ways to behave in white groups.

In her examination of the Gullah communities during slavery, Margaret Creel identified religious leaders who related in a variety of ways to Christianity and to African traditions. Among them were the "diviners," with the closest links to African practices; the "doctors" or "conjurers" who worked on the "periphery of Christianity" and who were highly regarded as a link with the African past as well as an active force in the present; and the "house elders" or "praise house watchmen." The latter were more definitely in alignment with the new religion, Christianity, and therefore lacked the connections to Africa which gave credibility to the others. However, Creel found that these elders were widely respected, "pillars of strength in the slave quarters," who for the most part used their power as white-connected spiritual leaders with "measure, fairness, and to the benefit of the slave community."[4] Slave testimony justifies extrapolating her conclusions about the slaves' respect for Christian elders to the slave communities beyond the Sea Islands. In their interviews, autobiographies, and narratives, former slaves recalled that they themselves often chose their religious leaders and that they chose those who could read. Simon Hare, a slave in North Carolina, remembered that "colored folks jes kinda raised 'em up a colored preacher ter preach ter 'em" and that these preachers were among the few slaves who could read and write. Preacher Peter Randolph was the sole individual among the eighty-one slaves on his Virginia plantation in the 1830s who could read. From his experience as one of 500 slaves on a Georgia plantation, Elisha Doc Carey agreed that "dem what could read was most allus called on by de others for preachin." Another former slave recalled that on many plantations the black preacher was "the onliest one who could read the Bible."[5]

The people in the slave community recognized the value of "God-made preachers" and sometimes demonstrated their support with concrete actions. For example, Byrd Day, a minister in Glennville, Georgia, recalled that when he was a slave, his fellow slaves chose to do extra work for him so that he could learn and pass on his knowledge to the community. He recalled that "we slaves were allowed night farms [which consisted of] an acre or so of land . . . given to each person wanting to work at night. Well, in order that I might study the Bible, the other slaves on the place worked my patch for me. So I studied the book and read it to them."[6]

Byrd Day's account is one of the scores written during and after slavery by prominent leaders of black churches, either as separate books or as brief autobiographies prepared for denominational histories or black histories. Added to narratives and interviews with former slaves, they form a picture of the fight for knowledge and self-fulfillment among enslaved African-Americans who felt they were chosen by God to lead their people. Their recollections reflect more of a sense of communal values than do typical white religious autobiographies, relating a quest for both individual and collective spiritual development which reaffirms the integral function of the black church as the core of the black community.[7]

As Elisabeth Schultz points out in her study of black autobiography, these nineteenth century life stories were written to inspire change or emulation: "as in a traditional church testimonial, the intention of the autobiographer's description of his experience is to bring his audience to a like action; consequently, the particular facts of personal experience are generalized through logic or exaggeration, so that listeners or readers may readily grasp their significance." Most of the autobiographies of religious leaders highlighted experiences which are common to heroic folklore: the death or separation from a beloved parent, the miraculous escape from slavery, the outwitting of white slaveowners, and, of course, the drama surrounding conversion to Christianity. Because the Bible was central to their leadership of the black community and to gaining the knowledge which would enable them to resist the oppression around them, the struggles by slave leaders to learn to read the Bible, as related in their autobiographies, take on this heroic character. Overcoming obstacles and successfully learning to read the Bible was an achievement to be emulated. One black preacher writing his story long after slavery had ended, for example, paused in his account of the many troubles he encountered in learning to read over a period of years with this plea to black children: "Boys and girls, grasp these golden opportunities which are now extended you from the school room. . . . My readers have better chances than I had. So I hope that they will make good use of their time."[8]

Religious leaders who wrote their autobiographies drew tightly the connection between religion and reading. They stated that they wanted to learn to read as a result of their conversion and their desire to preach. In his narrative, preacher Peter Randolph described his reaction to conversion at age ten:

> After receiving this revelation from the Lord, I became impressed that I was called of God to preach to the other slaves . . . but then I could not read the Bible, and I thought I could never preach unless I learned to read the Bible. . . . A friend showed me the letters and how to spell words. . . . Then I continued, until I got so as to read the Bible,—the great book of God,—the source of all knowledge.

Wilson Northcross, born a slave in 1840 in Colbert County, Alabama, became an ordained minister after slavery and, as pastor of the large First Baptist Church in Tuscumbia, wrote a brief autobiography in 1897 chronicling his achievements and the obstacles he had had to overcome. As a child he had received some religious information—but no literacy—from his owners. He began to lead prayer meetings when he was twenty, felt a call to preach, and fasted and prayed all night long that God would help him out of his ignorance. He recalled that "at this time I did not know A from B but I met a man who could read a little. This man liked me and promised to teach me how to read, provided I would keep it secret. This I gladly promised to do." Northcross described his efforts to "climb the mountain" of knowledge:

> I secured a blue-back speller and went out on the mountain every Sunday to meet this gentleman, to be taught.

> I would stay on the mountain all day Sunday without food. I continued this way for a year and succeeded well. I hired my own time and with my blue-back speller went to the mountain to have this man teach me. The mountain was the great school which I attended.[9]

Others wanted to learn to read after experience with preaching showed them what an essential skill reading was. Robert Grant was a blacksmith and miner for his master in Wilkes County, Georgia, in the 1840s. His master allowed him to hold religious services on the front porch. Conducting these services showed him how much he needed an education, so he made every possible effort to learn how to read. Noah Davis joined the Baptist church in Baltimore and tried to preach, but often felt embarrassed, though he could read a little: "My desires now increased for such a knowledge of the sacred Scriptures, as would enable me to read a chapter publicly to my hearers." The need for his own time for study speeded Davis' efforts, beginning in 1845, to buy his freedom and to become a full time missionary and preacher.[10]

Religious autobiographies and narratives by former slaves present the problem of gender bias in understanding the entire picture of literate slave religious leadership. Almost all the autobiographies of prominent nineteenth century black religious and political leaders were written by males, though nineteenth century black women also played prominent public roles. William Simmons' 1887 compilation of biographies entitled *Men of Mark—Eminent, Progressive, and Rising* was supposed to be followed by a companion volume entitled *Women of Mark,* but Simmons died before completing it.

Testimony by other less prominent former slaves also reflects this gender difference. Two thirds of the former slaves interviewed by the Federal Writers Project who stated that they had learned to read or write during slavery were male, though equal numbers of each sex were interviewed for the project. The reasons for this emphasis on literacy among males more than females are speculative. In traditional societies, males became literate before females did. This may also have been true in slave communities. West African traditional societies recognize a role for women as religious leaders, but emphasize the male role. The influence of Islam reinforced male dominance in religious leadership in Africa and nineteenth century white Christianity reinforced this in slavery. However, the emphasis on males as readers during slavery may be in part the result of biased sources. The tradition of male literacy may have been reflected in the topics former slaves selected to write about in their narratives or in topics abolitionists suggested for publication. It certainly may have been reflected in the questions asked by FWP interviewers of males rather than females in the 1930s.

In mid-nineteenth century America, however, women were being accepted more and more as literate and as teachers. The numbers and prominence of southern white women as religious educators on plantations and as schoolteachers were increasing rapidly as slavery came to an end. Evidence that African-American women also learned to read and to teach as slaves comes from Reconstruction, when educators from the North found many literate black women willing, able, and available to teach the freed peoples. The role of teacher predominates among literate women slaves; when former slaves did remember women who could read in the slave communities, these women were recalled as leaders and teachers who spread their knowledge to their families and other slaves, like "old lady Patsy," who was a nurse as well as a reader and who taught those around her. Some were religious leaders, like Susan Castle's "Aunt Vic," who was "one of the readers what read the Bible" on her Clarke County, Georgia, plantation of one hundred slaves and who read the Bible sometimes at Sunday School.[11]

Aunt Jane Lee was one of the notable African-American religious leaders who combined reading ability with religious devotion and piety, as she lived in the memory of Charlotte Brooks, who described her in the years shortly after slavery. Jane Lee was reared in Virginia, where she learned to read, and was sold to Louisiana. According to Brooks, Jane Lee "was the cause of so many on our plantation getting religion ... it was Aunt Jane's praying and singing them old Virginia hymns that helped me so much." Aunt Jane always brought her books to secret prayer meetings at Brooks' house: "She could read right good in the Bible and hymn-book, and she would read to me one or two hymns at a time. I remember she read to me about Daniel in the lions' den and about the king having the three Hebrew children cast in the fiery furnace. O, how Aunt Jane used to love to read about the Hebrew children!"[12]

As with Jane Lee, reading and preaching were closely connected. The religious leader wanted to be able to search the

Scriptures for herself or himself and not depend on others. The knowledge of print added to the religious authority of the leader and also provided practical benefits. One benefit was the ability to perform white rituals such as the marriage ceremony or the funeral service. Jennie Hill and her husband were married by another slave on their small farm in Boonesville, Missouri, one who could read and write and knew something of the Bible. As Jennie recalled, the slave preacher "said the same marriage ceremony for us that we had to say over again when we were freed."[13]

To the African-American religious leader, the ability to read was both spiritual and utilitarian, two functions which are not divided in the African religious view as they are in the European. African belief systems are not only integrative, but adaptive and practical. This is why, although many historians have described the separate churches in the plantation community— the black church, often secret, in the quarters, and the white church, sponsored by the slaveowner and sometimes supervised by the white family—slave religion was a mixture of both, a synthesis of selected Christian teachings and traditional African beliefs and practices. African-Americans preferred to hold their own worship services and observances free from white control, but they borrowed selectively from white theology and borrowed and adapted white hymns, sacraments, and liturgy.[14]

Members of both black and white churches valued the preacher's ability to read. Even though the advent of universal literacy had transformed European culture with the development of individual silent reading, oral reading was a centuries-old leadership practice in traditional cultures in Europe and Africa. In the African experience "speaking books," or sacred texts constantly recited, were familiar. West African cultures on the "margins of literacy," to use Goody's phrase, saw reading and writing as the path to contact with supernatural powers. African-American slave culture preserved an African oral tradition, but with respect for the text as authority. Therefore, according to Rhys Isaac religious learning was essential because it "consisted of the skills to interpret the Scriptures and other authoritative writings and to communicate to an audience the customary and indispensable knowledge that had been stored within these writings from ancient times." For African-Americans the sacred text, the Bible, spoke directly to their oppression through Jesus' suffering and through the Old

Testament captivity in Egypt. The words lived and the readers and listeners lived in them.[15]

The Bible was a tool for access to the practical and intrinsic facets of the white world as well as access to salvation and the support and guidance of Christianity. Their belief that reading the Bible was a way to gain power over their world is shown by the ways in which blacks used their blue-back spellers interchangeably with the Bible. Slaves recalled black preachers who preached out of blue-back spellers and conducted marriages using the speller as their guide. Northern observers during and immediately after the war noted that slaves treated the act of learning to read as a religious act. A Sea Islander, for example, described black children reciting the alphabet over a grave at a funeral in ritualistic style.[16]

Because the Bible was central to their leadership of the black community, and because writing had a magico-religious significance in the African world view, the ability to read the Bible took on a magical significance to religious leaders. African-Americans believed in a spirit world that played an active role in the earthly world, and their accounts of life in slavery include stories of ghosts or "haunts," witches, and spirits. Stories of how slaves learned to read reflected African traditions of spirit possession in a Christian context. As an example, Bartley Hamburg Townsley of Pike County, Georgia, was taken away from his mother in 1847 at the age of twelve to serve his young master as a "waitman." While there, he fulfilled his desire to read in an unusual way, as he related in the third person: "One night, when he had gone to bed and had fallen to sleep, he dreamed that he was in a white room, and its walls were the whitest he ever saw. He dreamed that some one came in and wrote the alphabet on the wall in large printed letters, and began to teach him every letter, and when he awoke he had learned every letter, and as early as he could get a book, he obtained one and went hard to work."[17]

George Washington Dupee learned to read, as he told it, with similar miraculous help. He was owned by a Baptist preacher in Gallatin County, Kentucky, and hired out to a brick yard and a carpenter. He wanted to become a preacher after his conversion at fifteen in 1842, "but not knowing how to read he thought preaching was out of the question." He learned the alphabet, however, and one rainy Wednesday he heard old father David Woods reading the New Testament. When he laid the book down, Dupee picked it up, wishing to read as he saw Father Woods read. He opened the book at the first chapter of John, saw the letters J-o-h-n, and said, "What did that fool put those letters that way for? They don't mean anything." He could not pronounce the name. But then he began to read over and over again the first three chapters of John. "When he realized that he could read the Word of God, he shouted, cried, and pressed the book to his breast in thankfulness to God for teaching him to read." Accounts like those of Townsley and Dupee dramatically demonstrate what scholars of the reading process would call "bringing meaning to the text"—the moment when, through inspired motivation, the readers combined the knowledge they carried inside them with the letters on the printed page.[18]

Slaves who became religious leaders and learned to read and write sometimes gained opportunities for leadership in the black community and chances to teach others to read through the actions of whites. White religious leaders, and those whites who supported an evangelical mission to slaves, found that they had to train and support black preachers in order for their missions to survive. Therefore, they trained black religious leaders, allowed them to teach within their churches, and tried to guard black churches from repression whenever possible.

When white Southerners began an evangelization campaign for slaves, they promoted it as a way of supplanting black preachers, which they admitted were numerous. At best, they said, black preachers were unable to undertake preparation and study; at worst, there was "too great a proneness to superstition among the most enlightened of them, to admit of their being entrusted with the care of souls." The reluctance to give blacks meaningful roles in church hierarchies permeated all American religious bodies, North and South. A Presbyterian leader cautioned that black preachers "should never be taken from among themselves," if only because "the circumstances preclude them from the preparation and study which such a charge involves." Several black men who applied to the Episcopal church's theological seminary in New York in the 1840s and 1850s were discouraged or refused outright. Methodists and Baptists allowed blacks more positions, but hesitated to give them much responsibility. One black Methodist bitterly complained that black denominations such as the A.M.E. and A.M.E. Zion churches gained hundreds of members because of the northern Methodist church's reluctance to ordain black preachers.[19]

White missionaries to the slaves always stressed the importance of white supervision over black religion. Evangelists assured the public that they could work with the prohibitions established by law against black preachers; in fact, the white evangelists would hasten the blacks' retirement. As Jones said in 1833, "The religious instruction of the Negroes by judicious, sensible, and acceptable white men, will destroy the *common colored* preaching in the country, or at least weaken its influence to a considerable extent."[20]

However, despite all these protestations, those white missionaries who actually worked successfully with black congregations quickly found it necessary and desirable to encourage blacks to take leadership positions. After he had been working with blacks for some years, Charles Colcock Jones took back his warning about black preachers; he told whites they had to encourage black leadership in the churches because it would emerge anyway:

> In all societies, some men possessing greater knowledge, zeal, and popularity of manners and excellency of character, than others, will become leaders *in fact*, whether they are made leaders by any *official act* of the societies in which they move or not. . . . Negro preachers and watchmen, regular and irregular, in their ecclesiastic connexions, have existed in our country ever since Christianity has had a footing among that class of people; and they will, in all probability, continue to exist either in one form or other.[21]

Holland McTyeire perceived that positions of religious leadership were necessary to provide an outlet for black aspiration because:

> The church is the only possible theatre for the slave's ambition. In the State he cannot rise, in the church he may. To him the church is eminently a social institution. At the chapel he makes acquaintances and meets friends. In the meeting, if he be a person of reputation and intelligence, he is accorded a distinction unknown elsewhere.[22]

Georgia planter Thomas Clay foresaw, furthermore, that channeling natural leaders into religion was a useful way to promote orderly conduct. Religious instruction, he observed, "draws together the well-disposed and orderly, and by their union gives force to their character and example; it establishes a *caste* among this people, always and in ages past held in respect by the young and the great mass of mankind; and it forms a body through which good principles and salutary regulations may be imparted to the whole community."[23]

Knowing this, and often maneuvered by able and ambitious slaves, white lay leaders and missionaries installed black leaders in churches and Sunday schools. Some of these black leaders taught their parishioners to read as well as to worship. Some of the denominations were moved by competition for converts to offer privileges to African-American slaves as proof of white sincerity.[24] Methodists, for example, who established the largest number of missions to slaves in the rapidly expanding frontier South, developed an effective system for incorporating black leadership into their church structure. Since their white ministers were few, they appointed blacks as local preachers, deacons, elders, exhorters, and class leaders.

African-Americans, either North or South, were seldom ordained as full Methodist preachers before the Civil War, but hundreds were appointed to be local preachers. Many others referred to as "black preachers" were actually exhorters, who were authorized to conduct prayer meetings and often preached at regular church services. Isaac Lane, for example, who taught himself to read and write, applied to the Methodist Church, South, in 1856 for permission to preach, but was licensed to exhort instead; he was only twenty-two. Several years later, the Methodist Church, South, did allow him to preach. Since Henry M. Turner was free as well as literate, on the other hand, he was licensed to preach in 1853 as an itinerant preacher. His connection with the Methodist Church, South, enabled him to travel through South Carolina, Georgia, Alabama, Louisiana, and to St. Louis to preach to both white and black congregations.[25]

Methodists insisted that in black missions or churches the class leaders should be black in order to foster close communion and sympathy for those relating religious experiences, and because "the negroes ordinarily know each others' moral character and conduct, even better than the owner." Autonomous black class leaders were an absolute necessity in southern Methodist churches because these churches claimed thousands of black members with only a few hundred white preachers to minister to them. This was particularly true by the 1850s, when the big Methodist mission campaign had amassed new black membership. For example, by 1858 Alabama had 24,000 black Methodist church members but only 202 fully ordained white preachers. South Carolina in the same year reported only 150 white preachers for 84,000 members, one for every 620 Methodists.[26]

Most of these churches had white preachers and nominal white supervision, but the sheer numbers of black members, the importance of their financial contributions to maintaining Methodism, and the Methodist structure of class leaders and exhorters gave black members considerable authority, allowing them to operate practically as churches within churches. In fact, in 1847, a white Charlestonian pointed out "it is not the white minister who is really the responsible instructor in any one of our churches which has a large black membership—the black class leaders are the real wire pullers."[27]

Since black leaders were so often in actual charge of whole congregations, their ability to read would be an asset for convenience as well as for spiritual benefits. Billy, for example, a plantation preacher in Tennessee, was a talented Methodist exhorter; he could read, and would read lines from hymns as a preface to relating his experiences. Another Methodist leader, Silas Philips, "had enjoyed both moral and religious advantages in his old home" and had been taught to read. According to the recollections of whites, Philips could "expound the scriptures with great clearness and force. He soon became a prophet among his people." Methodist missionaries saw from these and similar examples the value of training in literacy and allowed their black church members to learn from each other. Edwin Cook recalled that though his mission was supposed to be taught by oral instruction only, "many of the scholars . . . could read the catechism and Bible." Black preachers for the three churches Methodists founded in New Orleans were themselves slaves "who could read, and though colored, preach a fair sermon," according to a city newspaper.[28]

Methodists provided opportunities for black leadership within their church because of its carefully planned structure; Baptists because of the exact opposite. Complete independence of each church from another in the early years of the Baptist denomination, the absence of an obligatory creed, and a lay ministry facilitated the forming of new churches. In some racially mixed congregations, whites granted equal participation to blacks.

Black people also formed their own congregations and chose their own preachers. In addition, many southern black preachers preached to white congregations and converted whites. Many of these had acquired at least reading, if not writing skills.[29]

The black church was once called the "invisible church" in the slave South, but its existence is clearly a matter of record. Mechal Sobel has identified the existence of at least 130 formally constituted black churches in the South in the antebellum period in the Baptist denomination alone. These included autonomous black city churches which numbered membership in the thousands in Richmond, Savannah, Augusta, Lexington, and Petersburg, Virginia, as well as black branches of white churches. Thousands of black members in white Baptist churches made the black members of those churches practically autonomous also. Certainly this was true in Charleston's Baptist congregations, whose black membership totaled 5,502 blacks and 1,669 whites in 1850. Charleston whites nominally controlled the churches but divided black members into sections and appointed blacks as watchmen to actually supervise the members. Large Baptist churches in Savannah, Beaufort, South Carolina, Charleston, and Memphis established rural branches so that exhorters and watchmen could hold regular services for their far-flung membership.[30]

Black Baptists conducted affairs for the Sunbury Association, encompassing six Georgia counties which included a large slave population engaged in intensive rice and cotton agriculture as well as the city of Savannah. All but 435 of the 6,873 members of the Sunbury Association in 1841 were black. From 1818 to 1841, ten black men served as ordained ministers in the Sunbury Association. More than one-third of the association's ordained ministers were black in the 1840s and 1850s. In 1849, twelve of the twenty-five churches in the association were designated as "African." In addition, the association employed three black missionaries to preach to the slaves, two on the Savannah River and one on St. Simon's Island. In Florida, two of the six charter members of Bethel Baptist Church in 1838 were slaves, Bacchus and Peggie. By 1859 the church had 290 members of whom 250 were black. Other Florida churches also counted large numbers of black members, some of whom took leadership roles. When the Key West Baptist Church was without a pastor in 1845, black members held weekly prayer meetings and heard sermons by Austin Smith, a licensed Baptist slave preacher.[31]

Even in the most thoroughly white-dominated and controlled Baptist churches, black preachers and watchmen were appointed to administer separate discipline meetings. On the plantations, missionaries selected watchmen "from the most experienced, tried, and faithful" slaves. The watchmen not only supervised and reported delinquent members to the church, but also conducted nightly worship and were generally to "watch over the Church members." Large black churches like those in Savannah also appointed their own deacons. White churches with large black membership also gave their black members autonomy. In Richmond, the white-controlled First African Baptist appointed thirty black leaders, "men of discretion," to conduct the business of the church at monthly meetings with the white preacher in attendance. In addition, black members of the Richmond church conducted their own Temperance Society and the African Mission Society to which members pledged fifty cents per year.[32]

Sobel has noted that "of 284 antebellum black Baptist preachers for whom some biographical data are available, at least 106 were known to have been ordained, 57 of these in the South." She adds that hundreds more slaves served as black Baptist preachers, but that they were not likely to have had their names and vital statistics recorded. The earliest Afro-American Baptist preachers, including David George, George Leile, and Andrew Bryan, could read and promoted reading the Bible among their congregations, asking whites for contributions of reading material. Other literate black Baptist ministers who promoted reading included Gowan Pamphlet, Job Davis, and Lott Carey in the years before 1825. Autobiographies of many slaves who became black Baptist preachers after 1825 indicate that they, too, prized reading and fought to attain literate skills.[33]

Black members of other denominations also became literate religious leaders. Cumberland Presbyterians granted blacks permission to exhort, lead singing, hold prayer meetings, and read the Scriptures publicly. The Disciples of Christ even prepared blacks for the ministry through their college in Nashville. Episcopalians did not formally recognize blacks as their ministers in the antebellum South, but those Episcopal missionaries who had any success in evangelizing slaves used black leaders as helpers. In his Low Country parish, Alexander Glennie used plantation slaves who could read and were "of good character" to teach the catechism and liturgy to the black plantation communities in the evening and on Sundays. He also encouraged his black parishioners to assemble among themselves and read the prayer service. In the summer, in Glennie's absence, a Negro who could read taught the catechism and read the service. Catholic doctrine incorporated slaves into the church's membership and church rules ordered that they be provided with religion and education, which they were in cities. However, fulfillment of church prescriptions to provide religion and education to slaves on plantations was difficult to impossible because of the scarcity of priests and the resistance of many racist Catholic slaveowners. One priest complained that white-imposed restrictions on slave communion had so offended the slaves in his charge that they refused to attend services and began to read the Protestant Bible.[34]

Since both whites and blacks considered reading a valuable skill for a plantation preacher, owners employed literate slaves in that position. Recollections by former slaves corroborate the support of literate black preachers by slaveowners. The Tallahassee owners of "Father James Page," who could read and write, allowed him to visit all the area plantations once a month, where he would read the Bible, preach and sing, baptize the converted, and serve the sacrament. Owners allowed or commissioned preachers to teach also. James Southall of Clarksville, Tennessee, recalled that his owner "let us hav church in de homes. All of our cullud preachers could read de Bible. [His owner] let them teach us how to read iffen we wanted to learn."[35]

Henry Bohannon was a house boy on a 500-acre plantation east of Atlanta. In the 1850s his owner bought a black preacher and teacher who held church on Sundays and school during the week for the children too small to work in the field, where the black preacher taught them how to read and write. In Charlotte County, Virginia, also in the 1850s, Levi Pollard's master bought a slave who was a preacher and held school on Sunday evenings, where, Pollard recalled, "he [would] read de Bible en pray, den he use de New York Primmer with great big letters in hit. He show us how ter mak 'em en us wuz learnin' good."[36]

Slaves in unique positions were also able to carry on their teaching openly. According to his daughter's recollections, Little

Rock, Arkansas, butler William Wallace Andrews' English owner allowed Andrews and his wife to maintain their own home. They had permission to invite other slaves over for Sunday worship, where, as Andrews' daughter recalled, her father "taught not only the word of God by hearing but taught many eager friends to actually read the printed page."[37]

White religious leaders who allowed or encouraged black churches and literacy always risked community disapproval or worse and had little power to protect their churches. Southern whites in cities were constantly on guard in fear of African-American fraternizing, and more especially, against the growth of an organized black community. Since churches provided the best opportunity for this to occur, they were under suspicion during the entire slave era. The fact that black membership was so large, whites to supervise them so few, and that black leaders did therefore emerge, gave grounds for suspicion. Criticisms of churches filled southern newspapers, and city authorities periodically passed municipal ordinances restricting black congregations, black preaching, black learning and teaching. Occasionally mobs took or threatened to take more direct action against the churches and against Sunday schools, where learning was rightly suspected to be taking place.[38] And yet, black churches and Sunday schools continued to survive.

One of the reasons that white authorities allowed black churches to exist was expediency. In most cases, it was too much trouble to close a church and, more importantly, keep it closed. Churches which police closed tended to reopen in other buildings, or the congregations would meet in homes, as happened in New Orleans after city authorities closed the A.M.E. churches in 1858.[39] The problem of numbers was also an inhibiting factor in closing churches. More than 10,000 black Charlestonians belonged to the churches; there was danger and tension in completely and suddenly repressing their spiritual lives, or so the authorities calculated. Also, churches were not closed because whites would have objected. The feeling that there was something wrong in depriving human beings of religion and of the Bible was heightened through the decades of the antebellum period by mission evangelists, who had created a climate in which religion for blacks could be considered a positive value which followed in the tradition of their forbears. As a descendant of French Huguenots declared when a mob threatened an Episcopal mission church for slaves, blacks had a right to religion: "The liberty of teaching what was true and good to all men, why sirs, that was what brought many of our fathers here."[40]

If they moved carefully in this atmosphere of suspicion, Afro-American preachers could appeal to those whites with consciences, apply the skills of literacy to gain advantages for themselves in the white community, and at the same time mediate for their fellow slaves. An example of the way in which this interrelationship could work is seen in the autobiography of Elisha Green. For sixteen years Green, a slave hired out to a storekeeper in Maysville, Kentucky, was a sexton in a white Baptist church. Green's owner's young daughter taught him to write, beginning with the alphabet, and within a month he was able to write his brother a letter. He worked steadily to learn to read, keeping books in the third story of the store where he worked and in the summer, when his work was slack, going upstairs in the heat "endeavoring to study and read the Bible."[41]

In 1845 the white Baptists licensed Green to exhort and to travel to other towns to preach and conduct funerals for blacks. This was not without risk and difficulty; once he was stopped during a service in Georgetown, Kentucky, because there were no white men present. The next day, however, the pastor of the white Baptist church in Georgetown assured Green that he could stay there and preach as long as he wished. In 1853 Green began preaching on his own, with the support of whites who protected his travel and lent him Presbyterian, Church of Christ, and Baptist churches for his services. In the 1850s he bought himself and founded his own African Baptist Church in Maysville. In 1858, men in Maysville lent him $850 to purchase his wife and children.[42]

Elisha Green told his own story; many other black preachers who negotiated the fine line of behavior acceptable to whites to gain for themselves are seen only through white accounts. Jack, for example, was described in glowing terms by white religious leaders in Virginia in the early part of the nineteenth century. Jack was kidnaped in Africa and brought to Nottoway County, Virginia, at the age of seven. He learned to speak excellent English and, after his conversion to Christianity at the age of forty, learned to read through tutoring from his owner's children. He was licensed to preach to plantation slaves, but he also preached to whites, including "many of the most wealthy and refined people" of the county. A white preacher and professor described his distinctive and powerful use of language: "The acquaintance of this African preacher with the scriptures is wonderful. Many interpretations of obscure passages are singularly just and striking. In many respects indeed he is one of the most remarkable men I have known."

Whites also noted approvingly that Jack maintained order among his slave congregations, always dressed in slave clothes, and never "put himself on a level with the white race." He would never allow his congregation to "get happy," since he did not like "more sound than service" in the pulpit. After Virginia's 1831–32 legislation ostensibly barring blacks from reading or preaching, Jack quietly withdrew from public oratory, but his congregation raised a subscription to emancipate him.[43]

Other black leaders deemed remarkable by whites included George, chronicled in the *Southern Presbyterian Review,* who learned to read by his own efforts, assisted by his masters' children. By 1860 he traveled and preached a great deal, mostly to whites, who appreciated his expert use of the English language. George read his Bible and hymns quite well, subscribed to one or two religious periodicals, and used a dictionary to correct word pronunciation and usage. He was an excellent speaker and preacher, and in sum, according to whites, was a model of "piety . . . integrity . . . truth . . . humility [and] diffidence."[44]

Pompey, noted in the memoirs of a white Tennessee Methodist, was another able black preacher who gained benefits from his assimilation but learned to maintain a subordinate role. Pompey traveled with his master, an itinerant Methodist preacher, and became converted at a camp meeting, where he "felt a very great interest in his master's success as a minister of Jesus Christ." Like so many others after conversion, Pompey wanted to read, did so, and took great interest in reading the Bible. "He studied it day and night" and also "gave close attention to the expositions of Scripture as his master preached." After Pompey proved that he, too, could preach, his master freed him so that he might go where he pleased. Pompey chose to travel from North Carolina to middle Tennessee. There he was successful, according to accounts, because of the power, sincerity, and simplicity of his preaching.[45]

Pompey preached mostly to white congregations and even organized and presided over a camp meeting for white settlers in Mississippi in which he was the only preacher, with a white exhorter. He maintained his extraordinary success among whites through his awareness of what whites expected him to be, as related approvingly by a white southern minister: "Although so many would attend [Pompey's] ministry, and so many invite him to their houses, yet he was humble, respectful, and retiring. When invited by white persons to their homes (and many felt it to be an honor to have him go home with them), he would always go to the kitchen, or servants' house, unless they pressed him. . . . He would always say master, or mistress, when addressing white persons." Pompey was careful, also, not to show off his ability to read in front of whites who may have been illiterate themselves; the white minister recalled that "he had memorized so much of the Scriptures that I never knew him to take a Bible in his hand at family-worship."[46]

Former slaves who wrote their narratives and autobiographies in the United States seldom revealed the extent to which this conduct was a game. Thomas Johnson, however, who became a missionary in England and wrote his autobiography there, took on more of the role of the fabled trickster who is part of heroic folklore and told how he had fooled the whites around him in order to gain more and more knowledge of reading and writing and of the world around him.[47]

Few of those who learned to read as slaves were able to do so without earning the good will of some whites. Because literacy was a skill prized in both black and white communities, black leaders could exhibit qualities prized by whites without necessarily losing rapport with the black community. Their narratives show that slaves understood and sympathized with black preachers acting under white orders and appreciated the difficulties under which they worked. Those who assimilated could receive important privileges from masters or other whites for learning white skills but could also protect and benefit slaves on the plantation. Gerald Mullin calls these people "mediators, political go-betweens—what the anthropologist Malcolm McGee has called the '150 per cent acculturated man.'" Charles Joyner calls them "gifted," straddling the secular and sacred worlds, mediating between the slaves' Christian beliefs and the workaday world of oppression. These southern black leaders used the sacred texts they had learned to read to create a meaningful reality, "renewing and recycling the energies of the slave community." With their literate skills they fashioned slave religion into a progressive force and a shield against white domination.[48]

Chapter Five

■

"Bible Slavery":
The White Role in Slave Literacy

ORMER SLAVES WHO LEARNED TO READ AND WRITE
during slavery often recalled that whites had initiated
their learning.[1] Slaves remembered a variety of reasons
for this teaching by whites, some pragmatic, some ideological. A
few whites expressed libertarian outrage that the state would
dictate how they were or were not to treat their slaves. Samuel
Hall's owner, a teacher, taught his slaves to read out of opposition to the North Carolina law which forbade him doing so. He
preferred to perpetuate the state's tradition that masters
should teach apprentices to read and write. Even though this
feature of apprenticeship was no longer the law when Sam was
born in 1818, his master extended the definition of apprentices
to include slaves. Hall recalled that his owner "decided that his
Negroes should read and he gave us a chance to learn." Other
whites showed a belief in learning and a desire to extend it to
the people they controlled. Robert Laird's Mississippi owner had
his slaves taught to read and write, Laird recalled, simply because "he didn't want us not to know nothin'."[2]

Often, the reasons for white teaching were pragmatic: as
Texan Harrison Beckett succinctly stated, "Dey try not to let de
chilluns come up so ign'nant. Den dey could use 'em better for
dey own purpose." One such instructor was Washington Curry's
owner, a Mississippi doctor who owned about 100 slaves in the

1840s. Curry recalled that "there were so many folks that came to see the doctor and wanted to leave numbers and addresses that he had to have someone to 'tend to that and he taught my father to read and write so that he could do it." Similarly, on a very large plantation in Oglethorpe County, Georgia, in the 1830s, Adeline Willis' mistress taught her the letters on the newspapers and what they spelled so she could bring the papers they wanted. On a Texas plantation with over 100 slaves, Simpson Campbell's "Marse Bill" taught some of his slaves reading and writing so he could use them "bookin cotton in the field and sich like."[3] If there were few of these recollections of teaching for pragmatic reasons, most of the South was rural, literacy among the white population was far from universal, and much of the business of the farm and the plantation could be conducted without literate skills.

The slaveowners' belief that they could do what they wished with their slaves led to a curious variety of relationships, as recounted by former slaves and their descendants. Mamie Garvin Fields' great-great-uncle Thomas attended classes along with his young South Carolina charges, the Middleton sons, and then went with them to Oxford. He learned along with them, even studying Hebrew and Greek, and later taught his sons and daughters, who taught other slaves. Pauli Murray always believed that her great-grandfather Thomas Fitzgerald was born free until she found his emancipation papers in Wilmington, North Carolina. His Quaker owner never represented his slaves as such to the census taker and freed each of them when they reached twenty-four. He taught Thomas to read and write to prepare him for emancipation. Slave recollections of women teaching their house slaves as part of their household work together, or of teaching little slave children because they were "cute" gives some idea of the complexity of interactions between enslaved African-Americans and whites.[4]

Some white-initiated instruction of slaves was more widespread and purposeful, however. Southern white religious leaders and lay reformers, supported by a few large landowners, associated themselves with the benevolent movements so prominent in the antebellum North. One of the ways they saw themselves participating in these movements while living in the slave system was to establish systematic religious instruction for slaves on plantations and in cities, often in conjunction with the literary training which most of them felt was essential to understanding God's word. There were satisfying elements in providing religious instruction for slaves: it was supposed to be under the firm control of the slaveowner, thereby keeping his authority clearly in focus; its proven results were to improve the discipline of the plantation; and it made the slaveowner and his family feel that they were acting morally.

If we accept Paul Escott's interpretation of the plantation as "two worlds," the "slaveowner's world" justified teaching slaves for these "moral" purposes. White reminiscences written after slavery recalled that teaching slaves was a pleasant occupation, encouraged by "good" white families. Susan McPherson's children, for example, noted that she encouraged them to "teach the young negroes how to spell and read." The children even held regular schools for slaves from time to time "at which the young instructors did something else besides merely play at teaching." Susan Dabney Smedes' family held worship services and a Sunday school for their slaves in Virginia and Susan's brother Virginius taught those who cared to learn how to read, being paid by his slave pupils with two dozen eggs a month or occasionally a pullet. According to Smedes, five of his students learned to read so well that they became preachers. A Sea Island plantation owner recalled that "Jack could read and also August Baker our houseservant" because "our mother had given both of them Testaments and Prayerbooks."[5]

Moncure Conway's family was Methodist. Conway, later a critic of slavery, recalled that the family slaves were taught along with the white children, from the Bible. Conway taught one of his slaves to read in exchange for a new tie. Mary Chesnut and Atticus Haygood were among others who recalled teaching slaves to read. Mary Winans Wall, daughter of a Methodist leader, taught Sunday school for slaves as a young girl. When she married and moved to Clinton, Louisiana, she began another school for slaves and free blacks there. Two of her pupils became ministers. Thomas (Stonewall) Jackson, when a VMI cadet in Lexington, Virginia, began a Sunday school within his Presbyterian church for local African-Americans, including slaves, and personally reported each month to their owners on the progress of his students. Swedish traveler and writer Frederika Bremer reported this picture as the slaveowners wished to remember it; traveling in the South in the 1850s, she saw "some young girls, the daughters and sisters of planters, who are not ashamed of keeping schools themselves for the children of the slaves on the plantation."[6]

These images were used during slavery to justify its existence and mitigate its harshness; after slavery, reminiscences like these were added to the efforts to remember slavery times in a positive light. Therefore, justifiably, white claims of teaching slaves have always been open to skepticism. However, accounts by former slaves also recall some systematic white teaching for religious purposes. According to former slaves' recollections, owners gathered slaves in groups to catechize them and teach them to read the Bible, or built churches or schoolhouses for them and hired preachers and tutors. Near Birmingham, Alabama, for example, Andrew Goodman's "Marse Bob" built his slaves a church where a nearby slave, "a man of good learnin'," preached to them on Sundays; then on Sunday afternoons, Marse Bob taught them how to read and write, telling his slaves, "we ought to get all the learnin' we could." Nettie Henry's owner, a young widow, taught school in Meridian, Mississippi, in the late 1850s and early 1860s. She and her children tried to teach Nettie and her sisters from their blue-back spellers during the week. Then, on Sunday, Nettie and her sisters carried their spellers to Sunday school, where an old black Baptist preacher taught them to read.[7]

As Catherine Clinton has shown, recollections by both whites and former slaves "confirm that mistresses attempted to enforce Christian principles and to deal morally with a very brutal and dehumanizing system." Women were frequently the teachers or motivators for providing religious instruction and the teaching of reading. Typical of these was Alfred Jones' owner in Lowndes County, Alabama, in the 1830s and 1840s. Jones recalled that she would "load us all in a waggin and take us to meetin. She'd follow behine de waggin in her carriage so de patteroler wouln' bodder us." Jones added that "ole missus didn' sen' us to no school; she teach us herself. Onlies' book we had was de Blue Back Speller, but we had lessons in dat every day." Women sometimes had to overcome the opposition of their husbands in order to teach slaves. C. H. Hall's 1820s Maryland owner, "old madam Bean . . . belonged to the Baptist church [and] said we might all learn to spell and read the Bible. The old man fought against it for some time, but found it prevailed nothing."[8]

Some slaves learned to read in white churches. In Helicon Springs, Georgia, Alice Green recalled that she and her children "jined de white folks church and was baptized by de white preacher [who] larnt us to read de Bible." Mollie Mitchell, a field slave in Georgia after the age of seven, went to Sunday school where the slaves were taught "out of a blue-back speller." John Ellis' owner in Cleburne, Texas, in the 1850s was a preacher himself; Ellis recalled that "we had good bed and good food and he teached us to read and write too."[9]

Whites who were willing to allow slaves to read the Bible, however, often tried to limit any further reading. Mary Jones described such an effort to shield slaves from the possible liberating effects of knowledge. Her mother's owners in Gloucester County, Virginia, the Pages, descendants of early Virginia settlers, tried to carry on a tradition of *noblesse oblige* by funding special pews in Abingdon church for their slaves and by teaching them to read the Episcopal catechism and the Bible. They barred all other books but those two from their plantation, however. Similarly, North Carolina slaveowner Mary Ruffin Smith could not bear to ignore her brothers' children by Harriet, a slave woman. She raised them in her house and had them trained in her Episcopal faith. However, she allowed the governess to teach them only enough to read some of the Bible.[10]

Another measure of the conservatism of white religious instruction was the fact that a majority of whites who taught slaves for religious reasons taught reading only and not writing. In Missouri, Henry Bruce's owner, for example, was "glad his Negroes could read, especially the Bible, but he was opposed to their being taught writing," and Bruce did not learn to write until after slavery ended. Owners suspected, with justification, that slaves who learned to write would write their own passes and run away. Also, owners shared the traditional uneasiness about educating the working classes beyond their station: teaching workers to read would help inculcate morality, but teaching them writing might threaten the social order.[11]

Those southern whites who involved themselves with the systematic religious training of slaves were influenced by the great reform movements sweeping the nineteenth century western world. The rapid spread of organized benevolence in the century's second and third decades in the United States evolved from British models. Filled with the conviction that good will toward man was an essential Christian virtue, these societies worked outside regular church organizations to perfect society and to convert the nation to God. Theologically rooted both in Calvinism and the evangelicalism inspired by revivalist Awakenings, promoters of reform were concerned first and foremost with the individual sinner's search for personal holiness. However, reformers extended their focus to the individual's relationship with society. The views of society held by benevolent reformers were complex: on one hand, they wanted to preserve social order, which accepted inequality and hierarchy as inevitable; on the other hand their millennial base and emotional humanitarianism led the adherents of reform to attack and seek to solve social suffering. Reformers examined every American institution, every idea, every conceivable sin, evil, and burden.[12]

National organizations which had a connection with literacy were generally consolidations of local and regional efforts and included the American Bible Society (ABS), the American Tract Society, the American Sunday School Union, and the American Missionary Association. The American Bible Society was organized in a convention in 1816 which sought to integrate the efforts of previously organized local groups and to inspire new societies. The American Sunday School Union began in Philadelphia in 1817 as a businessmen's effort to supplement and expand denominational Sunday school movements. The American Tract Society was created in 1825 from a combining of groups promoting the distribution of religious literature in the major northeastern cities. Despite their northern orientation, these groups received support from those southern white churchmen and reformers who were interested in missions and benevolence. Bible Society directors included Carolina and Virginia ministers William Plumer, Benjamin Palmer, and William Meade, and prominent planters John Cocke and Charles Cotesworth Pinckney. Cocke, Meade, Plumer, and South Carolina Baptist leader Richard Fuller were also active in the Tract Society and the Sunday School Union. Their particular concern, in addition to their benevolent activities, was to be sure the South was not neglected in the associations.[13]

White southern support for benevolence was also shown by the number of Bible societies counted in southern states by 1814: eleven in Virginia, two each in Maryland and South Carolina, and others in North Carolina and Georgia. Charleston support for the evangelical and literary goals of the ABS and Tract societies is seen in the number of reform organizations which emerged in that city in the early nineteenth century, including the Charleston Bible Society, 1810; the Ladies Benevolent Society, 1813; the Religious Tract Society, 1815; the Congregational and Presbyterian Union Female Association,

1815; the Female Bible Society, 1816; the Sabbath School Association, 1816; the Marine Bible Society, 1818 [to give Bibles to seamen]; the Female Domestic Missionary Society, 1818; the Sunday School Union Society, 1819; the Elliott Society, 1819 [missions to Indians]; and the Associate Reading Society, 1819.[14]

The Charleston elite supported the Bible Society because their fathers had; the Charleston ministry, including William Capers, Benjamin Palmer, and William H. Barnwell, participated in the Tract Society also. Women were more active in the Tract Society than in the Bible Society. They ran female auxiliaries which raised money to publish tracts and also ordered large numbers of tracts which they personally distributed. Local Bible and Tract societies in the South undertook activities even when not affiliated with the national, northern-oriented organizations. Where local auxiliaries were absent in southern communities, individuals belonged to the national groups and shared their goals, depending on national journals and correspondence to justify altruistic activities.[15]

The American Bible Society, American Tract Society, and the American Sunday School Union emphasized the benefits of the printed page in the social improvement of the poor and degraded and in preparing the sinner for salvation. In a letter to the American Bible Society, a missionary to India expressed well the driving sentiments and goals of both these groups:

> Our own experience and that of others teach us that the Word of God is, and must be the great instrument of doing good among the people, of enlightening their minds, and of turning them to righteousness. Our ardent desire, therefore, is to supply, as far as our means and strength will permit, every family within our reach with a copy of the words of life. The truth and nothing but the truth as contained in the Scriptures, and accompanied by the quickening influences of the holy Spirit, we are convinced, ever can illumine the dark mind of man. The Gospel of Jesus Christ reveals the only remedy for a fallen world. May the nations of the earth soon possess and use it.[16]

The belief that knowledge of the Bible could control the dangerously disorderly poor is exhibited in the Sunday School Union's goals to "withdraw ignorant, neglected, and vicious children from the streets" and to produce from them an "orderly, responsible people."[17] However, the sentimentality towards the poor which was evolving in the industrial world in the early nineteenth century could also be seen in the pages of the societies' journals. Peddlers of devotional literature, called colporteurs, told of entering humble households where the poor received their Bibles and tracts with gratitude, models of faith among the lowly. In chronicles by mostly northern writers, African-Americans were particularly singled out among the poor as symbols of humble, simple devotion. They were favorite subjects for Sunday School Union claims of success: their "outcast and neglected" state aroused sympathy and their eagerness to learn gratified teachers and stimulated contributions. Their numbers added measurably to the claimed success of the Sunday School Union; in 1817 blacks constituted 25 percent of New York's pupils being educated by the Society. In 1819 about two thirds of almost 1,100 adults in Philadelphia's Sunday and Adult School Union were black. Southern cities, including Charleston, Nashville, and St. Louis, frequently included black pupils or black classes in their Sunday school reports.[18]

One of the most popular Tract Society pamphlets was *The Negro Servant,* an "authentic narrative of a young Negro, showing how he was made a slave in Africa; and carried to Jamaica, where he was sold to a captain in His Majesty's navy, and taken to America, where he became a Christian; and afterwards brought to England, and baptised." In the story, written in dialogue style, "William," the servant, relates his attraction to Christianity. When asked how he learned to read, William answered:

> God teach me to read. . . . God give me desire to read, and that make reading easy. Master give me a Bible, and one sailor show me the letters, and so me learn to read by myself, with God's goot help. . . . Me read all about Jesus Christ, and how he loved sinners, and wicked men kill him, and he died, and came gain from the grave, and all this for poor Negro.[19]

William's religious fervor and his reading ability, acquired at great cost and used to maintain his faith, showed tract readers that the most devout Christian could also be the least fortunate in society.

Another vignette featuring spiritually motivated black readers came from the 1840 campaign in which Charleston ministers and other Tract Society members undertook to visit every

1. Susie King Taylor, born a slave near Savannah in 1848, educator during and after the war and organizer of the Woman's Relief Corps. Taylor learned to read as a slave child in Savannah at a school kept by her grandmother's friend, a free black woman.

2. Thomas L. Johnson, born a slave in Richmond, Virginia, in 1840, became a missionary and evangelist in the United States, Africa, and the British Isles. Johnson often told how he learned to read as a boy and a young man while enslaved in Virginia.

3. Richard Fuller, Baptist minister and South Carolina plantation owner and slaveowner. Fuller, famous for his 1845 defense of slavery in a written debate with Francis Wayland, insisted on teaching his slaves to read, even when his petition to that effect was refused by the South Carolina legislature in 1850.

4. Rev. Joseph A. Booker, born a slave in Arkansas in 1859 and President of Arkansas Baptist College in 1880. Booker told how his father was whipped to death for knowing how to read and teaching others. Joseph's grandmother taught him to spell, read, and write before slavery ended.

5. Henry Bibb, born a slave in 1815 in Shelby County, Kentucky. After a number of failures and reenslavements, Bibb left slavery successfully for the North in 1845, where he wrote a narrative of his adventures. The American Missionary Association employed him in their "Bibles for Slaves" campaign in the late 1840s, to distribute Bibles in the border slave states; black abolitionists, led by Frederick Douglass, opposed the campaign and Bibb left for Canada in 1849.

6. William Jefferson White, born into slavery in Ruckersville, Georgia, 1831; cabinet maker, preacher, and teacher of a secret school for slaves. Became an organizer of schools for the Freedmen's Bureau, politician, and editor of the *Georgia Baptist*. White's mother taught him the alphabet and at the age of six he bought his own Webster's speller for twelve and one-half cents earned from gathering chestnuts. Hired out to factories, he studied from 1:00 to 2:00 A.M. every night and learned, one book at a time.

book, dôve, full, use, can, chaise, gem, thin, thou.

No. 26.—XXVI.

Words of two syllables, accented on the first.

Ba ker	tro ver	so lar	wo ful	pa pal
sha dy	clo ver	po lar	po em	co pal
la dy	do nor	lu nar	fo rum	vi al
ti dy	va por	so ber	sa tan	pe nal
ho ly	fa vor	pa cer	fu el	ve nal
li my	fla vor	ra cer	du el	fi nal
sli my	sa vor	gro cer	cru el	o ral
bo ny	ha lo	ci der	gru el	ho ral
po ny	so lo	spi der	pu pil	mu ral
po ker	he ro	wa fer	la bel	na sal
ti ler	ne gro	wa ges	li bel	fa tal
ca per	ty ro	ti ger	lo cal	na tal
pa per	bu bo	ma ker	fo cal	pe tal
ta per	sa go	ta ker	vo cal	vi tal
vi per	tu lip	ra ker	le gal	to tal
bi ter	ce dar	se ton	re gal	o val
fe ver	bri er	ru in	di al	pli ant
o ver	fri ar	hy men	tri al	gi ant

Bakers bake bread and cakes.
I like to play in the shady grove.
Some fishes are very bony.
I love the young lady that shows me how to read.
A pony is a very little horse.
We poke the fire with the poker.
The best paper is made of linen rags.
Vipers are bad snakes, and they bite men.
An ox loves to eat clover.
The tulip is very pretty, growing in the garden.
A dial shows the hour of the day.
Cedar trees grow in the woods.
The black-berry grows on a brier.

7b. First page of two-syllable words from Noah Webster's *The Elementary Spelling Book.* The "blue back" speller was the most frequently used aid to reading in the antebellum United States; slaves who learned to read often recalled "spelling to baker" or "reading as far as baker and shady."

"Let it hasten to those who wait for tidings."

"There is a Friend that sticketh closer than a brother."

7a. Letter from Private Spotswood Rice to his enslaved daughters, St. Louis, Missouri, Sept. 3, 1864. Rice, a tobacco roller and slave, joined the Union army in February 1864. "The first fourteen lines of this letter appear to be in Rice's handwriting, the remainder in another hand." (Courtesy of the National Archives. Notation from Ira Berlin, ed., *Freedom: A Documentary History of Emancipation, 1861–1867,* Cambridge, Eng.: Cambridge University Press, 1982.)

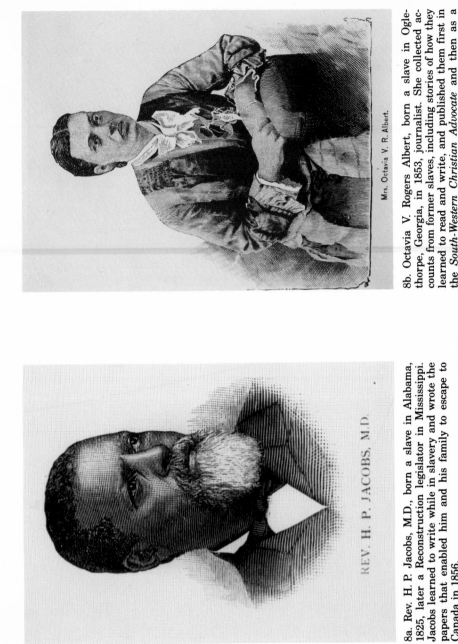

Mrs. Octavia V. R. Albert.

REV. H. P. JACOBS, M.D.

8b. Octavia V. Rogers Albert, born a slave in Ogle-thorpe, Georgia, in 1853, journalist. She collected ac-counts from former slaves, including stories of how they learned to read and write, and published them first in the *South-Western Christian Advocate* and then as a book collection.

8a. Rev. H. P. Jacobs, M.D., born a slave in Alabama, 1825, later a Reconstruction legislator in Mississippi. Jacobs learned to write while in slavery and wrote the papers that enabled him and his family to escape to Canada in 1856.

family in the city to offer Bibles. The Tract Society reporter told the following story from one of the volunteers:

> One distributor was repulsed by a family of great wealth and respectability, and when passing from the door, observed a colored man (a butcher) standing at the door of his little cottage. . . . The [black] man invited him into his house, and immediately paid for and took thankfully a family library of 15 volumes!—not the first instance where the Gospel has been welcomed in the abode of poverty, though excluded from the palace of plenty and pride.[20]

Following in this theme, the American Bible Society claimed that it had "always had a peculiar satisfaction in furnishing the Scripture, when in their power" to free blacks and slaves. Two Tract Society colporteurs became missionaries to slaves, "the most neglected part of our population," and the society hired a black colporteur, "an intelligent and pious colored man," to work in northern towns and cities among the black population.[21]

Presentation of African-Americans as "the poor," worthy and in need of aid, allowed white Southerners to justify furnishing slaves with religious materials and instruction in reading skills. White Southerners who were active in benevolent causes recognized that slaves played this role. In a sermon in Charleston, for example, John B. Adger asked, "Who are the Poor?" and answered:

> The poor of this city are easily distinguishable. They are in a class separated from ourselves by their color, their position in society, their relation to our families, their national origin, and their moral, intellectual and physical condition.[22]

White Southerners were also encouraged to educate slaves because of the inevitable progress of humanity which was assumed by leaders of the benevolent movement. Pervasiveness of millennial beliefs and of the conviction that the United States was specially chosen to achieve perfection in society permeated American reform movements. This conviction was echoed by white Southerners who viewed the progress of slavery with optimism. As evangelical Christians who accepted the Biblical version of creation, those white Southerners who were reform-minded could not accept theories of separate origins of the races which were being developed by Louis Agassiz and Josiah C. Nott, among others. On the other hand, Southern reformers' racism and the circumstances and rationalizations for slavery persuaded them that African-Americans were not their equals.[23] Their solution was to look on the slave as lower than the slaveowner on the scale of humanity at the present time— but moving up, with the help of their "superiors."

One origin of this perspective was the optimistic view of childhood which had developed since the eighteenth century. The Romantic vision of the child saw him as a rational, relatively innocent creature who could be "trained up in the ways of righteousness through education."[24] White Southern slaveholders, ministers, and missionaries who were interested in reform could make the leap from this condition of childhood to a similar condition in which they found slaves and could see slavery as a positive step in this training. Prominent South Carolina Presbyterian clergyman James Henley Thornwell postulated that for groups less advanced than his own, slavery could be, as Thornwell carefully put it, "a good, or to speak more accurately, a condition, though founded in a curse, from which the Providence of God extracts a blessing."[25]

One of the most forthright spokesmen in expressing a popular southern view of the positive prospects for slavery was Richard Fuller. Fuller was an energetic preacher and a prolific writer from a well-connected Beaufort, South Carolina, family which owned plantations and scores of slaves on the Carolina mainland and sea islands. A Harvard graduate in classics, Fuller had trained as a lawyer, but was converted in a famous Beaufort revival in 1832. In 1844, he used his position as one of the best-known Baptist preachers in the South to get involved in a literary debate over slavery with Francis Wayland, President of Brown University in Providence, Rhode Island.[26]

Wayland had proposed that slavery was inherently sinful and that all those who participated in the system as slaveholders were guilty of moral sin. Fuller undertook to respond to him and they exchanged a series of letters. In his responses, Fuller presented a beneficent picture of the slave system as it was practiced in the South. He thought it ironic that he found himself as the apologist for slavery, "the existence of which I lament; for the commencement of which I am not at all responsible; for the extinction of which I am willing to make greater sacrifices than any abolitionist." But Fuller was also an optimist, consistently cheerful—the kind of person who, according to a friend, would determinedly walk on the sunny side of the street, even on a steamy Beaufort summer afternoon. He refused, therefore, to see slavery as a disastrous situation for Africans or to bear its guilt. His descriptions of slavery in operation depicted lenient masters, slaves with light workloads and time and property of their own, and Christian missionaries bringing salvation and social order to the slave.[27]

Fuller's pleasant picture of slavery was based on his own experience. He owned from 150 to 200 slaves and declared that "their condition is as good as I can make it:" comfortable quarters, clothes and food and a light work schedule. He paid a missionary to teach and preach to them and refused ever to "sell human beings." Fuller, a wealthy man, donated his preacher's salary to pay missionaries to preach to slaves on outlying plantations and arranged for black exhorters to hold prayer meetings for them. A black colleague in the Baptist church once described him as "one of the best Masters in the state, and much loved by his slaves," an evaluation supported by the warm welcome he was given by his former slaves when he visited them shortly after the war. Black singers also incorporated his name into a well known spiritual, though whether because of his moral stature or his prominence is open to question.[28]

Like many other southern religious leaders, Fuller believed that "the whole human family have sprung from common parentage." He believed that African-Americans were capable of intellectual attainments, given the right circumstances, and that "everywhere the gospel requires of a master the moral and intellectual improvement of the slaves." Therefore, slaves as well as the white poor should be taught to read. Fuller insisted that laws barring slave assemblies and preaching were "a dead letter." He went further in his exchange with Wayland and proclaimed that South Carolina's law was regularly violated: "the most important law is that forbidding slaves being taught to read; yet how many are taught!" He concluded that "the condition of the African has been vastly improved, physically, intellectually, morally, and religiously, by his transportation to these shores."[29]

Fuller and other southern reformers admitted, however, that this improvement in the condition of the African had not yet been completed. It was the duty of white Southerners to fulfill the plan of God by advancing slaves into the next stages of civilization. Christian education would be the method for uplifting slaves, just as it was for the child. An Episcopalian priest portrayed himself and other southern ministers who taught slaves as "God's schoolmasters"; Presbyterian John B. Adger described southern slave society as "just a grand civilizing and Christianizing school."[30] By giving reformers hope and assurance that this "school of slavery" could be effected through use of the Bible, benevolent movements gave their southern adherents the encouragement they needed to promote literacy and religion for the slave population.

Thus justified, slaveowners and ministers in the South took advantage of the offer by Bible, tract, and Sunday school groups to distribute materials and asked for them for their slaves. Requests for reading materials came from slaveowners, ministers and missionaries teaching slaves even in Virginia, North Carolina, and Alabama, where such teaching was against the law. In addition to direct requests, many enslaved African-Americans "benefitted incidentally" from publications, according to the Tract Society, and Bibles and tracts were given covertly to black readers. In border states, Sunday schools maintained for whites and free and slave blacks were furnished with books.[31]

Even in Virginia and South Carolina, where teaching was illegal, Sunday schools for slaves were taught with books, catechisms, and hymnals. Sunday school teachers and ministers who had large black congregations in their churches and asked for hundreds of tracts must have been teaching blacks themselves or encouraging their reading. William Henry Ruffner organized a Sunday School in Lexington, Virginia, where hundreds of blacks were taught to read in the 1840s and 1850s. John B. Adger was in charge of a mission church for slaves established by Presbyterians in Charleston in 1849. Adger was an opponent of restriction on literacy for slaves and free blacks: he protested the laws, declared that they were constantly being violated, and let his children teach his own household slaves. A former missionary to the Armenians, where he used Charles Colcock Jones' catechism for slaves to teach his Armenian converts to read the Bible, Adger ordered and was sent 31,500 pages of tract literature for his black mission church in 1852. Almost certainly his slave congregation was using this literature in his church.[32]

White preachers and teachers were not enough to reach millions of slaves, and blacks preferred to choose religious leaders from among themselves. Caught up as they were in the convictions that their "school of slavery" was doing its best for the slave, that instruction was a guarantee of safety and stability in southern slave society, and that the slave's salvation depended on access to organized Christian religion, white reformers found themselves employing, encouraging, and protecting black leaders, schools, and churches in order to perpetuate their religious convictions and their dreams of maintaining their society.

Whites did, however, control another movement designed to promote benevolence, mission work, and literacy—colonization. White ministers, politicians, and professional reformers founded the American Colonization Society (ACS) in 1816. Its stated goals were to Christianize Africa through sending American free blacks and manumitted slaves to establish colonies in their land of origin and to witness to people there about the benefits of Christianity and civilization through example, preaching, and teaching.

The colonization movement actively publicized and promoted the idea of slave and free African-Americans being taught to read and write. The ACS assumed that if African-Americans were to Christianize and civilize Africa and establish businesses and trade, they would carry with them the skills of literacy. Colonization leaders and publication editors therefore promoted literacy and education projects for African-Americans, gave publicity to slaveowners who taught slaves to read and then emancipated them, identified numbers of literate emigrants, and printed letters from literate slaves.

Colonization was bitterly fought by antislavery groups, who rightly suspected that it aimed to divert reform energies from the complete abolition of slavery. This condemnation of colonization as a threat to the antislavery movement, however, has led historians to overlook general support for the movement among reform-minded white Southerners and to ignore ways in which the colonization goal was used to justify slave literacy and emancipation and black education.[33] Colonization aroused general suspicion in the white South because of its links with emancipation, but those southern reformers who were active in other benevolent causes considered colonization socially acceptable. Southern ACS supporters included church leaders Richard Fuller, William Meade, Benjamin Palmer, William S. Plumer, and Robert Breckinridge. Colonization societies were active in Kentucky, Mississippi, Missouri, Louisiana, and Georgia. Colonization was supported in New Orleans by Methodists Holland McTyeire, William Winans, and Benjamin Drake, and by Episcopal Bishop Leonidas Polk, president of the New Orleans Society in 1857.[34]

Some reform-minded slaveowners used colonization as an emancipation vehicle because they believed in African missions, they disliked slavery, their slaves begged them to be allowed to emigrate, or they were in financial trouble, which could be alleviated palatably by emancipating slaves rather than selling them. Several of Virginia's "First Families" participated in the colonization movement, first teaching some of their slaves to read and write and then emancipating them for emigration. Ann Randolph Page taught twenty-three slaves she owned, freed them for Africa, and furnished them with tools and a year's supply of provisions. Robert E. Lee emancipated his slaves and offered them the opportunity to emigrate; one family, William and Rosabella Burke and their four children, accepted. The Burkes could read and write and corresponded with the Lees from Liberia. Mary Berkeley Minor Blackford, who though a slaveholder was an outspoken critic of slavery and had taught slaves to read in Sunday school despite legal threats against her, freed slaves to be colonized in Africa. Blackford's son taught his manservant, James Cephas, to read and write and to run a printing business so that he could make a living in Liberia. John Hartwell Cocke established an infant and Sabbath school on his Bremo plantation where his wife taught reading, writing, and religion to his slaves. He constructed a complex plan to train slaves for emigration on a Alabama plantation bought for that purpose and equipped it with a school and a slave teacher. Several of his slaves learned to read and write and a few of them emigrated.[35]

Virginia's black communities also supported colonization. Black members of the Richmond Baptist Church funded the movement and sent several of their church members to Liberia as missionaries. For the most part, however, although earlier generations of African-Americans had devised "back to Africa" colonization and emigration plans, nineteenth century black spokesmen repudiated the goals of the American Colonization Society. The year the society was founded, three thousand African-Americans met in Philadelphia to protest the society's contention that blacks constituted a "dangerous and useless" class in the United States. They also objected to linking emancipation with colonization, which would break up families and fasten slavery more securely on those left behind. Colonization agents reported that there was a "general aversion" among African-Americans to going to Africa and indifference or hostility to the "detestable" colonization movement.[36]

Some free blacks did choose to emigrate. Their letters to the colonization society point to the reasons why: their despair over their economic and political prospects in the United States, their desperate desire to get an education for themselves and their children, and their mission to bring Christianity to Africa. As Peter Butler from Petersburg, Virginia, stated succinctly, "I have maid up my mind and wish to in form you that I wish to Go to Liberia So as I may teach Sinners the way of Salvation and also Educate my children and ingoy the Right of a man."[37]

Some slaves begged for the opportunity to emigrate to Liberia in letters to the ACS, whose records are a useful source for identifying literate slaves. A few slaves were regular subscribers to the ACS' publication, the *African Repository*. Several of these wrote asking for help in accumulating enough money to buy their freedom for emigration. They were disappointed; the ACS welcomed emancipation when initiated by owners, but not when initiated by slaves. The Society's policy was to use its funds to transport slaves, but not to actually buy and liberate them. The ACS did print letters from slaves asking for help. One who wrote often was James Starkey, a New Bern, North Carolina, barber. After he received some contributions, however, his owner raised his price, and he failed to raise enough money to be manumitted for emigration. Other slaves had a cruel choice: emancipated for emigration in wills, they either had to leave for Liberia or remain as slaves and be sold away from their families.[38]

Their only opportunity for freedom and the promise of schooling motivated some slaves to chance Liberia's unhealthy climate. Their letters home confirmed their faith in learning as a means to self-identity. A former slave wrote from Liberia that "I have found that a man must have an Edcation to be aman in enny country. . . . Please tell my friends that think of coming to Africa try an master thir Book."[39] Since many of the colonists were literate and prized literacy for their children as one of the benefits of freedom, many of their letters home appealed for books or writing materials, including "some Pencils and a slate and some Pens and paper and Ink." Over and over they wrote to family, friends, and former owners, "I wish you would send me some good books to read"; one, in thanking a book sender, confessed, "I was completely Dry for the Want of Something to Refresh my mind."[40]

While they worked hard as pioneers and fought debilitating disease and death, many emigrants to Liberia also took seriously their assignment to carry Christianity to the African population, together with the conviction that the native population should be taught to read the Bible. A few months after establishing a mission house for natives, an African-American teacher proudly reported progress: "Of the 28 boys there is but 5 that cannot read the word of God [and] 2 of the [three] girls can read the bible very well."[41]

The settlers viewed their own life style as progressive and worthy of African emulation; the Africans called the black Americans "white men," and attributed the cultural differences between them to literacy as well as other factors. One explained the difference between Africans and African-Americans in the guise of a folk tale which recalled the one told to Dutch trader Bosman on the Guinea Coast more than a century earlier. When asked why Africans "could not read & rite like white men . . . . he said that it was all their [Africans] own fault that God gave them the Choice either to learn book proper as they says or make Rice and they told god they had rather make rice." Under the tutelage of the black American emigrants, some Africans began to try to grasp skills in literacy. Seaborn Evans, a black American teacher for the Methodist Missionary Society, reported that the "poor African seem of late to be anxious to send the Children to school." In an ironic echo of the claims of the benefits of literacy made by white benevolent societies, black American emigrant Evans predicted that "the better it will be for us the Sooner we get the Africans civilized, and to lern them the book is the fastest way to do it."[42]

The Colonization Society and its members strongly encouraged these black American efforts to educate themselves and Africans. Gradually the Society began to promote training African-Americans as teachers not only in Liberia, but in "the West Indies, our own country, or other regions of the world." While the ACS worked for schools in Liberia and eventually for the founding of a college there, the *Repository*'s editor affirmed that "we would not allow our zeal for schools *in* Liberia to induce us to lose sight of the great importance of schools in this country for the education of colored persons *for* Liberia, previous to their emigration." In 1826, after urging by the ACS, the Society for the Education of African Youth was founded in Newark, New Jersey, for the purpose of educating free blacks for emigration to Africa. After another ACS appeal, the Episcopal Church of Connecticut founded the African Mission School Society which established a school in Hartford to train blacks to become "Missionaries, Catechists, and Schoolmasters in Africa." However, due to a scarcity of students and an uproar over an effort to establish a "Negro College" in New Haven, the Society abandoned its school and shifted support to missionary work in Africa.[43]

Colonizationists were instrumental in forming the African Education Society of the United States in Washington, D.C., in 1829. With the ACS director Robert Gurley as the coordinator, William Meade as president, and vice presidents which included such reformers and stalwart colonizationists as Francis Scott Key, William Winans, Charles Mercer, Gerrit Smith, and Theodore Frelinghuysen, the statements of the African Education Society were full of optimism. Founders assured the public that they underrated the "immense power of education" to bring the African from barbarism to civilization without the passage of the generations it had taken to accomplish this among Europeans. Specifically, the African Education Society proposed to educate slaves placed at the society's disposal by their masters on the condition of their emigrating to Africa. A slaveowner had donated a farm in the Washington, D.C., area for this purpose.[44]

The African Education Society promised to make their training of these emancipated slaves thorough and all-compassing, so it is interesting to see what kind of educational goals these advocates of colonization thought proper. In their prospectus, advocates promised that slaves would be trained up entirely from early childhood on the farm in a rigorous, paternalistic manner which reflected reformers' sweeping goals for educating the poorer classes everywhere. Their program began with basic literacy and included the following aims:

> To make constant and untiring inroads on their wrong habits and propensities; to subject them to a steady, mild and salutary discipline; to exercise towards them a kind and parental care . . . ; to give them an intimate practical acquaintance with agriculture, or some one of

the mechanic arts, most likely to be useful in Africa; to instruct them thoroughly in all the branches of a common school education; to endow them with industrious, active and manly habits; and to inspire them with virtuous, generous and honorable sentiments; in fine, to form their whole character, and render it, as far as possible, such as will qualify them to become pioneers in the renovation of Africa.

The secretary of the society, Isaac Orr, anticipated a question: what about the black person who, once educated, might choose to stay in the United States? The secretary admitted the question was valid, but this possibility had not deterred their direction toward black education; "The Board (of the Society) cannot yet discover sufficient reasons for changing their views."[45]

The African Education Society did not materialize after this initial pronouncement. A promised legacy was overturned in the courts and the Society promised to use money already collected "for the education of two or three worthy coloured men of promise." The ACS, however, continued to promote its goals for black learning. The *African Repository* served as a forum through which news of educational plans and efforts for African-Americans could be spread. For example, in 1850 J. W. Lugenbeel, a Methodist lay preacher who had spent five years as a doctor in the Liberian colony, proposed the establishment of a seminary in the United States to which blacks from both Africa and America could be sent to be furnished "with all needful facilities for receiving a thorough education" and then sent to Africa. In 1854 another Southerner offered through the *Repository* columns to raise money for a college for the education of young black men. He urged other friends of colonization to help him.[46]

In an effort to publicize the success of schooling for slaves, colonizationists pointed to the career of the famous "learned slave," Harrison Ellis. Ellis was a blacksmith, "intelligent, industrious, sincere, and ambitious," brought by his owners from Virginia to south Alabama in the 1830s. He already could read and had some knowledge of languages and religious training when he came to Alabama, where the Presbyterian synod purchased him, his wife, and two children to be prepared for emigration. Under the supervision of Rev. C. A. Stillman, Ellis was given the thorough education of a Presbyterian minister, ordained, and sent to Liberia as a missionary.[47]

The Society also supported African-American efforts to further their own education. The *Repository* noted with approval the opening of Ashmun Institute institute in Pennsylvania, designed to provide higher education for young black men. The journal also helped publicize Daniel Payne's plans for developing and expanding Wilberforce University as a college for black men and women under the auspices of the A.M.E. Church. The journal's editors also praised William Crane's building project in Baltimore. Crane provided space in his building for a large black Baptist church, school rooms, and lecture halls. In 1856 the building housed a pastor, school principal, and teachers at work.[48]

African-American educators who had no intention of emigrating to Liberia tried to use the colonization-inspired interest in black education to muster white support for black schools. When Arabella Jones proposed to open St. Agnes' Academy for colored girls in Washington, D.C., in 1852, she explained that the objectives of the school were to prepare skilled, industrious, and modest mothers of families and honest, sober household servants. She proposed that the school would also produce educated emigrants. She argued that "many of our citizens of color are emigrating to Liberia, and it is necessary, as well-wishers of our race, that our children be well educated, in order to impart their knowledge, to the illiterate. Shall we, my friends, go there to teach, or be taught? As emigrants from a land of intelligence, I answer, to teach."[49]

As colonization encouraged black education, it also encouraged those white Southerners who linked emancipation to literacy. The *Repository* gave a great deal of publicity to John McDonogh, the eccentric New Orleans slaveowner and colonization supporter who publicly and proudly proclaimed that he taught his slaves to read and write, sent scores of them to Liberia, and gave a few of them college training for mission work. Other individual slaveowners whose plans for literacy and emancipation were publicized in the *Repository* included Dr. Silas Hamilton, who decided to free his twenty-two slaves and proposed to purchase land in Illinois to build a "labor school" in which to qualify young slaves for usefulness in Africa through instruction in letters, agriculture, and the mechanical arts. Isaac Ross of Mississippi proposed that his slaves who were over twenty-one could decide whether to go to Liberia or remain slaves—if Liberia, his estate would be used to settle them and establish a school in the colony. (If they decided to remain slaves they as well as his land would be sold to build the school—a terrible choice.) The *Repository* editor himself suggested in 1852 that a school for promising young male slaves should be established to give them "a literary and scientific education, and a practical knowledge of some useful mechanical art" in preparation for their emancipation and emigration to Liberia. This school would enable benevolent slaveowners to both manumit and educate their slaves.[50]

The systematic training and general linking of education and emancipation promoted by the ACS encouraged other southern reformers to present organized proposals with political implications. Virginia Presbyterian leader Henry Ruffner recommended the establishment of a broad emancipation and education plan, including a requirement that owners give those slaves who were to be emancipated the rudiments of education while the church provided religious training. Similarly, Simeon Salisbury proposed that slaves should be liberated and then required to remain with their former masters for a period of training before emigration. Robert T. Breckinridge, who helped found both the Sunday school and public education systems in Kentucky, became convinced that "slavery is *the great* obstacle to general education" in the South, as it discouraged learning for both whites and blacks. In the 1830s Breckinridge supported colonization and insisted that emancipation should be its ultimate aim. This led the *African Repository* to publicize the emancipation plan fashioned by Breckinridge's Kentucky Union for the Moral and Religious Improvement of the Colored Race. The Union advocated preparation of slaves which would include instruction "in the common elementary branches of education" followed by a general emancipation. By the late 1840s, however, Breckinridge and other Kentuckians ceased to believe that colonization could be used to abolish the entire slave system and worked instead, unsuccessfully, to incorporate emancipation into the Kentucky constitution.[51] Colonization, like other benevolent movements in the South, was incapable of posing any meaningful challenges to the slave system. The publicity and implied approval the Society gave to black education and emancipation plans and its advocacy of slave literacy, however, seemed to reinforce the beliefs of southern white reformers in the morality of the "school of slavery." Colonization even offered a few of them a way out of their roles as slaveowners.

Chapter Six

■

"Only the Bible Can Save Us":
Literacy and National Survival

"**I**F OUR COUNTRY IS SAFE, IF THE UNION IS SAFE, IF the people are safe, if the Church is safe, the Bible must have a hand in all of it."[1]

This extravagant claim made in 1852 by New Jersey's Theodore Frelinghuysen, President of the American Bible Society, shows the burden being put on the "Word" in the late 1840s and 1850s. Southern African-Americans' rights to literacy were restricted in the 1820s and 1830s, but as sectional tensions accelerated with the Mexican War and the nation's two great popular churches, the Methodists and the Baptists, split over slavery-related issues, "Bibles for Slaves" became an appealing cry. It merged nicely with the benevolent societies' and educational reformers' belief that a reading and writing public was essential for a Christian and democratic nation. To offer "Bibles for Slaves," though, was also divisive. Every gesture which reminded the nation that blacks were humans and threatened slaveowner "property" rights stimulated southern opposition. In the 1850s the South became more defensive than ever before about slave rights vs. slaveowner property rights. Ironically, "Bibles for Slaves" also divided antislavery forces. Those who believed a focus on slaves' religious and literary rights would divert efforts from the fight for black freedom contested with others who saw literacy as the first step towards that freedom and "Bibles" as an attractive way to gain broader support among whites for black liberation.

Those benevolent societies supported by "moderate" Northern reformers and by white Southerners of the "school of slavery" inclination faced a dilemma in trying to negotiate literacy rights for African-Americans between both abolitionists and defenders of slavery. Literacy focused the dilemma on a concrete and emotional issue, with both nationalist and religious overtones. The need to teach all citizens to read and write as the best safeguard of a democracy had been a cherished goal of the American nation's founders, a goal which was reinforced by the leaders of the nineteenth century common school movement. Teaching the entire population to read was American as well as Christian. Benevolent societies felt motivated to do their country's bidding and to carry out God's will by encouraging reading among African-Americans as well as whites and by giving reading material to both groups. During the early nineteenth century, benevolent societies had called attention to the needs of black people for reading material and furnished it when possible; black religious leaders had participated in their efforts. The American Sunday School Union founded Sunday schools for blacks in the North and in the border southern states in which children and adults were taught to read and distributed instructional materials in reading to northern black churches. The American Bible Society made grants to northern black schools, to black emigrants in Liberia, to African-American colonies in Canada, which included numbers of escaped slaves, and to slaves in St. Croix and St. Thomas. The Tract Society printed material exclusively for the use of black groups, including its *Creole Harmony of the Gospels.* Through a Moravian missionary, Tract Society members distributed 20,000 copies of the *Creole Harmony* free to "all those of our colored population who are taught to read" in the Danish West Indies.[2]

While the ABS and the Tract Society were more timid in directly approaching the literacy needs of slaves in the southern United States, their journal editors did from time to time call attention to the slaves' need for the Bible and gave examples of how these needs were being met. In 1828, a North Carolina Bible Society reporter deplored the fact that many blacks "are not only without a Bible, but unable to read it." In the ABS journal, he challenged fellow Bible Society members with this question: "When and how can all these [black people] be furnished with the use of that chart which alone can direct them into the strait and narrow path that leads to life eternal?" A Kentuckian also pointed out in an ABS article that "the condition of our 100,000 slaves is . . . affecting to our hearts" and that "multitudes would gladly put the Bible into their hands." He also argued that "where these poor slaves have acquired (as many of them do) a knowledge of letters . . . the Bible is theirs of right and by divine commend." Therefore, when literate slaves were brought to the Society's attention, the Kentuckian claimed, "we have uniformly given them copies of the sacred word; subject, however, to the will of their masters." In Missouri, the Bible Society agent assured ABS members that "we constantly keep the wants of the colored population before our minds; and as there is no barrier here to their having and reading the Word of God, all who can read, or will promise to learn, are furnished with the blessed book."[3]

In 1847, the Tract Society went so far as to claim that slaves in the southern states were learning to read as a result of tract work:

> The access to the population is almost unrestricted by sect, color, or locality. Planters often assemble their servants and request the colporteur to address them, and supply them with Tracts and books so far as they are able to read. In some instances colporteurs have become permanent missionaries among the blacks, while the supply of religious publications in the families of planters is often the occasion of imparting instruction to the colored people, through some members of the families.[4]

Literacy continued to be a divisive reform goal, however. The northern orientation of the benevolent societies and their repeated emphasis on the value of reading for all people made them vulnerable to southern fears and suspicions. Despite the American Sunday School Union organizers' resolve not to mention education for blacks when they launched a "Southern Enterprize" in 1834, the effort was not very successful. Qualified missionaries were hard to find and got cool receptions. Sunday school agents reported that Southerners were suspicious of books published in Philadelphia and asked if southern books couldn't be obtained instead, and whether men from slaveholding states instead of Northerners couldn't be sent to the South as missionaries. One exasperated Northerner claimed that white Southerners' "inventive imaginations associate Northern influence—a rupture of our civil compact—dissolution of all social order—an armed host of incendiary *abolitionists*—blood and murder—and a thousand other hydra-headed gorgons dire, with the establishment of a Sabbath school." In the tense times of 1835, a gossip item in the *United States Telegraph* intimated that abolition pamphlets and tracts were being printed on American Bible Society presses, a rumor which was denied by the ABS but which was immediately seized upon by a South Carolina local Bible Society president.[5]

On the other hand, the societies were increasingly under attack by antislavery groups for their timidity in refusing to insist on the rights of slaves to have and to read the Bible. Antislavery groups put pressure on the ABS and Tract societies to be more insistent about literacy rights of slaves. In 1834, for example, the American Anti-Slavery Society offered to contribute $5,000 to the ABS to supply "every family of coloured persons in the United States not already supplied, with a copy of the Bible." The Bible Society's managers cautiously refused the offer, protesting that their function was "circulation of the Holy Scriptures without note or comment." Their excuse was that the Bible Society preferred to work through state and local societies who could develop their own "safe" distribution systems.[6] Since no such local or state distribution systems existed, this response outraged the antislavery groups.

In 1840 a group of antislavery black and white clergymen and wealthy New York merchants who disagreed with William Lloyd Garrison's decision to repudiate churches in the fight against slavery founded the American and Foreign Anti-Slavery Society. They planned to work within churches and with benevolent groups to convert them into active anti-slavery agents. These abolitionists declared their willingness to work with the American Bible Society, but they wanted to test ABS motives and courage on the issue of slave welfare. In 1847, the American and Foreign Anti-Slavery Society spearheaded a "Bibles for Slaves" campaign to raise large sums of money so they could insist that the Bible Society give Bibles to slaves on a wholesale basis. Joshua Leavitt, Congregationalist minister and editor of the Boston *Emancipator*, called for action by the Bible Society in editorials in his paper and in his pamphlet, "Shall We Give Bibles to Three Millions of American Slaves," printed and distributed by the American and Foreign Anti-Slavery Society.[7]

At first the ABS board responded by offering to fill any orders for Bibles for slaves "cheerfully and promptly . . . believing . . . that the word of God is intended for all men, and useful to them in every condition of life.[8] The cause was so popular among northern ministers and congregations as well as antislavery groups, however, that funds began to come in too quickly for the Bible Society to handle.

Suddenly, the ABS board recognized the dangerous implications of their commitment to Bibles for slaves for their standing in the South. The board discouraged further fund raising for slave Bibles and gave the following excuses to ABS members: first, the Bible Society was formed for the "purpose of circulating the Word of God without note or comment, as far as is practicable, among all classes and conditions of men who are capable of using it"; second, very few slaves could read, and the ABS was not directly involved in the teaching of reading; and third, the Bible Society and its auxiliaries did intend to continue distributing Bibles to those who could read: "so far as there are coloured freemen, or slaves . . . who are capable of reading the blessed word of God and are without, they should unquestionably be furnished with it as well as any other class of our ruined race." But while this duty was "plain and imperious," the ABS cautioned Northerners not to give money directly to that particular cause, "an object which can only be attained gradually, and the funds for which must remain in part unexpended."[9]

One of the aims of the 1847 "Bibles for Slaves" campaign was to expose the timidity of the American Bible Society and the refusal of its leaders to take a stand against slavery. However, those ABS leaders gained much of their support in the North from businessmen, religious professionals, and others who feared national division and possible civil war more than they disliked the continuation of slavery. During the 1850s those who saw themselves as "mediators" between the sections tried one avenue after another in an effort to keep the sectional rifts from widening. Among the efforts they made was to support benevolence and the Bible as a "last chance" for national unity. Therefore, the American Bible Society and Tract Society leaders sought desperately to preserve a presence in both the North and South in the 1850s.

Theodore Frelinghuysen, Bible Society president in the 1850s, promoted the Bible's power as a unifier, as he tried to appease both parts of the nation. To Northerners Frelinghuysen insisted that the American Bible Society gave Bibles to slaves, while he reminded white Southerners that literacy was the best guarantee of social order. In a typical speech in the South, he claimed:

> There are many gentlemen, who are not members of any church themselves, whom you could not persuade to withdraw from their slaves the use of the Bible, and the preaching of the Gospel to them by our missionaries. And why? Because they discover that whenever [slaves] believe what is said in that book, the greatest difficulty in the world is settled.[10]

Frelinghuysen told his northern audience about encountering many slaves who could read during his visit to South Carolina in 1851, where he preached to a camp meeting which included from 3,000 to 5,000 black people. He observed that "there were more books in [black] hands than in those of the white part of the congregation." African-Americans handed him contributions for the Bible Society, saying, "the Bible has blessed us, and we want to give it as a blessing to the world." Frelinghuysen concluded, "It may be thought by many that [slaves] have nothing to do with the Word of God. I am happy to tell you that that is a mistake. They had Bibles, and whenever they call for them we give them." He went on to claim extravagantly that "so far as I know, nobody has one word to say against their reading of the Bible."[11] His inaccurate and overstated claim shows the wishful thinking engaged in by mediators.

Some of the antislavery organizers, however, particularly those who had continued ties to organized religion, also believed in the power of the Bible to accomplish great things. Many still believed that the slaves' access to the Bible should be a priority in their movement. They were also aware that slave Bible reading was a more appealing cause than abolition to the general public in the North. When antislavery groups wanted to arouse public sympathy for the cause of the *Amistad* Africans, for example, they publicized the fact that the Africans were being taught to read and write English, studying the New Testament, and becoming "civilized" and, it was hoped, "Christian" men.[12]

When slaves learned to read the Bible, the antislavery groups promised, souls would be saved and literacy would be a step towards emancipation. Slaveholders would be reluctant to keep literate, Bible-reading slaves in bondage. Since the Bible Society refused to work with them, these advocates of "Bibles for Slaves" turned their campaign over to their own organization, the American Missionary Association. The American Missionary Association, the AMA, was an offshoot of the American and Foreign Anti-Slavery Society and an amalgam of antislavery missionary groups, including the Union Missionary Society, founded by northern black ministers in 1841. American and Foreign Anti-Slavery Society members initiated the AMA's Bibles for Slaves campaign in 1848, shortly after the ABS' declaration that they would not accept contributions to that cause. Henry Bibb, former Kentucky slave who had escaped North and begun antislavery work in the early 1840s, joined the cause. Even though Bibb himself had not learned to read until after he escaped, he contended that many slaves had learned to read secretly. The potency of the Bible as a weapon against slavery was obvious from the efforts of slaveowners to withhold it from slaves. Bibb also made the good point that a "Bibles for Slaves" campaign "takes well upon the public mind generally". People were more ready to hear about "this branch of the subject" of African Americans in bondage than about the naked facts of the oppressive slave system.[13]

Bibb's campaign began with a specific goal: the AMA would give a Bible or Testament to every slave who could read. Bibb and the American Missionary Association's campaign were attacked, however, by other black abolitionists, led by Frederick Douglass. Douglass, though he had himself learned to read and taught other blacks while a slave, denied that many slaves could read or that masters would permit Bibles to be given to them. He ridiculed Bibb's supposed claim that "if the slave had the Bible, the Lord would help him to read it." To Douglass, the Bibles for Slaves campaign had a positive side; it showed a growing interest by Northerners in the slaves' welfare. However, as a step to abolition of slavery, Douglass declared, "it seems to me a sham, a delusion, and a snare, and cannot be too soon exposed before all the people." The Word of God could not compromise with slavery: "The Bible is peculiarly the companion of liberty. It belongs to a new order of things—slavery is of the old—and will only be made worse by an attempt to mend it with the Bible." In fact, Douglass felt that distributing Bibles was a cruelty to the slave:

> Away with all trifling with the man in fetters! Give a hungry man a stone, and tell what beautiful houses are

made of it,—give ice to a freezing man and tell him of its
good properties in hot weather,—throw a drowning man
a dollar, as a mark of your good will,—but do not mock
the bondman in his misery, by giving him a Bible when
he cannot read it.[14]

The black abolitionists' division over the role of literacy and
the Bible in the antislavery movement resulted in destructive
confrontations in New York City in May, 1849. In the first,
Henry Highland Garnet and Samuel Ringgold Ward, prominent
black ministers who supported the "Bibles for Slaves" effort, debated Charles L. Reason, a black abolitionist in opposition to
Bibles for slaves. The next evening, Douglass debated Bibb and
Garnet at the Zion Baptist Church. Accounts from papers sympathetic to Douglass reported that Douglass effectively ridiculed and demolished Bibb's claims for the Bible and that
Garnet accused Douglass of being antireligious. The resulting
shouting match threatened to divide the black antislavery
movement. Bibb abandoned his work for the Slaves' Bible Fund
and emigrated to Canada.[15]

Whites continued to support the Slaves' Bible Fund, however.
From 1849 to 1854 contributions for the cause came in steadily
to the AMA from midwestern and New England states. Supporters argued that, while efforts to free slaves might take decades, the slaves' salvation required access to the Bible
immediately. Also, as Douglass himself said, the Bible was indeed subversive; as an AMA missionary argued, the slave who
could read the actual words in the Book would find that God
was not "a great Moloch delighting in the suffering of his voter-
ies, and conniving at the vilest system of oppression under the
sun." Spreading the truth, and the ability to read the truth, was
a revolutionary act in itself.[16]

The American Missionary Association, which did not admit
slaveowner members, was active in the border states. There,
AMA missionaries implemented the "Bibles for Slaves" mission
by distributing Bibles and testaments to slaves who could read.
They admitted, though, that since there were few slaves in the
areas where the AMA was most active, few Bibles were being
given out. Usually Bibles were given to slaves who could already
read, but on at least one occasion an AMA missionary first
taught the slave to read and them gave him a Bible.[17]

Opposition to AMA colporteurs, who made abolitionist literature as well as Bibles available to whites and blacks, always

limited their efforts. Colporteur James West, however, maintained that only non-slaveowners opposed the Slaves' Bible Fund; he claimed that he had not met an owner of slaves who was unwilling to have his slaves read the Word of God, "and some of them are willing to pay." Another missionary agreed, noting that "the slaves receive the Bible with marked thankfulness, and but few in northern Kentucky refuse to allow their slaves to have the Bible." He quoted a Kentucky woman who said to him that "all the slaves ought to be taught to read and to be supplied with the Bible."[18]

In their journals and papers, AMA missionaries combined appeals for support for the Slaves' Bible Fund with vignettes of devout slaves and with practical observations. One of the most memorable and prolific writers and workers for the Bible cause was John Fee, a Congregational minister from Kentucky recruited by an AMA agent for the project. Fee's antislavery views had alienated him from his family and his views on black equality set him apart from most white Americans. Fee also believed strongly in the value of education, so he distributed Bibles to slaves with enthusiasm. He told readers of AMA literature that there were slaves who could use Bibles if they were available; slaves, he had learned, were "being taught by other slaves and by children of their masters." He also found, "from reliable sources," that slave children were learning to read in Sunday schools in Kentucky towns.[19]

Matilda Fee, John's wife, was equally appreciative of African-Americans' respect for the Bible and perceptive about black needs. In AMA literature she portrayed grateful slaves thanking supporters for their Bibles. She also gave practical suggestions for more effective work: first, that "as slaves who can read are generally poor readers, they need Bibles with larger and clearer type"; second, that Bibles for slaves include a family record page since "slaves, like ourselves, have attachment for their children, and love to have their names to look upon, even if they cannot always retain their persons."[20]

Reports to AMA journals by John and Matilda Fee and others gave readers the impression that slaves in border Kentucky did have access to the Bible. These claims continued to irritate those abolitionists who insisted to the northern public that one of the evils of slavery was that the Bible was withheld from the slave. Frederick Douglass continued to remind AMA missionaries that they were playing into the hands of slaveowners and undermining the antislavery movement by supporting the South's claim that slaveowners allowed slaves to read. Douglass' objections to the Bibles for Slaves activity eventually convinced the AMA. After 1854 the Slaves' Bible Fund was seldom mentioned in AMA publications and special funding of the project ended, though AMA missionaries continued to give Bibles to slaves in border states. At the same time, though, the precarious position of the AMA in the South attracted more and more hostility from southern whites: AMA missionaries were attacked by mobs, whipped and jailed, and Fee's first school was burned. Finally, after they had expressed support for John Brown's raid in 1859, Fee and others were ordered to leave the South.[21]

In the 1850s, particularly after the enactment of the Fugitive Slave Law in 1852, African-Americans' discouragement with their status in the United States increased. Economic opportunities worsened in many northern cities and black political and legal status in the North improved little if at all. African-American efforts to expand literacy and schools in the North continued to grow, but at least one historian suggests that this belief in education was a "hope born of despair," an agonizing need to believe that at least this avenue of liberation was not closed to the black community as were other instruments of advancement.[22]

The desperation felt by many African-Americans is shown by their renewed discussions of emigration in the 1850s. Black leaders meeting in conventions began to consider plans for a separate black nation, either in the United States' "newly acquired territories" of the West; somewhere in Central or South America; Canada, where emigration of African-Americans totaled 20,000 by the 1850s; or Africa. Martin Delany proposed an exploration of the east coast of Africa for colonization and trade and organized a National Emigration Convention in 1854, with its strongest support from African-Americans in the midwest. Henry Highland Garnet and John Sella Martin, Boston minister and former slave, were major organizers of the African Civilization Society in 1858. The Society had white members but was run by blacks to promote "the civilization and evangelization of Africa" and to encourage black nationalism. It received some support from the American Colonization Society but condemnation from many black abolitionists.[23]

Even Liberia, long fought as an emigration site by African-American leaders, was reconsidered for black emigration.

Liberia's national independence in 1847 as well as the worsening situation for African-Americans led to reluctant support for emigration by some antislavery advocates. James G. Birney, white antislavery leader long opposed to the American Colonization Society, recommended in 1852 that free African-Americans consider emigration to Liberia because, he felt, white prejudice was unconquerable in the United States. Members of a Free Colored People's Convention in Maryland reached the same conclusion; "in the face of growing prejudices" they had little choice but to emigrate. Other groups of blacks meeting in conventions disagreed, but blacks continued to emigrate. Despite the horrendous death toll and other hardships colonists faced in Liberia, the American Colonization Society continued to receive applicants for emigration, particularly southern blacks.[24]

The numbers of talented, literate African-Americans who emigrated has been deplored by Carter Woodson, who noted how much American society could have used their leadership in the decades afterwards. The quality of southern black leaders lost to American society is shown in the list of African-American emigrants to Liberia from 1849 to 1851, during a period when the ACS kept statistics on the emigrants' literacy. A total of 789 free blacks and 743 freed slaves were listed as leaving for the African colony during those two years. About one-third of the free blacks and one-fourth of the freed slaves could read or read and write. Among these were a single shipment of 181 black people who sailed from Savannah on the *Huma* in May 1849. They included leaders of the Charleston and Savannah black religious communities and skilled workers and seamstresses. The same families contained both free blacks and slaves who bought their freedom or were manumitted for the effort. A high proportion could read and write: for example, among the Savannah adults, almost three-fourths of the free blacks and over half of the freed slave emigrants could read. From their later letters from Liberia, it is clear that while their desire to mission to Africans was one reason for the emigration of these Charleston and Savannah African-American leaders, other reasons predominated. The chance for freedom for the enslaved members of the group and the general "crisis mentality" justifiably emerging among free blacks in the Deep South were factors which influenced their decision to leave as a group and to establish a Liberian colony.[25]

The Colonization Society offered the emigration option, however unattractive, for African-Americans to escape their situation in the United States. The ACS also continued in the 1850s to offer a chance for northern reformers to do something, however small, about slavery and sectional tensions. Even though colonization was under renewed suspicion in the South in the 1850s, Southerners offered publicly to ship their slaves to coastal ports for emigration when their own states forbade manumission. The ACS raised money in the North to help them. When William McLain, ACS Secretary, asked 426 ACS members, almost all in the North, to send ten dollars each to fund passage to Liberia for seventy-one manumitted slaves to be freed by a Virginia minister and his family, northern Colonization Society members responded quickly. The money was successfully raised and the former slaves, described as "industrious, intelligent . . . several of them can read, some can write . . ." were on their way to Liberia. Letters by northern contributors showed their concern about the situation of slaves and their continued hope that slave education, manumission and colonization might be the path to peace.[26]

In the tension of the late 1840s and 1850s, southern whites who tried to protect black literacy faced new challenges. African-American literacy was, of course, the most vulnerable target for militant proslavery politicians, though the movement for white universal literacy and common schooling in the South was also damaged by rabid advocates of southern nationalism and slavery. Whitemarsh Seabrook became Governor of South Carolina in 1848. In 1849 he and other fire-eaters tried to flame enthusiasm for a secession convention. They used the same tactics which had resulted in passage of anti–black literacy laws in 1834, generating suspicion of worship and reading for blacks in the state and especially in Charleston. The result in 1849 was similar to that in 1835: a mob threatened to destroy an Episcopal mission church being built for slaves in the city and had to be deterred by the city's religious and civic leaders. To assuage suspicions about the dangers of black religion, a Charleston committee investigated the state's religious opportunities for slaves. One of the questions the committee asked all those whose churches included black members was whether religious instruction was oral or printed and "what proportion of colored [church] members could read?" The responses that numbers of black church members in the state could read and were being encouraged and taught by whites confirmed fears and heightened tensions.[27]

Suspicion of Northerners and criticism of any Southerner who spoke of black rights to worship or read increased in the 1850s. In 1856, for example, a northern Sunday school missionary told his colleagues that he had had to be introduced to his southern audience by a Southerner, and that the Southerner had been sure to mention that the missionary was actually born in the South. The same year, when the American Tract Society offered to publish the best essay on the "Duties of Masters," southern religious journal editors protested the implication that masters had duties, or needed to be told about them. Several journals withdrew their support for the Tract Society. William Meade, longtime Episcopal reformer, joined in the criticism, but was excoriated himself for supposedly speaking in a sermon "in a way calculated unduly to elevate the slaves, socially and politically, and of course to render them dissatisfied and lead to insurrection." Meade denied it, but was only one among prominent ministers open to suspicion; a longtime white Richmond Baptist preacher was accused of "insidiously and fiendishly insinuating" abolitionist "poison" into his sermons. Some of the fears, as usual, centered on slave literacy. In March 1860 a writer demanded the investigation of the common practice of "illegally selling books to slaves." In September 1860 a Penfield, Georgia, woman accused a local white man of taking blacks into the woods on Sundays and "teaching them to read and cipher." Fear culminated in violence. George Daughaday was "beaten by a mob and then held under a pump" for conducting a black Sunday school. In 1860 a Texas mob hung Anthony Bewley, a white Methodist minister. While he represented the northern wing of the Methodist church, the crowd's action signified the vulnerability of the entire white ministry to suspicion.[28]

Some southern reformers spoke out for literacy rights for African-Americans in this tense time. When the Memphis city government prohibited all literacy instruction for Memphis blacks in 1856, Edward Porter of the First Presbyterian Church defended his church's practice of teaching blacks to read the Bible. In 1857 Richmond ministers defended the white preacher who supervised the First African Baptist church when he was labeled an abolitionist because he supported blacks' right to worship.[29]

Richard Fuller also spoke out. He had backed down on defending black literacy in the early 1840s, when he had prepared a speech for a local Carolina agricultural society in which he had planned to protest the state's law which forbade teaching slaves to read. He was asked not to give the speech for fear of arousing opposition and had acquiesced, blaming "abolitionist pressure" for the request. The incident, however, contributed to his decision to leave South Carolina for a border Baltimore pastorate in 1845. From that location Fuller continued to come into conflict with South Carolina authorities over slave reading. He still owned property and slaves in the state. In 1850 he petitioned the South Carolina state legislature for permission "privately and on his plantations to give instruction to his slaves—so that they may be able to read the word of God—." A legislative committee refused him, but the language of his petition suggests that Fuller may have determined to ignore the refusal. He made the significant claim that while he always obeyed the laws of the state, he owed "a higher and paramount allegiance to the law of God, and these laws require him to instruct his slaves so that they may be able to read the Scriptures." When he criticized the literacy prohibition again in a speech to the American Colonization Society in 1851, he was informed that he was no longer welcome to speak in his South Carolina hometown.[30]

Another white protest against South Carolina's literacy restrictions for blacks, this one couched in strong and vigorous language, emerged from upcountry South Carolina in the 1850s and received national attention from the American Bible Society. The protest was in the form of a speech given by Robert Fair, a young South Carolina attorney, at the annual meeting of the Abbeville Bible Society.[31] Fair's audience, from an area which had petitioned against the literacy bans several years earlier, may have been sympathetic and encouraged his forthright language, but the tone of Fair's address was unusually frank and passionate.

Fair deplored the South Carolina law barring the teaching of blacks to read as "unbecoming the South . . . and a slur upon the christian age in which we live." He effectively contrasted southern reluctance to teach the slave at home with the eagerness to teach the illiterate foreigner in overseas missions. Some Southerners assured the North that slaves could become Christians without reading the Bible themselves; on the other hand, in foreign missions, "we argue the perfect impotency of oral instruction, and call loudly for the school-house and the printing press, even at the cost of immense expenditures." Slave-owners were justly afraid that if slaves read the Bible, slaves would realize just how short owners fell of their duty to those dependent upon them; nevertheless, it was owners' responsibility to teach slaves according to God's will. Fair went far beyond any other white southern speaker, and beyond most white Northerners: he insisted that slaves should be taught even if learning brought about slave revolt. It was better, Fair insisted, to "risk the dangers . . . of an indiscriminate massacre" than to risk "the danger of the wrath of an incensed God. . . . Better to suffer the utter destruction of the body, than that the soul should dwell in eternal burnings."[32]

This was strong language anywhere and at any time—but in South Carolina in the 1850s, it's amazing that Fair was allowed to speak. His speech did arouse attention and opposition. The editor of the *Southern Presbyterian Review* criticized him bitterly, insisting "that the laws in question are imperiously demanded by a regard to public safety," and asking, "is there any great moral reason why we should incur the tremendous risk of having our wives and children slaughtered in consequence for our slaves being taught to read incendiary publications?" Fair had dared to answer this question directly in his speech: there was indeed such a great moral reason. He obviously had some local support in a district where sixty-two men had signed a protest against South Carolina's literacy restrictions for slaves more than ten years before. Members of the Abbeville Bible Society voted to print and distribute Fair's volatile speech.[33]

The distribution of Fair's speech did not stop with the Abbeville Bible Society; the Society's national parent organization, the American Bible Society, also printed the entire address in the *Bible Society Record*. Why did its editors do so? By the mid-1850s sectional tensions had intensified to such an extent that the publication of "Our Slaves Should Have the Bible" may have been a desperate effort to appeal to white Southerner's consciences and to show Northerners that there were strong voices in the South supporting slaves' access to the Bible.

The Bible Society made another move to bring North and South together over "Bibles for Slaves." The Society designated Joseph C. Stiles as a "special secretary" for southern work. Stiles had connections with conservatives in both sections of the country. He was a native Georgian, a graduate of Andover and Yale, and an esteemed evangelist who had helped fellow Presbyterian Charles C. Jones pioneer the slave mission movement in the early 1830s. Stiles, however, had taken the "New

School" side of the Presbyterian split in 1837, was suspended by the Old School Presbyterians after a bitter squabble in 1841, and moved North. As a New York preacher he gained support from New York businessmen and others concerned about preserving ties with the South.[34]

Like Theodore Frelinghuysen, Stiles sought to assure the North that the Bible was not withheld from the slave, regardless of abolitionists' accusations. Like the ABS president, Stiles tended to overstate, however, perhaps because as a northern resident he was removed from the immediate reality of the system he sentimentalized. In an 1857 article in *DeBow's Review*, Stiles told of planters who worshiped with their slaves and of a slaveowner who paid Stiles for five hundred Bibles to be distributed among his and his neighbors' slaves. In a typical speech in the North, he claimed:

> It has long been a common spectacle to see the children of a southern family at night, or on the Sabbath, employed in teaching the servants to read. It is many years since night-schools, in which Colored adults taught Colored children to read, were common in all our Southern cities, and I believe well known to city authorities, and generally unmolested by them.[35]

Stiles believed that "God has made me useful in healing breaches among the brethren." He perceived his main task for the ABS as serving as an ambassador of goodwill to the South, and he claimed considerable success in retaining Southerners' allegiance to the national Bible Society. He also worked at "healing breaches" through the Southern Aid Society, created in 1854 by conservative northern reformers, politicians, and commercial leaders who included Anson G. Phelps, William E. Dodge, and J. H. Dulles. The Southern Aid Society sought to maintain peace with the South and sent money to needy southern churches to foster religion and education. Among the churches aided were a few black congregations; the Society claimed to be the entire support for the First Colored Church of Washington, D.C.; its minister, William Catto, a former slave; and its 170 members, twenty-five Sunday school teachers, and library of books.[36]

By 1860, however, the Southern Aid Society disbanded. The commercial depression of the late 1850s dried up northern contributions and the "bitter sectional animosity" which followed

John Brown's raid and reprisals produced opposition to the enterprise. Northern businessmen, led by Samuel F. B. Morse, tried once more to continue building bridges through an "American Society for the Promotion of National Unity" in early 1861, but without success.[37] Neither the conservative Southern Aid Society nor the antislavery American Missionary Association had been any more successful than the ABS or the Tract Society in maintaining national unity through a belief in the power of the Bible and of the printed word.

Epilogue:

■

Black Literacy in the
Aftermath of War

"TRULY THEIR HEAVENS ARE OPEN AND THIS IS their shining hour." This is the way an educator in Washington, D.C., in 1864 characterized African-Americans who were gathering in schools for freedmen after the war, all ages from the old to the infant classes, "all learning from the same beautiful primer, and all improving with diligence."[1]

After war came to the South and slavery began to end in one region after another, freed slaves enthusiastically grasped opportunities to learn to read and write openly and legally. Black soldiers, most of whom were former slaves, petitioned for regimental schools, bought their own books, and paid for their own teachers or taught each other, drawing on the knowledge of those who had already learned the basics of literacy. "Cartridge box and spelling book are attached to the same belt," noted one chaplain.[2]

Both the former slaves themselves and northern missionaries described the "greed for letters" shown by African-Americans in the South. As Booker T. Washington, who had been prevented from learning while he was a slave, recalled, "few people who were not right in the midst of the scenes can form any exact idea of the intense desire which the people of my race showed for education." According to Washington, "it was a whole race trying to go to school. Few were too young, and none too old, to make the attempt to learn."[3]

Northerners who came South as missionaries and educators echoed Washington's impressions. As early as 1861, a teacher of contraband slaves in Virginia found that "men, women, and children evince an ardent thirst for knowledge." A Bible Society agent was impressed with the earnestness of "these new readers, who may be seen in groups and squads in the streets, roads, and in plantations with their books, reading to one another." In Alabama, a missionary reported, " to open a school has been to have it filled." In Norfolk, an A.M.E. missionary kept her school open all summer because the pupils begged her to do so. Another reported that "the children . . . hurry to school as soon as their work is over. The plowmen hurry from the field at night to get their hour of study. Old men and women strain their dim sight with the book two and a half feet distant from the eye, to catch the shape of the letter. I call this heaven-inspired interest."[4]

African-Americans showed a ready grasp of the practical benefits of reading and, especially, writing. Soldiers, including former slaves, wrote home to their families and members of their families wrote to them. Soldiers also wrote to Washington to complain of brutal medical treatment, to ask for protection for families still enslaved, for discharge papers, or for promised bounties.

As Edmund Drago points out in his study of Reconstruction Georgia, the ability to read was also crucial for the freed peoples as they became involved in labor contracts and as they tried to acquire property. Former slaves recognized the importance of being able to read contracts, as one recalled, "so they would know how to keep some of them white folks from gittin land 'way from 'em if they did buy it." Freed slave Robert Cheatham recalled how his ability to read kept fellow freedmen in his community from being tricked into signing an indenture just after the war.[5]

Newly freed slaves, particularly the elderly, wanted to learn to read so that they could read the Bible. According to the superintendent of an adult night school in Macon, "the eagerness of the older ones to learn is a continual wonder to me. The men and women say, 'we work all day, but we'll come to you in the evening for learning and we want you to make us learn.' " Booker T. Washington recalled that "the great ambition of the older people was to try to learn to read the Bible before they died. With this end in view, men and women who were fifty and seventy-five years old, would be found in night-schools." Teachers also charted the eagerness with which freed slaves seized the chance to read the Bible for themselves. A Virginia teacher described the new readers' "ardent thirst for knowledge, especially Scriptural knowledge" and reported that "as soon as they can spell out words they want a Testament." Missionary Lucy Chase told her friends of a woman who came to school every day and told her, "I feel so anxious to learn! Every once in awhile I come to the name of God,—and the love of it, the name is so sweet, I can't help trying to learn!"[6]

Responding to this enthusiasm and glad for a new cause, the American Tract Society opened schools during the war for black refugees in Washington, D.C., and Alexandria, Virginia, and the American Bible Society began a new campaign to provide Bibles for freed slaves. The enthusiasm with which the campaign was launched suggests the societies' long-held frustration with their limitations in the antebellum South, when they had had to be circumspect about providing Bibles for slaves.[7]

The Bible Society's inflated prewar claims for the power of "Bible literacy" to foster unity and social order were perpetuated after the war by missionaries and their northern financial supporters. John W. Alvord, Freedmens' Bureau general superintendent, attributed black peoples' eagerness for literacy to the "natural thirst for knowledge common to all men" and explained that African-Americans had "seen power and influence among white people always coupled with *learning*—it is the sign of that elevation to which they now aspire." But the conflicting functions of literacy—the "double-edged sword" of liberation and control—created confusion. As Ronald Butchart has observed, one wing of the freedmen's aid movement urged black learning to "liberate men from the mental shackles of slavery," but other powerful voices in the education movement urged the use of schooling as an essential tool to moderate the threat arising from "an inferior, dangerous addition to the republic." However, whether they stressed the goals of liberation or control, Northerners believed that education was the way to solve the crucial problems of integrating a previously enslaved racial minority into a racist American society.[8]

This northern belief in education as a panacea was not necessarily shared by black Southerners, despite their eagerness for schooling. One freedman spoke for many when he declared, "I tink we better not wait for education" and urged fellow African-Americans to make a separate life in the South. When questioned by Sherman and Stanton in January 1865, a group of literate Savannah black ministers and community leaders agreed; they stated that the best way for blacks to survive was to live separately from whites, to be placed on land with the opportunity of buying it, and to labor for their own profit. Knowing, in Butchart's words, that "education alone has probably never been liberating for a group, social class, or race, when the ends, methods, and curriculum have been defined and controlled by others," the Savannah ministers created a Black Education Association to found their own schools, hire their own teachers, and determine their own curriculum. Within two years they had organized 120 black schools in forty percent of Georgia's counties, staffed entirely with black teachers.[9]

Northerners did not share the black Savannah leaders' conviction that African-Americans could run their own literacy program. Northern educators and missionaries, both black and white, were often appalled at the cultural differences between themselves and some of the former slaves. They were also surprised to find church leaders and other African-Americans in the South with literacy skills, to discover that a number of schools had already been conducted in the South under slavery, and to be able to hire capably educated southern blacks as teachers. Wesley Gaines, an African Methodist Episcopal bishop who had learned to read and write as a slave, described the astonishment of northern missionaries when "it was found there were many of the young who had secretly learned from the forbidden books, and were soon made ready for advanced work." An 1870 survey of black ministers who were associated with the Methodist Church, South, under slavery showed that most of them could read; fewer could read and write, but only a small minority were completely illiterate.[10]

Northerners were impressed with the fact that black schools had been held in southern cities during slavery and described those they found in Richmond, New Bern, Charleston, Savannah, New Orleans, and elsewhere. Laura Haviland told of a "drill school" for slaves which Milla Granson, a slave herself, had conducted in Natchez for several years. An AMA missionary encountered two ex-slaves conducting a school for freedmen in an old Atlanta church. When AMA missionary Lewis Lockwood arrived in Hampton, Virginia, with the first Union troops, he met several black teachers, including Mary Peake, a free black woman who had taught slave and free blacks for years, despite Virginia laws which forbade her.[11]

Though Northern missionaries and freedmen's aid societies preferred to employ northern teachers, in their necessity they found and used literate southern blacks as teachers. The AMA commissioned dozens of native teachers throughout the South, usually placed in rural areas where no educational opportunity would otherwise have been available. One of these was Lily Granderson, whose prior experience was teaching a secret school for slaves at night. In Alabama black teachers were frequently used as assistants to white teachers, while other African-Americans served as the primary or the only teachers in small town schools, in Sunday schools where elementary education was taught, and in small "paying" schools. John Alvord of the Freedmen's Bureau told of a school in Goldsboro, North Carolina, where "two colored young men, who but a little time before commenced to learn themselves, had gathered 150 pupils, all quite orderly and hard at study." Teachers also reported to the Freedmen's Bureau that hundreds of Georgia black women and men conducted schools immediately after the war. Among them was Harriet Brent Jacobs, author of *Incidents in the Life of a Slave Girl*, who was taught to read as a slave by her mistress but who hid from her master's sexual advances for years before she escaped to the North. Jacobs and her daughter made a poignant return to the South and taught in Savannah for a year.[12]

In South Carolina, southern black people joined northern teachers to establish a school system. Among the Charleston natives who participated were Francis and Thomas Cardozo, Frances Rollins, and Mary and William Weston, whose family had supported black schools and Methodist Sunday schools for decades. Mary had taught a black school for several years. William, a bookkeeper, "had been educated in common branches and in such advanced subjects as logic, rhetoric, algebra, geometry, surveying, astronomy, Greek, and Latin," showing Northerners that antebellum Charleston schools for blacks had advanced beyond basic literacy. Herbert Gutman chronicled the establishment of schools for ex-slaves by African-Americans in rural northeastern South Carolina and in Camden, Sumter, Marion, Darlington, Florence, and other South Carolina towns.

The first postbellum teachers in Promised Land, an upcountry colony of freed slaves, were members of the colony who apparently received their literacy education as slaves on antebellum plantations.[13]

Tensions developed in the postwar educational efforts when the freed African-Americans made clear their preference for black teachers, either by open expression or by forsaking white-taught schools for private ones taught by blacks. As black minister Richard H. Cain said, "We must take into our hands the education of our race. Though honest, dignified whites may teach ever so well, it has not the effect to exalt the black man's opinion of his own race." African-Americans suspected that whites were willing to settle for lower qualifications than they were. The African Methodist Episcopal Church found that this was true for literacy among preachers. Despite the crucial need for ministers to the freedmen, the A.M.E. Church refused to relax its requirement that its ministers know how to read and write. Henry M. Turner explained, "the simple titles of preacher, deacon, and elder are not enough to satisfy those who are thirsting for moral and religious knowledge. We must be able to impart the same, otherwise . . . our preaching will be little more than the low of an ox or the bray of an ass." In contrast, the white Methodist Episcopal Church, North, eager to take advantage of the Southern opportunity, licensed thirty black men to preach to the freed slaves, only four of whom could read and none could write. This effort to outflank black churches by stressing emotion over learning was scorned by the A.M.E. Church.[14]

As education for freedmen proceeded, southern whites were forced to confront in new ways the realities of their changing situation. When the war began, southern white ministers and reformers had rallied to the cause of independence, based on the virtues of the southern way of life and the slave system. However, as the war dragged on they began to reexamine their beliefs and acknowledged that slavery should have been conducted differently. In "An Address to Christians Throughout the World" in 1863, for example, a group of prominent ministers proclaimed their support for the Confederacy, decried the Emancipation Proclamation, and asserted that "the South has done more than any people on earth for the christianization of the African race," but also promised to work to better the legal status of the slave. In their wartime meetings, members of the

Confederate Episcopal Church resolved to remove "unchristian features" from slave codes and southern Presbyterians considered proposals to recognize slave marriages legally, to prohibit separation of slave families, and to remove restrictions against literacy for slaves. Some Baptist spokesmen advocated similar changes.[15]

In the midst of wartime these resolutions and discussions came to nothing, but as war turned into tragedy, the tone of reformers turned accusatory. In 1864 an educator suggested that the Confederacy was being chastised because of the evil nature, not of slavery *per se*, but of the way it was conducted in the South. A contributor to the *Confederate Union* speculated that the prevention of slave literacy "is one of the many reasons why God is withholding, in a degree, his smiles from the righteous struggles we are waging with our cruel foes." A Georgian accused his fellow whites of making slavery "a stumbling block over which men fall into hell," and declared that the evils of slavery "must be speedily corrected or God will blot us out from among the nations of the earth."[16]

White Southerners, however, still believed that their guidance was needed to control African-Americans. In 1861 Joseph Stiles, who left the North to become a self-appointed "evangelist" to Confederate troops, insisted that blacks "possess no present qualifications for freedom. . . . Christianity rather decides, that for the present, *progressive social and religious improvement of the slave is his* SUPREME GOOD." Even those who believed that Negroes were potentially as capable as Caucasians felt that they still had a distance to go to be "elevated." John B. Adger, who conceived of slavery as "just a grand civilizing and Christianizing school," concluded wistfully after the war that "when emancipation was suddenly forced upon us, it found a good many pupils in the school of slavery who were ready to be graduated." He further speculated that "one hundred years more of the school of slavery might have fitted them all for graduation,"[17] voicing a common white Southern postwar theme.

Richard Fuller also deplored the precipitous end of white control over African-Americans. Fuller, a native South Carolinian ministering in the border state of Maryland, had angered both sections during the war: the South with his criticisms of slavery, his defiance of laws against teaching his slaves to read, and his loyalty to the Union, and the North because he chaired a committee of Southern Baptists which expressed sympathy with the Confederacy. Fuller's South Carolina plantations were occupied by Union soldiers early in the war and he wrote letter after letter to his friend Samuel Chase, in which he deplored the seizure of his property and the "moral desolation" of his slaves: "Their masters & religious teachers & overseers have all gone, & the Negroes have pillaged & are pillaging wherever they can." Fuller grimly predicted that "unless they be placed at once under strict regulations, they will swiftly degenerate into hordes of vagrant & forever irreclaimable outlaws." At the end of the war he wrote Chase about the degradation into which, from his perspective, his former slaves had fallen.[18]

In the ensuing years, Fuller tried to reestablish the support and guidance which he believed blacks still needed from white Southerners. He led the reconciliation between border and Deep South whites in the Southern Baptist Convention and urged the Baptists to concentrate their money and effort on home missions, including those "among the colored people," insisting that "the South is our own country, and the people our people."[19] On the whole, though, even Fuller's kind of missionary-minded Southerner was unwilling or unable to support postbellum black education, even for basic literacy. Leaders of southern white churches and denominations did believe in the usefulness of education; they passed resolutions which favored teaching freedmen "at least to read and write" and called for support for church schools and teachers who would present "good, sound theological instruction" for blacks. However, even such resolutions were seldom followed with concrete actions. While some penurious southern whites took jobs teaching the freedpeople, the planter class as a whole did not encourage the literacy effort. One Georgia planter who did teach African-Americans to read described a Sunday school he conducted with "over 100 pupils, mostly adults, 75 of them have already purchased the National Primer and all are anxious to learn." A.M.E. leader Theophilus G. Steward also praised Marion, South Carolina, planters who financed Steward's church and his school.[20]

Most of the teaching, though, was done by African-Americans themselves. Despite the credit for southern black education which is often given to northern missionaries and philanthropists, black people themselves were responsible for founding and perpetuating most of their educational efforts in the South. In fact, according to James Anderson, ex-slaves were the leaders most responsible for the entire late nineteenth century public education movement in the South. Universal education was never popular among southern whites, who followed the planters' reluctance to let the state intervene in their social and economic relationships. Instead, the public school system for blacks and white children was brought about in the southern states primarily by the efforts of African-Americans, who carried with them from slavery into freedom the belief in universal learning as a necessary basis for freedom and citizenship.[21]

The experiences of generations of African-Americans who endured the slave experience sparked the drive for literacy after slavery and perpetuated education as a cherished value and a basis for freedom within the black community. Many black leaders in the ministry, government, and education in the first decades of freedom had learned to read and write as slaves. Others carried with them from slavery a resentment that literacy had been withheld from them. The belief in the value of literacy and education was instilled deep within the African-American consciousness and took shape during the slave experience as a form of resistance to oppression and a maintenance of psychological freedom. Literacy's significance to the African-American community has helped shape the American South in freedom as it did in slavery.

NOTES

Abbreviations

ABS   Annual Reports of the American Bible Society

ACS   Papers relating to the American Colonization Society, Library of Congress

AR   African Repository and Colonization Journal

ASSU American Sunday School Union Annual Reports

JNH   Journal of Negro History

Rawick, ed. George L. Rawick, ed., *The American Slave: A Composite Autobiography.* Vols. 1–19. Greenwood Press, Westport, Conn., 1972. Supplement, Series 1, Vols. 1–12. Greenwood Press, Westport, Conn., 1977. Supplement, Series 2, Vols. 1–10. Greenwood Press, Westport, Conn., 1980.

Tract Society Annual Reports of the American Tract Society

Introduction

1. Frederick Douglass, *Life and Times of Frederick Douglass* (Hartford, Conn., 1881; facsimile ed., 1983), 75.

2. Charles T. Davis and Henry Louis Gates, Jr., *The Slave's Narrative* (Oxford, 1985), xvi.

3. James Olney, " 'I Was Born': Slave Narratives, Their Status as Autobiography and Literature," Davis and Gates, 153; Vincent P. Franklin, *Black Self-Determination: A Cultural History of the Faith of the Fathers* (Westport, Conn.: Lawrence Hill, 1984), 161.

4. Lucius Holsey, *Autobiography, Sermons, Addresses, and Essays* (Atlanta, Ga., 1898), 16; Rawick, ed., Georgia, XII (2), 34.

5. Roger Chartier, "The Practical Impact of Writing," in Roger Chartier, ed., *A History of Private Life, Vol. III: Passions of the Renaissance,* gen. eds., Philippe Aries and Georges Duby, trans. Arthur Goldhammer (Cambridge, Mass., 1989), 116–117; Paul Saenger, "Silent Reading: Its Impact on Late Medieval Script and Society," *Viator* 13, 1983, 367–414; Harvey J. Graff, ed., *Literacy and Social Development in the West: A Reader* (Cambridge and London: Cambridge U. Press, 1981), 1; Jack Goody and Ian Watt, "The Consequences of Literacy," in Jack Goody, ed., *Literacy in Traditional Societies,* (Cambridge, 1968), 67; Lawrence A. Cremin, *Traditions of American Education* (New York, 1977), 32–35.

6. Franklin, 6, 8, 24; Graff, *The Literacy Myth: Literacy and Social Structure in the Nineteenth Century City* (New York, 1979), 28, 314–15; Roger Schofield, "The Measurement of Literacy in Pre-Industrial England," in Goody, ed., 312–13.

7. John Blassingame, ed. *Slave Testimony: Two Centuries of Letters, Speeches, Interviews, and Autobiographies* (Baton Rouge: LSU Press, 1977), 710–12; Margaret Washington Creel, *"A Peculiar People": Slave Religion and Community-Culture Among the Gullahs* (New York: NYU Press, 1988), 267; James McKaye, *Mastership and its Fruits: The Emancipated Slave Face to Face with his Old Master* (New York, 1864), 7.

8. Charles H. Long, "Perspectives for a Study of Afro-American Religion in the United States," *History of Religions,* 11:1 (Aug. 1971), 59, 62; Rhys Isaac, "Books and the Social Authority of Learning: The Case of Mid–Eighteenth Century Virginia," William L. Joyce, David D. Hall, Richard D. Brown, and John B. Hench, eds., *Printing and Society in Early America* (Worcester, Mass., 1983), 232.

9. Creel, 274–75, 209; Franklin, xii, 176, 50–51.

10. Kenneth A. Lockridge attributes the initial rise of mass literacy in the Atlantic world to "intense Protestantism," whose primary purpose was "pious conformity." (Lockridge, *Literacy in Colonial New England: An Enquiry into the Social Context of Literacy in the Early Modern West,* [New York, 1974], 98–100.) Harvey Graff notes that the early nineteenth century American public school movement fostered traditional Protestantism; its architects were clergymen, its publicists were the religious press, and its major goals included the inculcation of morality (Graff, *Literacy Myth,* 28.)

11. Janet Duitsman Cornelius, "God's Schoolmasters: Southern Evangelists to the Slaves, 1830–1860," Ph.D. Diss., U. of Ill., Urbana, 1977; Erskine Clark, *Wrestlin' Jacob: A Portrait of Religion in the Old South* (Atlanta, 1979); Milton Sernett, *Black Religion and American Evangelicalism: White Protestants, Plantation Missions, and the Flowering of Negro Christianity, 1787–1865* (Metuchen, N.J., 1975); Charles Colcock Jones, *The Religious Instruction of the Negroes in the United States* (Savannah, 1842; reprint, 1969); Creel, *op. cit.*

12. Max Warren, *Social History and Christian Mission* (London, 1967), 135–36.

13. For the teaching of reading but not writing in religious education in seventeenth century Sweden, see Daniel P. Resnick and Lauren B. Resnick, "The Nature of Literacy: An Historical Exploration," *Harvard Educational Review* 47: 3 (Aug. 1977), 374. For a similar practice in late eighteenth and early nineteenth century England, see Michael Sanderson, "Literacy and Social Mobility

in the Industrial Revolution in England," *Past & Present*, 56 (Aug. 1972), 81; John McLeish, *Evangelical Religion and Popular Education: A Modern Interpretation* (London, 1969), 95; Philip McCann, "Popular Education, Socialization, and Social Control: Spitalfields, 1812–1824," and Simon Frith, "Socialization and Rational Schooling: Elementary Education in Leeds before 1870," Frith, ed., *Popular Education and Socialization in the Nineteenth Century* (London, 1977), 11–12, 81–82.

14. J. A. Hutton, *Caste in India*, 3rd ed. (Oxford, 1961), 92–93; Roger Schofield, "Measurement of Literacy," 313.

15. Graff, *Literacy Myth*, 314–15; Cremin, 32–35; David B. Tyack, ed., *Turning Points in American Educational History* (Waltham, Mass., 1967); Merle Curti, *Social Ideas of American Educators* (Totowa, New Jersey, 1968), 36; Frederick Rudolph, ed., *Essays on Education in the Early Republic* (Cambridge, Mass., 1965), 5, 66.

16. William R. Taylor, "Toward a Definition of Orthodoxy: The Patrician South and the Common Schools," *Harvard Educational Review*, 36:4 (Sept. 1966), 412–16.

17. Benjamin Drew, *The Refugee: or the Narratives of Fugitive Slave in Canada Related by Themselves* (Boston, 1856); William Still, *The Underground Rail Road* (Philadelphia, 1872); Octavia V. Rogers Albert, *The House of Bondage or, Charlotte Brooks and Other Slaves* (New York, 1890; reprint 1972); Laura Haviland, *A Woman's Life-Work* (Chicago, 1887); McKaye, *op. cit.;* Gustavus D. Pike, *The Jubilee Singers and their Campaign for Twenty Thousand Dollars* (Boston, 1893).

18. For a complete listing of individual biographies which include accounts by former slaves of how they learned to read during slavery, see Chapter Three, footnote 7. Compilations of biographies include William Simmons, *Men of Mark: Eminent, Progressive, and Rising* (Cleveland, O., 1887; reprint 1968); Monroe A. Majors, *Noted Negro Women: Their Triumphs and Activities* (1893; reprint Freeport, N.Y., 1971); Daniel Culp, *Twentieth Century Negro Literature* (Naperville, Ill., 1902; reprint 1969); Charles Octavius Boothe, *The Cyclopedia of the Colored Baptists of Alabama: Their Leaders and Their Work* (Birmingham, Ala., 1895); Edward R. Carter, *Biographical Sketches of our Pulpit* (Atlanta, 1888; reprint, 1968); A. W. Pegues, *Our Baptist Ministers and Schools* (Springfield, Mass., 1892); Alexander Wayman, *Cyclopedia of African Methodism* (Baltimore, 1882).

19. Rawick, ed.; Charles L. Perdue, Jr., Thomas E. Barden, Robert K. Phillips, eds., *Weevils in the Wheat: Interviews with Virginia Ex-Slaves* (Charlottesville, Va., 1975). For evaluations of the Federal Writers Project accounts and comparisons with other accounts by former slaves, see Blassingame, ed., "Introduction," *Slave Testimony*, xvii–lxv; David Thomas Bailey, "A Divided Prism: Two Sources of Black Testimony on Slavery," *Journal of Southern History*, XLVI: 3 (Aug. 1980), 381–404; William L. Van Debrug, *The Slave Drivers: Black Agricultural Labor Supervisors in the Antebellum South* (Westport, Conn.: Greenwood Press, 1979), 77–94; Thomas L. Webber, *Deep Like the Rivers: Education in the Slave Quarter Community, 1831–1865* (New York, 1978), 131–38.

20. Rawick, ed., Georgia, XIII (4), 270; Texas, IV (1), 167; Mississippi, Suppl., Series 1 (2), 365.

21. Schofield, "The Measurement of Literacy," 313–15; Chartier, "The Practical Impact of Writing," 112.

22. Resnick and Resnick, "The Nature of Literacy," 371. Graff, "Literacy Past and Present: Critical Approaches in the Literacy-Society Relationship," *Interchange* 9 (1978), 8–9; Lee Soltow and Edward Stevens, *The Rise of Literacy and the Common School in the United States: A Socioeconomic Analysis to 1870* (Chicago, 1981), 4.

23. W. E. B. DuBois, *Black Reconstruction* (1935; reprint, New York: Harcourt, Brace, 1963), 638; Carter Woodson, *Education of the Negro* (Washington, D.C., 1921), 228. Eugene Genovese used the five percent estimate, but cautioned that this might be too low (*Roll, Jordan, Roll: The World the Slaves Made,* [New York: Pantheon Books, 1974], 563).

24. Cornelius, "We Slipped and Learned to Read: Slave Accounts of the Literacy Process, 1830–1865," *Phylon,* XLIV:3 (Sept. 1983), 186.

25. Ivan McDougle, "Slavery in Kentucky," *JNH* III:3 (Jul. 1918), 289; Still, *op. cit.*

26. James D. Anderson, *The Education of Blacks in the South, 1860–1935,* (Chapel Hill: U. of N. Carolina Press, 1988), 6.

27. Edmund Drago, *Politicians and Reconstruction in Georgia* (Baton Rouge, 1982), appendix; Joe M. Richardson, *Christian Reconstruction: The American Missionary Association and Southern Blacks, 1861–1890* (Athens: U. of Ga. Press, 1986), 27; Robert C. Morris, *Reading, Writing, and Reconstruction: The Education of Freedmen in the South, 1861–1870* (Chicago: U. of Chicago Press, 1982), 92.

Chapter One

1. William Bosman, *New and Accurate Description of the Coast of Guinea* (London, 1705), 146–47.

2. Creel, 37–42; Allen D. Austin, *African Muslims in Antebellum America* (New York, 1984), 25–36; Charles T. Davis and Henry Louis Gates, Jr., *The Slave's Narrative,* (New York, 1985), 328–30; Goody, ed., "Introduction," 4–5.

3. Mitford M. Mathews, *Teaching to Read Historically Considered* (Chicago, 1966), 19; Lawrence Stone, "Literacy and Education in England, 1640–1900," *Past and Present,* 42 (1969), 77–83; Marcus Jernegan, "Slavery and Conversion in the American Colonies," *American Historical Review,* 21 (Apr. 1916), 508.

4. *Ibid.;* William Stevens Perry, *Historical Collections Relating to the American Colonial Church,* I (Hartford, Conn., 1870–1878), 3–8; Frank J. Klingberg, *Anglican Humanitarianism in Colonial New York* (Philadelphia, 1940), 6; David Brion Davis, *The Problem of Slavery in Western Culture* (Ithaca, 1966), 211; H. P. Thompson, *Into All Lands: The History of the Society for the Propagation of the Gospel into Foreign Parts, 1701–1950* (London, 1951), 62.

5. Creel, 85–86; Alan Gallay, "Planters and Slaves in the Great Awakening," in John Boles, ed., *Masters and Slaves in the House of the Lord: Race and Religion in the American South, 1740–1870* (University Press of Kentucky: Lexington, Ky., 1988), 23; Perry, *Historical Collections,* I, 344; H. P. Thompson, 12; George C. Rogers, Jr., *Charleston in the Age of the Pinckneys* (Norman, Okla., 1969), 91.

6. Arthur Lyon Cross, *The Anglican Episcopate and the American Colonies* (Harvard Hist. Studies, IX, 1902; reprint 1964), 4–5; Perry, *Historical Collec-*

tions, I, 346–47; Philip Alexander Bruce, *Institutional History of Virginia in the Seventeenth Century,* I (N.Y., 1910), 125, 127, 193; Carl Bridenbaugh, *Mitre and Sceptre: Transatlantic Faiths, Ideas, Personalities and Politics, 1689–1775* (N.Y., 1962), 179; Peter H. Wood, *Black Majority: Negroes in Colonial South Carolina from 1670 through the Stono Rebellion* (N.Y., 1974), 135–142; David Brion Davis, *Problem of Slavery in Western Culture,* 217; Klingberg, 28–30; H. P. Thompson, 45; Faith Vibert, "The Society for the Propagation of the Gospel in Foreign Parts: Its Work for the Negroes in North American before 1783," *JNH,* XVIII:2 (Apr. 1933), 194; Carter Woodson, *Education of the Negro Prior to 1861* (Washington, D.C.; reprint 1968), 38–39.

7. Cross, 124–25; J. Harry Bennett, Jr., "The S.P.G.'s Plantations," Samuel Clyde McCulloch, ed., *British Humanitarianism: Essays in Honor of Frank Klingberg* (Philadelphia, 1950), 17–24; Woodson, *Education of the Negro Prior to 1861,* 363–64; C. F. Pascoe, *Two Hundred Years of the S.P.G.: An Historical Account of the Society for the Propagation of the Gospel in Foreign Parts, 1701–1900* (London, 1901), 200.

8. Wood, 137; Winthrop Jordan, *White Over Black: American Attitudes toward the Negro, 1550–1812* (Chapel Hill, 1968), 136–78; Davis and Gates, xxv.

9. Wood, 142. A typical S.P.G. missionary reported that he had difficulty getting permission to catechize slaves because many of the slaveowners thought baptism "hurt [slaves] by giving them better Notions of themselves than is consistent with their state of Slavery and their duty to their Masters." (Jordan, 182–83.)

10. James Gronniosaw, *A Narrative of the Most Remarkable Particulars in the Life of James Albert Ukawsaw Gronniosaw* (Bath, 1770).

11. Davis and Gates, xxvii; Goody, "Restricted Literacy in Northern Ghana," in Goody, *op. cit.,* 206; Jupiter Hammon, *Address to the Negroes in the State of New York* (New York, 1787).

12. E. T. Thompson, *Presbyterians in the South* (Richmond, Va., 1963) 52–60; Andrew Murray, *Presbyterians and the Negro—a History* (Philadelphia, 1966), 10–11; Perry, *Historical Collections,* I, 369.

13. Herbert Aptheker, ed., *A Documentary History of the Negro People in the United States,* I (New York, 1951), 1–4. Angelo Costanzo, *Surprizing Narrative: Olaudah Equiano and the Beginnings of Black Autobiography* (New York, 1988), 35–37; Creel, 75.

14. Klingberg, 113–34; 2 *Brevards Digest,* 243, quoted in George M. Stroud, *A Sketch of the Laws Relating to Slavery in the Several States of the United States of America* (Philadelphia, 1856), 60.

15. H. P. Thompson, 62; Albert J. Raboteau, *Slave Religion: The "Invisible Institution" in the Antebellum South* (Oxford, 1978), 118–19; *Cobb's Digest of the Laws of Georgia,* vol. 2, 1851, 57.

16. Woodson, *Education of the Negro,* 45–46; Bruce, *Institutional History of Virginia,* 243; Thomas E. Drake, *Quakers and Slavery in America* (New Haven, 1950), 5–8.

17. Jordan, 213; William Warren Sweet, *Religion on the American Frontier, Vol. I: The Baptists,* 4–13; Wesley Gewehr, *The Great Awakening in Virginia, 1740–1790* (Gloucester, Mass., 1965), 169–70; J. H. Hartzell, "Methodism and the Negro in the United States," *JNH,* VIII:3 (Jul. 1923), 301.

18. Luther P. Jackson, "Religious Development of the Negro in Virginia from 1760 to 1860," *JNH,* XVI:2 (Apr. 1931), 174.

19. Sweet, *The Baptists,* 21.

20. Mechal Sobel, *Trabelin' On: The Slave Journey to an Afro-Baptist Faith* (Westport, Conn., 1979), 139–49; William L. Lumpkin, *Baptist Foundations in the South* (Nashville, 1961), 147–50; Donald G. Mathews, *Religion in the Old South* (Chicago, 1977), 23–27; James D. Tyms, *The Rise of Negro Education Among Negro Baptists* (New York, 1965), 97–102.

21. Owen D. Pelt and Ralph Lee Smith, *The Story of the National Baptists* (New York, 1960), 35; James D. Simms, *The First Colored Baptist Church in North America* (Philadelphia, 1888; reprint 1969), 14–30.

22. Walter H. Brooks, "The Priority of the Silver Bluff Church and its Promoters," *JNH,* 7:2 (Apr. 1922), 172–75; *Baptist Annual Register, 1790–93,* 332–37, quoted in "Early Negro Churches in Kingston, Jamaica and Savannah, Georgia," *JNH,* 1:1 (Jan. 1916), 69–75; Philip Curtin, *Two Jamaicas* (Cambridge, Mass., 1955), 33; Leonard E. Barrett, *Soul Force: African Heritage in Afro-American Religion* (N.Y., 1974), 112–13.

23. "Early Negro Churches in Kingston, Jamaica and Savannah, Georgia" *JNH,* 1:1 (Jan. 1916), 87; John W. Davis, "George Liele and Andrew Bryan, Pioneer Baptist Preachers," *JNH* III:2 (April 1918), 119–27; Creel, 133–34; Gallay, 23–32.

24. Richard M. Cameron, *Methodism and Society in Historical Perspective* (N.Y., 1961), 38, 114, 129–30; Sweet, *The Methodists,* 45; Mathews, *Religion in the Old South,* 30–31; Woodson, *Education of the Negro,* 73; *Doctrines and Discipline of the Methodist Episcopal Church* (Cincinnati, 1854), 30–31; *Doctrines and Discipline of the Methodist Church, South* (Nashville, 1866), 87–88, 95–96, 106, 241–45; *Proceedings of the Meeting in Charleston, S.C., May 13–15, 1845 on the Religious Instruction of the Negroes* (Charleston, 1845), 23–43; *Public Proceedings Relating to Calvary Church and the Religious Instruction of Slaves* (Charleston, 1850), 39, 42, 46, 47. John Wesley's system of "bands" of a few persons, which he established to create a closely supervised fellowship in a hostile world, were used by slaves to provide the aid, welfare, and mutual support which they needed so desperately. (Woodson, *History of the Negro Church* [Washington, D.C., 1921], 57–61; Curtin, 33; Barrett, 118–19; Woodson, *Education of the Negro,* 74.)

25. E. T. Thompson, 135; Sidney Ahlstrom, *Religious History of the American People* (New Haven, 1972), 445; B. W. McDonnold, *History of the Cumberland Presbyterian Church* (Nashville, 1893), 432–34; R. Douglas Brackenridge, *Voice in the Wilderness: A History of the Cumberland Presbyterian Church in Texas* (San Antonio, 1969), 77–78.

26. Aptheker, *Documentary History,* I, 11; Marion Wilson Starling, *The Slave Narrative: Its Place in American History* (Boston, 1981), 5; Franklin, 85–86.

27. Robert McColley, *Slavery in Jeffersonian Virginia* (Urbana, Ill., 1964), 144, 157; Woodson, *Education of the Negro,* 74; John C. Fitzpatrick, ed., *Writings of George Washington,* 37 (Washington, D.C., 1940), 276–77; Benjamin Franklin, *Letters,* vol. 8, 425; vol. 9, 174; vol. 10, 396.

28. Merle Curti, *Social Ideas of American Educators* (Totowa, N.J., 1968), 36; Benjamin Rush, "Plan for the Establishment of Public Schools," in Frederick Rudolph, ed., *Essays on Education in the Early Republic* (Cambridge, Mass., 1965), 5; Noah Webster, "On the Education of Youth in America," *Ibid.,* 66; *The American Convention of Abolition Societies,* 1794: 20; 1779: 41; 1797: 36. (facsimile ed., I: 1794–1805, New York, 1969).

29. "Minutes of the Proceedings of the 10th Annual Convention for the Abolition of Slavery, 1805", *JNH*, VI:1 (Jan. 1921), 105–11.

30. *William Patton, A Sermon, with the Constitution of the African Benevolent Society* (Newport, R.I., 1808).

31. Daniel Payne, *Recollections of Seventy Years* (Nashville, 1888; reprint 1968), 13–16; Maria Wikmaranayake, *A World in Shadow: The Free Black in Antebellum South Carolina* (Columbia, S.C., 1973), 84–86.

32. Mathews, *Slavery and Methodism*, 20–21, 26; Trinity College Historical Society, *Historical Papers*, Series IX, 1912, 94.

33. John Scott Strickland, "The Great Revival and Insurrectionary Fears in North Carolina: An Examination of Antebellum Southern Society and Slave Revolt Panics," *Class, Conflict, and Consensus: Antebellum Southern Community Studies*, eds. Orville Vernon Burton and Robert C. McMath, Jr. (Westport, Conn., 1982), 60, 62, 77, 81–82.

34. Mathews, *Religion in the Old South*, 65; David Brion Davis, *Problem of Slavery in the Age of Revolution* (Ithaca, 1975), 206–7.

35. Woodson, *Education of the Negro*, 55; E. T. Thompson, 324; Cameron, 196; Donald Mathews, *Slavery and Methodism: A Chapter in American Morality, 1780–1845* (Princeton, 1965), 14–16; Mathews, *Religion in the Old South*, 254.

36. Mathews, *Slavery and Methodism*, 22–25.

37. Ira Berlin, *Slaves Without Masters: The Free Negro in the Antebellum South* (N.Y., 1975), 396–99; Davis, *Problem of Slavery in the Age of Revolution*, 121–22.

38. Berlin, *Slaves Without Masters*, 55.

39. *Minutes of the Annual General Conferences of the Methodist Episcopal Church*, II: 1829–1839; Ahlstrom, 436–45; Berlin, *Slaves Without Masters*, 70.

40. Jackson, 18, 194, 203; Charles S. Sydnor, *The Development of Southern Sectionalism, 1819–1828: A History of the South, Vol. 5* (Baton Rouge, 1948), 89–103; Starkey, 17.

41. Leon F. Litwack, *North of Slavery* (Chicago, 1961), 66–67, 75, 79, 97, 114.

42. Zephaniah Kingsley, *A Treatise on . . . Slavery . . .* (1829), 13; Philip Foner, *History of Cuba* (New York, 1962), 121; Herbert Aptheker, *American Negro Slave Revolts* (New York, 1943), 265.

43. *An Account of the Late Intended Insurrection Among a Portion of the Blacks of the City* (Charleston, 1822; reprint, 1970); William W. Freehling, *Prelude to Civil War: The Nullification Controversy in South Carolina, 1816–1830* (New York, 1966), 54–61; Daniel Alexander Payne, *History of the African Methodist Episcopal Church* (Nashville, 1891; reprint 1969), 45, 53–54; Aptheker, *Slave Revolts*, 269; Robert Starobin, ed., *Denmark Vesey: The Slave Conspiracy of 1822* (Englewood Cliffs, N.J., 1970), 40, 48, 53.

44. Betty Fladeland, *Men and Brothers: Anglo-American Antislavery Cooperation* (Urbana, Ill., 1972), 177, 185, 49, 201–202. For examples of white southern sensitivity to the famed Wedgewood medallion featuring a shackled slave, see William Capers, "American Methodism," *Wesleyan-Methodist Magazine*, 51 (1828), 626–27; Pinckney, *Address*, 7; *Methodist Magazine and Quarterly Review*, 13 (1831), 313.

45. Wilmore, 36–38.

46. David Walker, *Walker's Appeal in Four Articles* (Boston, 1830; reprint 1969), 16, 41–42.

47. Aptheker, *Slave Revolts*, 281–290; Clement Eaton, *The Freedom-of-Thought Struggle in the Old South* (New York, 1964), 91.

48. Henry Irving Tragle, *The Southampton Slave Revolt of 1831; A Compliation of Source Material* (Amherst, Mass., 1971), 91–92, 276; *Confessions of Nat Turner* (Baltimore, 1831; reprint, 1969), 5; Curtin, 83–88.

49. Mary Turner, *Slaves and Missionaries: The Disintegration of Jamaican Slave Society, 1787–1834* (Urbana, 1982), 148–52.

50. *Digest of the Laws of Georgia* (Philadelphia, 1831), 316–317; *Acts of the State of Louisiana*, 1830, 96; North Carolina, *Revised Statutes*, 1837, 209, 578; *Code of Virginia*, 1849, 747–48; John G. Aiken, *A Digest of the Laws of Alabama* (Philadelphia, 1833), 397; John Codman Hurd, *The Law of Freedom and Bondage in the United States*, II (New York, 1862; reprint 1968), 9, 93, 87–88, 105–6, 151, 161–62; George M. Stroud, *A Sketch of the Laws Relating to Slavery in the Several States* (Philadelphia, 1856), 61.

51. Aiken, 397–409; William Birney, *James G. Birney and His Times* (New York, 1890), 104.

52. Elsa V. Goveiea, "The West Indian Slave Laws of the Eighteenth Century," *Slavery in the New World*, eds. Laura Foner and Eugene Genovese, (Englewood Cliffs, N.J., 1969), 133; Edward Laurens, "Address before the Agricultural Society of South Carolina, Sept. 18, 1832," *Southern Agriculturist*, V (1832), 565; Kingsley, 13; *An Account of the Late Intended Insurrection among a Portion of the Blacks of the City*, 29–30; Aptheker, *Slave Revolts*, 269; Tragle, 91–92.

53. North Carolina, *Revised Statutes*, 1837, 209, 578; 1854, 218–219; Stroud, *Sketch of Laws Relating to Slavery*, 58–63; *Code of the State of Georgia* (Atlanta, 1861), 1878–1879; *Code of Virginia*, 1849, 747–48; *Digest of the Laws of Alabama* (Tuskaloosa, 1843), 543; John P. Ormond, Arthur P. Bagley, George Goldthwaite, *The Code of Alabama* (Montgomery, 1852); *Louisiana Digest of the Penal Law* (New Orleans, 1841), 126; *Acts of the State of Louisiana* (New Orleans, 1855), 377–91; *Revised Statutes of Louisiana* (New Orleans, 1856); *Code of Mississippi*, 1798–1848, 534; *Maryland Code*, 1860, 462; *Missouri Laws*, 1847, 103–104; *Missouri Revised Statutes*, 1856.

54. J. Withers, *State v. Boozer*, 5 Strobhart 21, May 1850, in Helen Catterall, *Judicial Cases Concerning American Slavery and the Negro*, II (Washington, D.C., 1929), 417.

55. Margaret Douglass, *The Personal Narrative of Mrs. Margaret Douglass* (Boston, 1854), 5–51. A search of collections on slave jurisprudence, including Catterall, *Judicial Cases*, and Michie's *Jurisprudence* did not uncover additional cases concerning prosecutions of violations of literacy restrictions.

56. Moncure D. Conway, *Autobiography, Memories, and Experiences of M. D. Conway*, I (Boston, 1904; reprint, 1969), 5–7.

57. William S. Jenkins, *Pro-Slavery Thought in the Old South* (Chapel Hill, 1935), 72; Charles Colcock Jones, *Religious Instruction*, 69–70.

58. Charles Cotesworth Pinckney, *An Address Delivered in Charleston before the Agricultural Society of South Carolina* (Charleston, 1829), 4–18; Marvin R. Zahniser, *Charles Cotesworth Pinckney* (Chapel Hill, 1967), 272–73.

59. Mary Jones to Charles Colcock Jones, Oct. 24, 1827, Charles Colcock Jones to Elizabeth Maxwell, Mar. 28, 1828, Sept. 19, 1828, Charles Colcock

Jones to Mary Jones, June 20, 1829, Jul. 9, 1829, Aug. 24, 1830, Mar. 19, 1830, Charles Colcock Jones Papers, Tulane University; William P. Harrison, *The Gospel to the Slaves* (Nashville, 1893, reprint 1971), 194; Thomas M. Clay, *Detail of a Plan for Religious Instruction of Slaves* (Charleston, 1832); Charles Colcock Jones, *Religious Instruction*, 72–80; Robert J. Breckinridge to Propper Hodge, July 2, 1833, Breckinridge Papers, Library of Congress; Roger Crook, "The Ethical Emphasis of the Editors of Baptist Journals Published in the Southeastern Region of the United States up to 1865" (Th.D. diss., Southern Baptist Theological Seminary, Louisville, 1947); *New York Christian Advocate*, Jan. 14, Feb. 7, Apr. 11, May 2, 1834.

60. *Presbyterian Magazine*, 1 (Apr. 1851), 199–200; John Robinson, *The Testimony and Practice of the Presbyterian Church in Reference to American Slavery* (Cincinnati, 1852), 256; *DeBow's Review*, 21 (Dec. 1856), 609; 24 (Sept. 1858), 326; David Christy, *Pulpit Politics; or, Ecclesiastical Legislation on Slavery* (Cincinnati, 1862), 23; Daniel Hundley, *Social Relations in our Southern States* (New York, 1860), 297.

61. Charles Colcock Jones, *Religious Instruction*, 229–30; Robert Manson Myers, *The Children of Pride: A True Story of Georgia and the Civil War* (New Haven, 1972), 168; Robert Starobin, *Blacks in Bondage* (New York, 1974), for letters written by Jones' slaves.

Chapter Two

1. Harriott Horry Ravenel, *Eliza Pinckney* (New York, 1896; reprint 1967), 24, 29, 189; Zahniser, 272–73.

2. St. Philip's Church Parish Records, 1814, South Carolina Historical Society, Charleston; South Carolina Episcopal Diocese, *Journal*, 1851, 18, 28; Charleston Baptist Association Minutes, 1828, 1829, 1835; Minutes of the Annual Conference of the Methodist Episcopal Church, 1829–1839; Payne, *History of the A.M.E. Church*, 31–45.

3. Duncan Alexander Reilly, "William Capers: an Evaluation of his Life and Thought" (unpubl. Ph.D. Diss., Emory U., 1972), 82, 107; Albert Sidney Thomas, "Christopher Edward Gadsden," *Historical Magazine of the Protestant Episcopal Church*, 20 (Sept. 1951), 294–97; Nathaniel Bowen, *A Pastoral Letter on the Religious Instruction of the Negroes* (Charleston, 1835); William Weatherford, *American Churches and the Negro* (Boston, 1957), 148–49; Louisa Manly, *The Manly Family* (Furman U., 1930), 77–78; John Tracy Ellis, ed., *Documents of American Catholic History* (Milwaukee, 1956), 234.

4. Freehling, 61; George C. Rogers, *History of Georgetown County, South Carolina* (Columbia, S.C., 1970), 236–37; *An Account of the Late Intended Insurrection among a Portion of the Blacks of the City*, 29–30; Charleston Baptist Association Minutes, 1829, 1835; Minutes of the Annual Conference of the M.E. Church, South, 1845–1851, 1858–1865.

5. C. W. Birnie, "Education of the Negro in Charleston, South Carolina, Prior to the Civil War," *JNH*, XII:1 (Jan. 1927), 15; Daniel Payne, *Recollections of Seventy Years* (Nashville, 1888; reprint 1968), 13–16; Wikmaranayake, 84–86.

6. "Bishop Daniel Alexander Payne's Protestation of American Slavery," *JNH*, LII:1 (Jan. 1967), 59–64.

7. Freehling, 340–48; Savage, 44–45.

8. Petitions by sixty-four "citizens of St. Helena Parish" and ninety-five other unidentified South Carolinians asking that the state's free Negroes be enslaved or removed to Liberia. Petitions on Slavery, South Carolina State Archives, Columbia, S.C.

9. *Southern Agriculturalist,* II (Mar. 1829), 111; *The National Cyclopaedia of American Biography,* 12 (New York, 1906), 170; *South Carolina Historical and Geneological Magazine,* 17 (Apr. 1916), 70–71; Whitemarsh Seabrook, "Remarks on the General Unsuccessfulness of Sea Island Planters," *Southern Agriculturalist,* VII (Jan. & Apr. 1834), 9–12, 177–78; Samuel Gaillard Stoney, ed., "Memoirs of Frederick Augustus Porcher," *South Carolina Historical and Geneological Magazine,* 46 (Jul. 1945), 151–53.

10. *Southern Agriculturalist,* VII (Apr. 1834), 178; Whitemarsh Seabrook, *Essay on the Management of Slaves* (Charleston, 1834), 9–13; *Ibid.,* 4, 7, 9–13. This address has been cited as supporting or representing advocates of religious instruction for slaves, but it was actually an attack on the project.

11. Seabrook, *Essay,* 15, 20, 31, 7, 20.

12. *Journal of the General Assembly of the State of South Carolina, 1835* 3–10; Petitions on Slavery, South Carolina Archives, Columbia, S.C.; Seabrook, *Essay,* 8; *Journal of the General Assembly of S.C., 1833,* 13, 15, 48; Freehling, 109, 114, 335.

13. *Charleston Courier,* quoted in H. M. Henry, *Police Control of the Slave in South Carolina* (1914; reprint 1968), 167.

14. *Journal of the General Assembly of S.C., 1834,* 52–53, 74.

15. David Grimstead has compiled evidence of twenty incidents of popular violence between 1828 and 1833, sixteen in 1834, and thirty-seven in 1835. Most of the latter were concentrated in the summer and fall of that year. Grimstead, "Rioting in its Jacksonian Setting," *American Historical Review,* 77 (Apr. 1972), 362–64.

16. Clement Eaton, *The Freedom-of-Thought Struggle in the Old South,* (New York, 1964), 95–97; Ulrich Phillips, *American Negro Slavery* (New York, 1918), 484–86; Aptheker, *Slave Revolts,* 325–29.

17. Savage, 14–15.

18. *Ibid.,* 44–45.

19. Freehling, 340–44.

20. John England to Dr. Cullen, Feb. 23, 1836, *American Catholic Historical Society Records,* 8 (1897), 215–29.

21. Peter Guilday, *The Life and Times of John England, 1786–1842,* II (New York, 1927), 176–83, 218.

22. Frank Otto Gatell, ed., "Postmaster Huger and the Incendiary Publications," *South Carolina Historical and Geneological Magazine,* LXIV (Oct. 1963), 194–95.

23. England to Cullen, *American Catholic Historical Society Records,* 220–21.

24. Charles Colcock Jones, *Religious Instruction,* 97–98.

25. John G. Jones, *Methodism in the Mississippi Conference,* II (Nashville, 1908), 346–47; Harrison, *Gospel Among the Slaves,* 194–95.

26. Andrew Murray, *Presbyterians and the Negro—A History* (Philadelphia, 1966), 66–68; Ernest Trice Thompson, I: 338; Donald Mathews, *Slavery and*

Methodism: A Chapter in American Morality, 1780–1845 (Princeton, 1965), 55–56.

27. Betty Fladeland, *James Gillespie Birney: Slaveholder to Abolitionist* (Cornell, 1955; reprint, 1969), 1–90; Dwight L. Dumond, ed., *Letters of James Gillespie Birney, 1831–1857,* I (Gloucester, Mass., 1966), 56, 77, 85, 89, 147.

28. *An Address to the Presbyterians of Kentucky* (Cincinnati, 1835); "Kentucky Union for the Moral & Religious Improvement of the colored Race," *African Repository,* 11 (Nov. 1835), 268; William E. Arnold, *Methodism in Kentucky,* II (Louisville, 1936), 143–45.

29. Charleston Baptist Association, Minutes, 1835; Minutes of the General Assembly of the Presbyterian Church, 1835, 38; John G. Jones, *Methodism in Mississippi,* II, 500; Weatherford, 143; Statement issued by Whitefoord Smith and William Capers [Methodists], Whitefoord Smith papers, Duke University, Aug. 10, 1835; Bowen, *Pastoral Letter,* 6–11.

30. Ryland, V; Jones, *Catechism;* Trapier; Winkler, x; William Plumer, ed., *Thoughts on the Religious Instruction of the Negroes of this Country* (Princeton, 1848), 49; Robert Manson Myers, 16, 168; John B. Adger, *My Life and Times, 1810–1899* (Richmond, 1899), 100–101; John E. Hughes, Th.D. Diss., 81.

31. Duncan A. Reilly, "William Capers", 152–53.

32. Eugene D. Genovese, *Roll, Jordan, Roll: The World The Slaves Made* (New York, 1974), 186–87.

33. Suzanne Keller, *Beyond the Ruling Class: Strategic Elites in Modern Society* (New York, 1964), as interpreted by Donald Mathews, "Religion in the Old South: Speculation on Methodology," *South Atlantic Quarterly* (Winter 1974), 49–50.

34. John G. Jones, *Methodism in Mississippi,* II, 488–89.

35. James O. Andrew, "The Southern Slave Population," *Methodist Magazine and Quarterly Review,* 13 (1831), 315.

36. Harry V. Richardson, *Dark Salvation: The Story of Methodism as it Developed Among Blacks in America* (New York, 1976), 116; Payne, *Recollections,* 10–25.

37. Payne, *Recollections,* 30.

38. *Dictionary of American Biography,* I, 466–67; *Evangelical Review,* 1 (Apr. 1850), 605–6; 7 (Jan. 1856), 400–412; H. Shelton Smith, *In his Image, But . . . Racism in Southern Religion, 1780–1910* (Durham, N.C., 1972), 155–64; Andrew, "Southern Slave Population," 317; J. H. Thornwell, *A Sermon Preached . . .* (Charleston, 1850), 11; Adger, 162.

39. Payne, *Recollections,* 44.

40. Payne, "Bishop Daniel Alexander Payne's Protestation," 61.

41. *Ibid.* plus Payne, *Recollections,* 25, 44.

42. "Autobiography of Francis Asbury Mood," Francis Asbury Mood Papers, South Caroliniana Library, University of South Carolina.

43. Payne, *Recollections,* 34–35.

44. *Ibid.,* 36–38.

45. *Ibid.,* 39.

46. Clifford Geertz, *The Interpretation of Cultures: Selected Essays* (New York, 1973), 103, 131.

47. George Freeman, *Rights and Duties of Slaveholders* (Charleston, 1837), 22.

48. Bowen, 6, 23.

49. Geertz, 124.

50. Payne, *Recollections,* 38.

51. *Southern Presbyterian Review,* 2 (Mar. 1849), 582–83.

52. John Belton O'Neall, "Slave Laws of the South," *The Industrial Resources, etc. of the Southern and Western States,* ed. J. D. B. DeBow, II (New Orleans, 1853), 278–79.

53. Petitions by sixty-two Abbeville residents; thirty-six citizens of Chester, November, 1838; forty-one "sundry citizens of Sumter", Nov. 20, 1838. Petitions on Slavery, South Carolina State Archives, Columbia, S.C.

54. George Howe, *History of the Presbyterian Church in South Carolina,* I (Columbia, 1870), 241; Douglas Sumner Brown, *A City Without Cobwebs: A History of Rock Hill, South Carolina* (Columbia, 1953), 4–5, 37–39; Edwin Gaustad, *Religion in the South,* 169.

55. U.S. Census Office, *7th Census, 1850* (Washington, D.C., 1853), 128–31, 237, 350, 452, 552–57.

56. Freehling, 213, 237; Rosannah P. Rogers to David L. Rogers, Oct. 29, 1831, William W. Renwick Papers, Duke University.

57. Freehling, 335; *Acts of the General Assembly of South Carolina, 1830–39.*

58. Petitions on Slavery, South Carolina State Archives, Columbia, S.C.

59. *Ibid.*

60. *Ibid.*

61. *Ibid.*

62. *Ibid.*

63. *Ibid.*

64. *Ibid.*

65. *Proceedings of the Meeting in Charleston, S.C., May 13–15, 1845, on the Religious Instruction of the Negroes* (Charleston, 1845), 5; Rawick, ed., South Carolina, III (3), 53, 119, 167–69; South Carolina, III (4), 52, 154; Herbert Gutman, "Observations on Selected Trends in Working-Class Historiography," quoted in James D. Anderson, *The Education of Blacks in the South, 1860–1935,* (Chapel Hill, 1988), 8.

Chapter Three

1. Thomas Johnson, *Twenty-Eight Years a Slave* (Bournemouth, England, 1909), 14, 17.

2. *Ibid.,* 3, 5, 6, 18.

3. *Ibid.,* 18.

4. *Ibid.,* 3, 13, 11–12.

5. *Ibid.,* 29–30.

6. Paul D. Escott, *Slavery Remembered: A Record of Twentieth Century Slave Narratives* (Chapel Hill, 1979), 2–3; Vincent P. Franklin, *Black Self-Determination, 161.*

7. The most numerous accounts of slaves who learned to read or read and write are found in the Federal Writers Project (FWP) interviews as collected and published in the following: Perdue, Barden, and Phillips, eds., *Weevils in the Wheat;* George L. Rawick, ed., *The American Slave: A Composite Autobiography,* 19 vols. (Westport, Conn., 1972); Supplement, Series 1, 12 vols. (Westport, Conn., 1977); Supplement, Series 2, 10 vols. (Westport, Conn., 1980). For evaluations of the merits and problems in the FWP interviews, see William L. Van Deburg, *The Slave Drivers: Black Agricultural Labor Supervisors in the Antebellum South* (Westport, Conn., 1979), 77–94; David Thomas Bailey, "A Divided Prism: Two Sources of Black Testimony on Slavery," *Journal of Southern History,* XLVI: 3 (Aug. 1980), 381–404; Paul D. Escott, *Slavery Remembered: A Record of Twentieth-Century Slave Narratives* (Chapel Hill, 1979); Thomas L. Webber, *Deep Like the Rivers: Education in the Slave Quarter Community, 1831–1865* (New York, 1978), 131–38. Autobiographies and narratives by former slaves who learned to read or to read and write during slavery include the following: Octavia V. Rogers Albert, *The House of Bondage or, Charlotte Brooks and Other Slaves* (New York, 1890; reprint 1972); Sam Aleckson, *Before the War, and After the Union: An Autobiography* (Boston, 1929); Henry Bibb, *Narrative of the Life and Adventures of Henry Bibb* (New York, 1850; reprint 1969); Leonard Black, *Life and Sufferings of Leonard Black* (New York, 1947); John W. Blassingame, *Slave Testimony: Two Centuries of Letters, Speeches, Interviews, and Autobiographies* (Baton Rouge, 1977); Charles Octavius Boothe, *The Cyclopedia of the Colored Baptists of Alabama: Their Leaders and Their Work* (Birmingham, Ala., 1895); Levi Branham, *My Life and Travels* (Dalton, Georgia, 1929); Hallie Q. Brown, *Homespun Heroines and Other Women of Distinction* (Xenia, Ohio, 1926); Henry Clay Bruce, *The New Man. Twenty-Nine Years a Slave. Twenty-Nine Years a Free Man* (York, Pa., 1895; reprint 1969); Edward R. Carter, *Biographical Sketches of our Pulpit* (Atlanta, 1888; reprint, 1968); Daniel W. Culp, ed., *Twentieth Century Negro Literature* (Naperville, Ill, 1902; reprint, 1969); Noah Davis, *A Narrative of the Life of Rev. Noah Davis, A Colored Man, Written by Himself, at the Age of 54* (Baltimore, 1859); Frederick Douglass, *Narrative of the Life of Frederick Douglass* (Boston, 1845); Benjamin Drew, *The Refugee: or the Narratives of Fugitive Slaves in Canada Related by Themselves* (Boston, 1856); Orville Elder and Samuel Hall, *The Life of Samuel Hall, Washington, Iowa: A Slave for Forty-Seven Years* (Washington, Ia., 1912); Elisha Green, *Life of the Rev. Elisha W. Green* (Maysville, Ky., 1888); Laura Haviland, *A Woman's Life-Work* (Chicago, 1887); Lucius Holsey, *Autobiography, Sermons, Addresses, and Essays* (Atlanta, Ga., 1898); Louis Hughes, *Thirty Years a Slave* (Milwaukee, 1897); Thomas L. Johnson, *Twenty-Eight Years a Slave* (Bournemouth, England, 7th ed., 1909); Thomas Jones, *The Experience of Thomas Jones, Who Was a Slave for Forty-Three Years* (Boston, 1862); Isaac Lane, *The Autobiography of Bishop Isaac Lane* (Nashville, 1916); Monroe A. Majors, *Noted Negro Women: Their Triumphs and Activities* (1893; reprint Freeport, N.Y., 1971); Elijah P. Marrs, *Life and History of the Rev. Elijah P. Marrs* (Louisville, Ky., 1885; reprint 1969); A. W. Pegues, *Our Baptist Ministers and Schools* (Springfield, Mass., 1892); Gustavus D. Pike, *The Jubilee Singers and their Campaign for Twenty Thousand Dollars* (Boston, 1873); Peter Randolph, *Sketches of Slave Life* (Boston, 1855); William J. Simmons, *Men of Mark: Eminent, Progressive, and Rising* (Cleveland, Ohio., 1887; reprint 1968); William Still, *The Underground Rail Road*

(Phila., 1872); Susie King Taylor, *Reminiscences of My Life in Camp* (Boston, 1902; reprint 1968); Alexander Wayman, *Cyclopedia of African Methodism* (Baltimore, 1882).

8. For my analysis of 272 accounts by former slaves of the ways they learned to read see Janet Cornelius, "We Slipped and Learned to Read: Slave Accounts of the Literacy Process, 1830–1865," *Phylon*, XLIV:3 (Sept. 1983), 186.

9. William H. Heard, *From Slavery to the Bishopric in the A.M.E. Church* (1924; reprint, New York, 1969), 31.

10. John McKivigan, "The Gospel Will Burst the Bonds of the Slave: The Abolitionists' Bibles for Slaves Campaign," *Negro History Bulletin*, 45:3 (1982), 63.

11. Carter Woodson, *Education of the Negro Prior to 1861* (Washington, D.C., 1919; reprint 1968), 85, 228.

12. Rawick, ed., Alabama & Indiana, VI, 302.

13. Pegues, 371–74; Cornelius, 185.

14. Rawick, ed., Alabama and Indiana, VI, 410.

15. Blassingame, *Slave Testimony,* 347–54; Marrs, 14; Rawick, ed., South Carolina, III (4), 52.

16. Conway, *Autobiography,* I, 21; Rawick, ed., Georgia XII (2), 226.

17. Green, 15; Bibb, 21; Rawick, ed., Oklahoma and Mississippi, VII, 78–79.

18. Rawick, ed., Arkansas, I (3), 311; Rawick, ed., Georgia, XIII (4), 201.

19. Pegues, 62–63; Rawick, ed., Mississippi, Suppl. 1, VIII (3), 1329; Black, 18–19.

20. Rawick, ed., Oklahoma and Mississippi, VII, 78–79. Rawick, ed., Mississippi, Suppl. 1, VI (1), 10; Elder and Hall, *Life of Samuel Hall;* Rawick, ed., Georgia, XIII (4), 305.

21. Blassingame, *Slave Testimony,* 643.

22. Margaret Spufford, "First steps in literacy: the reading and writing experiences of the humblest seventeenth-century spiritual autobiographers," Graff, ed., *Literacy and Social Development,* 125–50; David Cressy, *Literacy and the Social Order: Reading and Writing in Tudor and Stuart England* (Cambridge, 1980), 41.

23. Cornelius, "We Slipped . . . ," 186.

24. Spufford, 127; Holsey, 15–18; Thomas Johnson, 3; Carter, 23; Marrs, 12.

25. S. Jay Samuels and Michael L. Kamil, "Models of the Reading Process," in P. David Pearson, ed., *Handbook of Reading Research,* (New York and London: Longman, 1984), 197.

26. Holsey, 18; John Brother Cade, *Holsey—The Incomparable* (New York, 1974), 5–6.

27. Thomas G. Sticht and James H. James, "Listening and Reading" in Pearson, *op. cit.,* 294.

28. Blassingame, *Slave Testimony,* 709; Pike, 57–58.

29. Noah Webster, *The Elementary Spelling Book* (Cincinnati, 1848); Hugh Banton Smith, *American Reading Instruction* (Neward, 1965), 44–50; Jennifer E. Monaghan, *A Common Heritage* (Hamden, Conn., 1983).

30. Rawick, ed., Arkansas, X (5), 319; Mississippi, Suppl. 1, IX (4), 1620–1621; Holsey, 18; Thomas Johnson, 3.

31. Webster, 25.

32. Thomas Jones, 76–79;

33. Webster, 91–92; Edward Fry, "A readability formula that saves time," *Journal of Reading,* II (1968), 513–16, 575–77.

34. Samuels & Kamil, 206; Ernest R. Hilgard, "The place of Gestalt psychology and field theories in contemporary learning theory," *Theories of Learning and Instruction* (Chicago, 1964), 70–76.

35. Rawick, ed., Mississippi, Suppl. 1, 7 (2), 365.

36. Blassingame, 710–11; Samuels and Kamil, 206.

37. Cressy, 23–25. More slaves in the FWP interviews reported that they learned to read than to write.

38. Rawick, ed., Mississippi, Suppl. 1, IX (4), 1664–65; Randolph, 11; F. Douglass, *Narrative of the Life,* 65; Hughes, 54.

39. H. Alan Robinson, *Reading and Writing Instruction in the United States: Historical Trends* (Urbana, Ill., 1977); Cressy, 22; Spufford, 129–31.

40. Rose-Marie Webber, "Reading," Ronald Wardhaugh and H. Douglas Brown, eds., *A Survey of Applied Linguistics* (Ann Arbor, 1976), 96; Parveen Adams, ed., *Language in Thinking* (Harmondsworth, Middlesex, England, 1972), 217–35. For a recent examination of word separation by beginning writers in societies based primarily on oral communication, Paul Saenger, "Physiologie de la lecture et separation des mots," *Annales,* 44:4 (July–Aug. 1989), 939–52.

41. Thomas Johnson, 12–13; Douglass, *Narrative,* 43; Noah Davis, *Narrative,* 17; Drew, 185–86.

42. Drew, 185–86; Albert, 111–113, Blassingame, *Slave Testimony,* 643.

43. Holsey, 16, Thomas Jones, 75.

44. Holsey, 17.

45. Rawick, Texas, V, 213.

46. Holsey, 16–18; Blassingame, *Slave Testimony,* 131.

47. Rawick, ed., S. Car. II (2), 50; Drew, 45; Simmons, 291–92.

48. Rawick, ed., Fisk University, *Unwritten History of Slavery,* XVIII, 57; Rawick, ed., Alabama, VI, 30–302.

49. J. William Harris, "A Slaveholding Republic: Augusta's Hinterlands Before the Civil War" (Unpubl. Ph.D. Dissertation, Johns Hopkins University, 1981), 268; Rawick, ed., North Carolina & South Carolina, Suppl. 1, II, 264–265; Rawick, ed., South Carolina, II (2), 32, Blassingame, *Slave Testimony,* 45; F. Douglass, *Narrative of the Life,* 52.

50. Gerda Lerner, *The Grimke Sisters from South Carolina* (New York: Shocken Books, 1967), 23.

51. Rawick, ed., Oklahoma, Suppl. 1, XII, 297–299.

52. Rawick, ed., North Carolina, XIV (1), 268.

53. Rawick, ed., Georgia, XII (2) 34; Pegues, 195.

54. Rawick, ed., Indiana and Ohio, V (suppl. series 1), 197.

55. Albert, 102; *JNH,* VIII:3 (Jul. 1923), 335–37; Payne, *History,* 428; Holsey, 11–13.

56. Rawick, ed., Mississippi, XIII (Suppl. Series 1), 1210; Oklahoma, XII (Suppl. Series 1), 371.

57. Rawick, ed., Indiana, VI, 211; Bruce, 29–30; Branham, 10; Rawick, Georgia, XIII, 212.

58. Jack Goody, "Restricted Literacy in Northern Ghana," Goody, ed., *Literacy in Traditional Societies*, 215.

59. John Hope Franklin, *The Free Negro in North Carolina* (1943; reprint 1969), 129–30; John Henderson Russell, *The Free Negro in Virginia, 1619–1865* (Baltimore, 1913), 139–40; Henry E. Sterkx, *The Free Negro in Ante-Bellum Louisiana* (Cranbury, N.J., 1972), 268; Berlin, *Slaves Without Masters*, 282–83.

60. Rawick, ed., Alabama & Indiana, VI, 319; Boothe, 22; Simmons, 460–474.

61. Simmons, 908–9; Monroe A. Majors, *Noted Negro Women: Their Triumphs and Activities* (Freeport, N.Y., 1893; reprint 1971), 112–13; Anjanette Sophie McFarlin, *Black Congressional Reconstruction Orators and their Orations* (Metuchen, N.J., 1976), 54, 87.

62. Leonard P. Curry, *The Free Black in Urban America 1800–1850: The Shadow of the Dream* (Chicago: U. of Chicago Press, 1981), 148–49; Morgan Goodwin, "Schools and Education of the Colored Population," *Special Report of the Commissioner of Education on the Improvement of Public Schools in the District of Columbia* (Washington, D.C., 1871; reprint 1969), 211–99; Birnie, *JNH*, XII:1 (Jan. 1927), 18–20; Henry L. Swint, ed., *Dear Ones at Home* (Nashville, 1966), 155; J. C. Napier to Monroe N. Work, *JNH*, V: 1 (Jan. 1920), 116–17.

63. "Autobiography of Francis Asbury Mood," Francis Asbury Mood Papers, Columbia, S.C.; Horace Mann Bond, *Negro Education in Alabama: A Study in Cotton and Steel* (1939; reprint 1969), 9–10, 15; Berlin, *Slaves Without Masters*, 304.

64. Simmons, 545–46; Susie King Taylor, 5–7; Joe M. Richardson, *Christian Reconstruction: The American Missionary Association and Southern Blacks, 1861–1890* (Athens: U. of Ga. Press, 1986), 194.

65. Color segregation had been encouraged in the French West Indies by the Code Noir, which forbade the education of slave children but allowed schools for mulattos. Shelby T. McCloy, *The Negro in the French West Indies* (Lexington, Ky., 1966), 182–90; Payne, *Recollections*, 13–16; Wikmaranayake, 85.

66. Herbert S. Klein, *Slavery in the Americas* (Chicago, 1967), 101; John T. Gillard, *The Catholic Church and the Negro* (Baltimore, 1929), 18–19; Berlin, *Slaves Without Masters*, 278, 282; John T. Gillard, *Colored Catholics in the U.S.* (Baltimore, 1941), 197–99; Miriam T. Murphy, "Catholic Missionary Work among the Colored People of the U.S., 1766–1866," *Records of the American Catholic Historical Society*, 35 (June 1941), 114–25.

67. Southern Baptist Convention, Minutes, 1853, 17; Walter B. Posey, *Frontier Mission: A History of Religion West of the Southern Appalachians to 1861* (Lexington, Ky., 1966), 194–95.

68. U.S. Census Office. *9th Census, 1870* (Washington, D.C., 1870), 394–97.

69. Jane H. Pease and William H. Pease, *They Who Would be Free: Blacks' Search for Freedom, 1830–1861* (New York, 1974), 144–56; Woodson, *Education of the Negro*, 234–40; William and Jane Pease, "Negro Education in Canada," *JNH*, XLVII:1 (Jan. 1962), 25; *Anglo-African Magazine*, 1 (Jul. 1859), 222–24; Curry, 148; Linda Perkins, "Quaker Beneficence and Black Control: The Institute for Colored Youth, 1852–1903," in Vincent P. Franklin and James D. Anderson, eds., *New Perspectives on Black Educational History* (Boston: G. K. Hall, 1978), 21.

70. Creel, 267.

71. *Anglo-African Magazine,* 1 (Jul. 1859), 339; David E. Swift, "Black Presbyterian Attacks on Racism: Samuel Cornish, Theodore Wright, and their Contemporaries," David W. Wills and Richard Newman, eds., *Black Apostles at Home and Abroad: Afro-Americans and the Christian Mission from the Revolution to Reconstruction* (Boston, 1982), 56; Pease & Pease, *They Who Would be Free,* 134–37.

72. Payne, *Recollections,* 75–79, 122–30; Payne, *History of the A.M.E. Church,* I, 335, 397, 399–400; Clarence E. Walker, *A Rock in a Weary Land: The African Methodist Episcopal Church During the Civil War and Reconstruction* (Baton Rouge: LSU University Press, 1982), 77, 90.

73. Aptheker, *Documentary History,* I, 228.

74. Joel Schor, *Henry Highland Garnet* (Westport, Conn., 1977), 56.

75. Rawick, ed., Georgia, XII (1), 257; Arkansas, IX (3), 28–29; Vincent Harding, *There is a River: The Black Struggle for Freedom in America* (New York: Harcourt Brace, 1981), 74.

76. James McKaye, *Mastership and its Fruits: The Emancipated Slave Face to Face with His Old Master* (New York, 1864), 7.

Chapter Four

1. John B. Cade, "Out of the Mouths of Ex-Slaves," *JNH,* XX:3 (Sept. 1935), 330; Creel, 4.

2. Drew, 333–34; Rawick, ed., Oklahoma, VII, 69.

3. Creel, 206–7; Vincent P. Franklin, *Black Self-Determination,* 67; Orville Vernon Burton, *In My Father's House Are Many Mansions: Family and Community in Edgefield, South Carolina* (Chapel Hill, 1985), 154, 249; Escott, 76; James Cone, *A Black Theology of Liberation* (Philadelphia, 1970), 69, 75–76; Gayraud Wilmore, *Black Religion and Black Radicalism: An Interpretation of the Religious History of Afro-American People* (Maryknoll, N.Y.: 2nd ed., 1983), xii, 36.

4. Creel, 57–58, 284.

5. Rawick, ed., Mississippi, Suppl. 1, VIII (3), 914; Randolph, 10–11; Rawick, ed., Georgia, XII (2), 5; Georgia, XIII, 291.

6. Boothe, 69–70; Katharine L. Dvorak, "After Apocalypse, Moses", in John B. Boles, ed., *Masters & Slaves in the House of the Lord: Race and Religion in the American South, 1740–1870* (Lexington, 1988), 175.

7. Costanzo, 9. For cited autobiographies see Chapter 3, endnote 7.

8. Randolph, 10–11; Rawick, ed., Georgia, XII (1), 180; Elizabeth Schultz, "'To Be Black and Blue: The Blues Genre in Black American Autobiography," *Kansas Quarterly* 7:3 (Summer 1975), 84; Rawick, Alabama & Indiana, VI, 302.

9. Randolph, 25; Rawick, Alabama & Indiana, VI, 299.

10. Carter, 53–54; Noah Davis, *A Narrative,* 21.

11. Rawick, ed., Georgia, XII (1), 180; Mississippi, Suppl. Series 1, IX (4), 1674.

12. Albert, 10–11.

13. Blassingame, *Slave Testimony,* 591–92.

14. Albert J. Raboteau, *Slave Religion: The "Invisible Institution" in the Antebellum South* (Oxford, 1978), 44–92; Basil Davidson, *The African Genius* (Boston, 1969), 30–31, 146; Melville Herskovitz, *The Myth of the Negro Past* (New York, 1941), 140–42; Robin Horton, "African Traditional Thought and Western Science," *Africa,* 37:1 (Jan. 1967), 58–65; Thomas L. Webber, 63–70.

15. Isaac, 232; Long, 59, 64; Goody, 202, 205; Chartier, Vol. III, 126–27.

16. Rawick, ed., Arkansas, X (6), 83; Mississippi, Suppl. 1, VIII (3), 978; Mississippi, Suppl. 1, IX (4), 1670; Georgia, XIII (3), 134; Mississippi, Suppl. 1, VIII (3), 914; Lawrence W. Levine, *Black Culture and Black Consciousness: Afro-American Folk Thought from Slavery to Freedom* (Oxford, 1977), 156; Rawick, ed., Mississippi, Suppl. 1, VI (1), 307; *The American Missionary (Magazine),* V:11, 257.

17. Carter, 113; Rawick, ed., Alabama, VI, 300; Goody, 201.

18. Pegues, 177–78; S. Jay Samuels and Michael L. Kamil, "Models of the Reading Process," *Handbook of Reading Research,* ed. P. David Pearson (New York and London: Longman, 1984), 206. For an account of acquisition of reading skills through miraculous intervention by an antebellum free black female religious leader, see Jean M. Humez, "Visionary Experience and Power: The Career of Rebecca Cox Jackson," Wills and Newman, eds., 113.

19. Andrew Murray, 62; J. H. Thornwell, *Collected Writings,* IV, 396, in Murray, *Ibid;* Robert A. Bennett, "Black Episcopalians," *Historical Magazine of the Protestant Episcopal Church,* 43 (Sept. 1974), 236–38; William Manross, *The Episcopal Church in the U.S., 1800–1840: A Study in Church Life* (New York, 1938), 70, 130.

20. Charles Colcock Jones, *Third Annual Report of the Association for the Religious Instruction of the Negroes* (Savannah, 1835), 13.

21. William L. Plumer, ed., *Thoughts on the Religious Instruction of the Negroes* (Princeton, 1858), 18.

22. *DeBow's Review,* 30 (Sept. 1860), 365.

23. *Proceedings of the Meeting in Charleston . . . on the Religious Instruction of the Negroes* (Charleston, 1845), 58.

24. Clarence L. Mohr, "Slaves and White Churches in Georgia," in Boles, *op. cit.,* 157.

25. *Proceedings, Charleston, 1845,* 23–43; Lane, 15; M. M. Ponton, *Life and Times of Henry M. Turner* (Atlanta, 1917; reprint 1970), 34–40.

26. *Public Proceedings Relating to Calvary Church and the Religious Instruction of Slaves* (Charleston, 1850), 42, 46, 47; *Minutes of the Annual Conferences of the Methodist Episcopal Church, South, 1858* (Nashville, 1859), 92.

27. Richard C. Wade, *Slavery in the Cities: The South, 1820–1860* (N.Y., 1964), 83.

28. Harrison, 290, 342, 280; Robert C. Reinders, "The Churches and the Negro in New Orleans, 1850–1860," *Phylon,* XXII:3 (Fall 1961), 244.

29. William Hicks, *History of Louisiana Negro Baptists from 1804 to 1914* (Nashville, 1918), 31; James M. Simms, *The First Colored Baptist Church in North America* (Philadelphia, 1888; reprint 1969), 14–30; *Baptist Home Missions in North America: Jubilee Meeting, 1832–1882* (New York, 1883), 389.

30. Sobel, 286–356; J. H. Cuthbert, *Life of Richard Fuller, DD* (New York, 1878), 105; Charleston Baptist Association, Minutes, 1835; David M. Tucker, *Black Pastors and Leaders: Memphis, 1819–1972* (Memphis, 1975), 5.

31. Sunbury Baptist Association, Minutes, 1841–1858; Simms, 97; Josiah Law, *Sixth Annual Report of the Association for the Religious Instruction of the Negroes*, 2–8; Minutes of the First Baptist Church, Savannah, Georgia (typed copy, Georgia Historical Society), 628, 873; *Proceedings, Charleston, 1845*, 27 ff; *Public Proceedings Relating to Calvary Church*, 63; Robert L. Hall, "Black and White Christians in Florida" in Boles, ed., 85, 87.

32. *Public Proceedings Relating to Calvary Church*, 48–49; First Baptist Church of Richmond, Minutes, 1830, 57.

33. Sobel, 235; Owen D. Pelt and Ralph Lee Smith, *The Story of the National Baptists* (N.Y., 1960), 35; Simms, 14–30; Walter H. Brooks, "The Priority of the Silver Bluff Church and its Promoters," *JNH*, 7:2 (Apr. 1922), 172–75; Barrett, 112–13; "Early Negro Churches in Kingston, Jamaica, and Savannah, Georgia," *JNH*, 1: 1 (Jan. 1916), 69–75, 87; John W. Davis, "George Liele and Andrew Bryan, Pioneer Baptist Preachers," *JNH*, III:2 (Apr. 1918), 119–27; Sobel, 235, 306–7; C. C. Adams and Marshal A. Talley, *Negro Baptist and Foreign Missions* (Phila. 1944), 13–17; Boothe, *The Cyclopedia of the Colored Baptists*; Carter, *Biographical Sketches;* Pegues, *Our Baptist Ministers and Schools.*

34. B. W. McDonnold, *History of the Cumberland Presbyterian Church* (Nashville, 1893), 434; R. Douglas Brackenridge, *Voice in the Wilderness: A History of the Cumberland Presbyterian Church in Texas* (San Antonio, 1969), 77–78; J. C. Napier to Monroe N. Work, *JNH*, V:1 (Jan. 1920), 116–17; *Proceedings, Charleston, 1845*, 36–37; South Carolina Diocese of the Protestant Episcopal Church, *Journal*, 1851, 44; Randall M. Miller, "Slaves and Southern Catholicism," in Boles, ed., 135.

35. Rawick, ed., Florida, XVII, 245; Oklahoma & Mississippi, VII, 308.

36. Rawick, ed., Alabama, Suppl. 1, I, 65; Perdue, et. al., 58.

37. Hallie Q. Brown, *Homespun Heroines and other Women of Distinction* (Xenia, O., 1926), 35.

38. Wade, 160–61, 256; Robert F. Durden, "The Establishment of Calvary Protestant Church for Negroes in Charleston," *South Carolina Historical Magazine*, 65 (Apr. 1964), 63–84.

39. New Orleans *Daily Crescent*, June 28, 1858, quoted by Robert C. Reinders, 246.

40. Durden, 72; Adger, 174.

41. Elisha W. Green, 15.

42. *Ibid.*, 21.

43. Luther P. Jackson, "Religious Development of the Negro in Virginia from 1760 to 1860," JNH, XVI:2 (Apr. 1931), 185–86.

44. *DeBow's Review*, 30 (1860), 352.

45. John B. McFerrin, *History of Methodism in Tennessee*, II (Nashville, 1873), 388.

46. *Ibid.*, 391.

47. Thomas Johnson, 12–13.

48. Gerald Mullin, *Flight and Rebellion: Slave Resistance in Eighteenth Century Virginia* (New York, 1972), 37; Malcolm McGee, *American Anthropologist,* 70 (1968), 1096–1103; Escott, 116; Charles Joyner, "Slave Language and Slave Thought in Antebellum Charleston," *Intellectual Life in Antebellum Charleston,* eds. Michael O'Brien and David Moltke-Hansen (Knoxville, 1986), 277; Creel, 195, 284.

Chapter Five

1. According to accounts by 272 former slaves who learned to read and write during slavery, over half of their beginning efforts to learn to read and write were initiated by whites. Cornelius, "We Slipped and Learned to Read," 186.

2. Elder and Hall, n.p.; Rawick, ed., Mississippi, Suppl. 1, VIII (3), 1292.

3. Rawick, ed., Texas, Suppl. 2, II (2), 224; Texas, IV (1), 55, 192; Georgia, XIII (3), 163; Arkansas, VIII (2), 84; Georgia, XIII (3), 163; Texas, IV (2), 112.

4. Mamie Garvin Fields, *Lemon Swamp and Other Places: A Carolina Memoir* (New York: Free Press, 1983), 2–3; Pauli Murray, *Proud Shoes: The Story of an American Family* (1956; reprint New York, 1978), 60–61; Rawick, ed., Mississippi, Suppl. Series 1, IX, 1792; Arkansas, VIII (1), 198; Texas, IV (2), 103–4; South Carolina, III (3), 53.

5. Escott, 2–3; Harrison, 364; Susan Dabney Smedes, *Memorials of a Southern Planter* (Baltimore, 3rd ed.: 1888), 65; Creel, 301–2.

6. Moncure D. Conway, *Autobiography: Memories and Experiences of M. D. Conway,* I (1904; reprint 1969); Mary Chesnut, *A Diary from Dixie,* ed. Ben Ames Williams (Boston, 1949), 292; Harrison, 304; *Proceedings of the National Convention of the Protestant Episcopal Church,* 1856, 242–47; Frank E. Vandiver, *Mighty Stonewall* (New York, 1957), 110; Frederika Bremer, *Homes of the New World,* II (New York, 1853), 434–37.

7. Rawick, ed., Texas, IV (2), 76; Mississippi, Suppl., Series 1, VIII (3), 978.

8. Catherine Clinton, "Caught in the Web of the Big House," *The Web of Southern Social Relations: Women, Family, & Education* eds. Walter J. Fraser, Jr., R. Frank Saunders., Jr., Jon L. Wakelyn (Athens: U. of Georgia Press, 1985), 30; Rawick, ed., Alabama, Suppl., Series 1, I, 222; Blassingame, *Slave Testimony,* 416–18.

9. Rawick, ed., Georgia, XII (2), 42; Georgia, XIII (3), 134; Texas, IV (2), 22.

10. Pauli Murray, 52–53; Perdue, et. al., 187.

11. Bruce, 25. English reformers who advocated literacy for the working class often limited this advocacy to reading and did not recommend the teaching of writing. McLeish, 95; William Bean Kennedy, *The Shaping of Protestant Education . . . 1789–1860* (New York, 1966), 58; McCann, "Popular Education, Socialization, and Social Control: Spitalfields, 1812–1824," 11–12 and Frith, 81–82 in McCann, ed., *Popular Education and Socialization in the Nineteenth Century* (London, 1977); Harvey Graff, "Literacy Past and Present: Critical Approaches in the Literacy-Society Relationship," *Interchange* 9 (1978), 11.

12. Anne C. Loveland, *Southern Evangelicals and the Social Order, 1800–1860* (Baton Rouge, 1980), 111; Clifford S. Griffin, "Religious Benevolence as Social Control, 1815–1860," *Mississippi Valley Historical Review,* 44 (Dec. 1957), 423–44; Gilbert Barnes, *The Anti-Slavery Impulse, 1830–1844* (New York, 1933;

2nd ed. 1964), 17–18; Timothy L. Smith, *Revivalism and Social Reform* (New York, 1957), 150–51.

13. Kuykendall, 22–26, 104–5; Richard Fuller, *Speech of Dr. Fuller at the Anniversary of the American Tract Society* (New York, 1860); J. H. Cuthbert, *Life of Richard Fuller* (New York, 1878), 201; Tract Society, 1826–1860; ABS, 1826–37, 1839–42, 1846–55.

14. George Howe, *History of the Presbyterian Church in South Carolina*, II (Columbia, S.C., 1870), 228–29.

15. Tract Society and ABS, *op. cit.; Encyclopedia of Southern Baptists*, 817–19; Joe M. King, *A History of South Carolina Baptists* (Columbia, S.C.), 182–96, 242–50.

16. ABS, 1834, 37.

17. Robert W. Lynn and Elliott Wright, *The Big Little School: Sunday Child of American Protestantism* (New York, 1971), 14; ASSU, 1854, 14, 62; William J. Peterson, *A Brief History of the American Sunday School Union* (Philadelphia, 1969), n.p.

18. Anne M. Boylan, *Sunday School: The Formation of an American Institution, 1790–1880* (New Haven: Yale U. Press, 1988), 23; ASSU, 1826, 62; Lynn & Wright, 15.

19. Marion Wilson Starkey, *The Slave Narrative: Its Place in American History* (Boston, 1981), 84–86.

20. Tract Society, 1840, 48–49.

21. ABS, 1828, 74; Tract Society, 1845, 84.

22. Adger, 166–67.

23. H. Sheldon Smith, 155–61; Thornwell, *Sermon Preached*, 11; McTyeire, *et. al.*, 105, 123–24; Freeman, 28.

24. Thomas Laqueur, *Religion and Respectability: Sunday Schools and Working Class Culture, 1780–1850* (New Haven, 1976), 10–11.

25. Richard Fuller and Francis Wayland, *Domestic Slavery Considered as a Scriptural Institution* (New York, 1845), 128, 131–32; Thornwell, *Sermon*, 33.

26. Fuller and Wayland, 222; Cuthbert, 18–22, 37, 76; Creel, 251.

27. Fuller and Wayland, 128, 131–32; Cuthbert, 106.

28. Miles Mark Fisher, *Negro Slave Songs in the United States* (Ithaca, N.Y., 1953; reprint, 1978), 180; Fuller to Samuel Chase, Jan. 9, 1862, Jan. 14, 1862, in David Rankin Barbee, "Lincoln, Chase, and the Rev. Dr. Richard Fuller," *Maryland Historical Magazine*, 46:2 (June 1951), 117; Cuthbert, 104–5; Harrison, 15.

29. Fuller, *Our Duty to the African Race: An Address Delivered at Washington, D.C., January 21, 1851* (Baltimore, 1851) [an address to the American Colonization Society], p. 5; Fuller and Wayland, 207, 128.

30. Joseph C. Stiles, *Speech on the Slavery Resolutions* (N.Y., 1850), 14; Freeman, 36; Adger, 162; Willie Lee Rose, *Rehearsal for Reconstruction: The Port Royal Experiment* (Indianapolis, 1964), 231.

31. ABS, 1847, 58–59; 1852, 78; Tract Society, 1840, 49; *Minutes of the Annual Conferences of the Methodist Episcopal Church, South* (New York, 1858), 10, 16; Episcopal Diocese of Kentucky Annual Report, 1845, 27; Episcopal Diocese of Tennessee, Annual Report, 1846, 25; *Proceedings of the National Conven-*

tion of the Protestant Episcopal Church, 1856, 242–47; Morgan B. Godwin, *Special Report of the Commissioner of Education on the Improvement of Schools in the District of Columbia, 1871* (Washington, D.C., 1871; reprint, 1969), 217–20.

32. George Lewis, *Impressions of America and American Churches* (Edinburgh, 1845), 66; South Carolina Episcopal Diocese, Annual Report, 1855, 46–47, 53, 57, 68–71, 29; Tract Society, 1830, 18; 1845, 84; 1853, 30; ABS, 1847, 58–59; Charles William Dabney, *Universal Education in the South,* Vol. I (Chapel Hill, 1936), 145.

33. Berlin, *Slaves Without Masters,* 396–99; Philip J. Staudenraus, *The African Colonization Movement, 1816–1865* (N.Y., 1961), 1–31; Minutes of the General Assembly of the Presbyterian Church, 1832, 326; *Methodist Magazine* (Jan. 1824), 29–30; Donald Mathews, *Slavery and Methodism,* 90–94.

34. *AR,* vols. 11; 21; 29 (Jul. 1853), 219; Timothy Reilly, "Religious Leaders and Social Criticism in New Orleans, 1800–1861," (Ph.D. Thesis, U. of Missouri, 1972), 75; William M. Polk, *Leonidas Polk: Bishop and General,* I (N.Y., 1915), 194–199, 226–227; Andrew Murray, 77; John Johns, *A Memoir of the Right Reverend William Meade* (Baltimore, 1869), 77; Staudenraus, 27–28, 70–72; Blake Touchstone, "Planters and Slave Religion," in Boles, ed., 111.

35. Bell I. Wiley, ed., *Slaves No More* (Lexington, Ky., 1979), 100–101, 188, 176.; L. Minor Blackford, *Mine Eyes Have Seen the Glory: The Story of a Virginia Lady* (Cambridge, Mass., 1954), 23, 60–61; Blassingame, *Slave Testimony,* 65–82; Clement Eaton, *Growth of Southern Civilization, 1790–1860* (New York, 1961), 292; John H. Cocke to Charles Colcock Jones, Jones Papers, Tulane University; John Cocke to Wm. McLain, June 25, 1855, ACS papers; Randall Miller, ed., *Dear Master* (Ithaca, N.Y., 1978), 35–36, 183–90.

36. Philip Slaughter, *The Virginian History of African Colonization* (Richmond, 1858; reprint Freeport, N.Y., 1970), 4–10, 75, 102; Owen D. Pelt and Ralph Lee Smith, *The Story of the National Baptists* (N.Y., 1960), 26. Gayraud S. Wilmore points out that "it was the arrogance of the whites, their miscalculation of the self-esteem of free blacks and their feeling of solidarity with the slaves, rather than the aversion to the idea of emigration that made black leaders repudiate the ACS." Wilmore, 102; Floyd J. Miller, *The Search for a Black Nationality: Black Emigration and Colonization, 1787–1863* (Urbana, 1975), 8–13; Dorothy Sterling, ed., *Speak Out in Thundertones: Letters and Other Writings by Black Northerners, 1787–1865* (Garden City, 1973), 7–12; Vincent P. Franklin, *Black Self-Determination,* 85–86; Pease and Pease, *They Who Would be Free,* 22; David Christy to Wm. McLain, Dept. 4, 1849, ACS papers.

37. Carter G. Woodson., ed., *The Mind of the Negro as Reflected in Letters Written During the Crisis 1800–1860* (Washington, D.C., 1926), 93.

38. B. W. Mann to American Colonization Society, Aug. 3, 1849, ACS papers; Woodson, *Mind of the Negro,* 15–47, 76–81.

39. *AR,* 26 (Sept. 1850), 259–60.

40. Henry B. Stewart to Charles Colcock Jones, Apr. 7, 1851; Peggy Potter to Mrs. Sarrah Andrews, Dec. 29, 1847; Seaborn Evans to Josiah Sibley, Nov. 5, 1856; Harrison W. Ellis to William McLain, Apr. 15, 1850; John M. Page, Jr. to Charles W. Andrews, May 7, 1849; Peyton Skipwith to John H. Cocke, June 25, 1846; James C. Minor to John Minor, Feb. 11, 1833; Henry B. Stewart to Ralph R. Gurley, July 16, 1858. All in Wiley, ed., 3–7, 17, 64, 285, 105, 110, 270, 232–33, 301. See also Julia Smith to John McDonogh, Jul. 1, 1848; Simeon Jackson

to John McDonogh, Jul. 3, 1848, McDonogh papers; Willis Helm, Monrovia, Liberia, to Dangerfield Lewis, Feb. 12, 1846, ACS papers; James N. Riddle to ACS, June 2, 1830; David Floyd to Wm. McLain, Apr. 10, 1859, ACS; Joseph Cortner to Wm. McLain, Feb. 1, 1853, ACS papers.

41. Washington McDonogh to John McDonogh, Feb. 7, 1844, McDonogh papers; Robert Leander Sterdivant to John H. Cocke, June 11, 1846, Wiley, ed., 62–63.

42. Diana Skipwith James to Sally Cocke Brent, March 6, 1843, Wiley, ed., 57; Seaborn Evans to Josiah Sibley, Nov. 5, 1856, Wiley, ed., 270.

43. *AR,* 33 (May 1857), 157; *Report of the Proceedings of the Formation of the African Education Society, Washington, Dec. 28, 1829* (Washington, D.C., 1830).

44. *Ibid.*

45. *Ibid.;* WIlliam Winans to ACS, May 15, 1830, ACS papers.

46. *AR,* 30 (Jul. 1854), 195–96.

47. *AR,* 25 (June 1849), 28; George C. Whatley, "The Alabama Presbyterian and his Slave, 1830–1864," *Alabama Review,* XIII (Jan. 1960), 48.

48. *AR,* 32 (Sept. 1856), 284; 32 (Mar. 1856), 91.

49. Goodwin, 222.

50. William Allan, *Life and Work of John McDonogh and Sketch of the McDonogh School* (Baltimore, 1886), 52–53; James T. Edwards, ed., *Some Interesting Papers of John McDonogh* (McDonogh, Md., 1898), 47–56; Sara Bella McLean to John McDonogh, Jan. 17, 1845, Mar. 12, 1846; McDonogh to Charles Colcock Jones, Jan. 26, Apr. 20, May 11, 1835; Charles Colcock Jones to John McDonogh, Dec. 22, 1843; John McDonogh to John H. Cocke, Mar. 20, 1846; John H. Cocke to John McDonogh, Oct. 19, 1845; McDonogh papers, Tulane; William D. Hoyt, Jr., "John McDonogh and Colonization in Liberia," *JNH,* XXIV: 4 (Oct. 1939), 448; *AR,* 11 (Nov. 1835), 336–37. McDonogh intended the balance of his estate to be used to fund the emigration of the rest of his slaves and to finance the colonization of other slaves through the ACS. Though his will was challenged and only a fraction of the estate went to the ACS, forty-two more of his slaves were manumitted and sent to Liberia in 1859 after his death in accordance with his wishes. Edwards, ed., *Papers of John McDonogh,* 92–95, 78–79; *AR,* 14 (1838), 312; 11 (Nov. 1835), 268; 6 (Feb. 1831), 378; 12 (May 1836), 235; 28 (Sept. 1852), 270–71; 18 (Aug. 1842), 263–64.

51. *AR,* 11 (Nov. 1835), 268; Dwight L. Dumond, ed., *Letters of James Gillespie Birney, 1831–1857,* I (Gloucester, Mass., 1966), 183–84; Staudenraus, 146. R. J. Breckinridge (RJB) to Samuel Steel, Apr. 17, 1849; W. M. O. Smith to RJB, Apr. 7, 1849; W. L. Breckinridge to RJB, Feb. 6 & 14, 1849; John Clarke Bayley to RJB, Jan. 7, 1849, Breckinridge papers.

Chapter Six

1. ABS, 1851, 111–112.

2. Curti, 36; Benjamin Rush, "Plan for the Establishment of Public Schools," in Frederick Rudolph, ed., *Essays on Education in the Early Republic* (Cambridge, Mass., 1965), 5; ASSU, 1825, 12, 86–87; Peterson, *Brief History of the American Sunday School Union,* n.p.; John B. McFerrin, *History of Method-*

ism in Tennessee, II (Nashville, 1873), 156; Michael Patrick Williams, "The Black Evangelical Ministry in the Border States: Profiles of Elders John Berry Meachum and Noah Davis," Wills and Newman, eds., 88–90; Luther P. Jackson, "Religious Development of the Negro in Virginia from 1760 to 1860," *JNH,* XVI: 2 (Apr. 1931), 231; Daniel Payne, *History of the A.M.E. Church,* I, 182–96; Richard Robert Wright, Jr., ed., *Encyclopedia of the African Methodist Episcopal Church* (Phila., 1947), 14; ASSU Ledgers, Presbyterian Historical Society, Philadelphia. In 1844 Philadelphia's black Zoar Sabbath School library included: 14 Bibles, 42 Testaments, 65 library books, 18 hymn books, 74 spelling books, and 75 primers (Records of Zoar Sabbath School, Pennsylvania Historical Society, Philadelphia.)

3. Boylan, 83; ABS, 1847, 58–59; 1828, 74; 1826, 80; 1852, 78.

4. Tract Society, 1847, 64.

5. *The Southern Enterprize* (Philadelphia, 1833), 12–13; Kuykendall, 79, 137–38.

6. Charles I. Foster, "Colonization of Free Negroes in Liberia," JNH, XXXVIII:1 (Jan. 1853), 61; ABS, 1845, 29.

7. Bertram Wyatt-Brown, *Lewis Tappan and the Evangelical War Against Slavery* (Cleveland, 1969), 294; *The American Missionary (Magazine),* III:11 (Nov. 1859), 248; John D. McKivigan, "The Gospel Will Burst the Bonds of the Slave: The Abolitionists Bibles for Slaves Campaign", *Negro History Bulletin* 45: 3 (July–August–September 1982), 62–64; Anne C. Loveland, "Evangelism and Immediate Emancipation in American Anti-Slavery Thought," *Journal of Southern History,* XXXII (May 1966), 180–88.

8. ABS, 1847, 58–59.

9. *Ibid.*

10. ABS, 1851, 111–12.

11. *Ibid.,* 46–52.

12. Howard Jones, *Mutiny on the Amistad: The Saga of a Slave Revolt* (New York: Oxford University Press, 1987), 149.

13. Bibb, 178–87; McKivigan, 64.

14. Philip S. Foner, ed. *The Life and Writings of Frederick Douglass,* I (New York, 1950), 253–55.

15. McKivigan, 63–64.

16. *American Missionary* (Magazine), III (Nov. 1859), 162.

17. *Ibid.*

18. *American Missionary* (paper) VI (Jul. 1852), 68; VIII (Jul. 1854), 79.

19. *American Missionary (Magazine),* III:11 (Nov. 1859), 256–57; Green, "Northern Missionary Activities," 153; *American Missionary* (paper), XI (Jan. 1857), 19; (Aug. 1857), 87; (Nov. 1857), 3. Fee carried out his convictions about racial equality in religion and education by founding nonsegregated congregations and schools "opposed to slavery *and caste,*" first a meeting house where classes were attended by both whites and blacks and then a "Literary Institution" which became Berea College.

20. *American Missionary* (paper), XI (Nov. 1856), 14.

21. McKivigan, 62–64; *American Missionary* (paper), XI (Jan. 1857), 19; Green, "Northern Missionary Activities," 159–61.

22. Curry, 148.

23. Floyd Miller, *The Search for a Black Nationality,* 192.

24. Pease and Pease, *They Who Would be Free,* 255–72; Joseph Tracy (Boston agent for the ACS) to Gurley, April 5, 1859, ACS papers.

25. Woodson, *The Mind of the Negro,* 116; Clarence L. Mohr, *On the Threshold of Freedom: Masters and Slaves in Civil War Georgia* (Athens, Ga., 1986), 14; List of emigrants deporting Savannah on the *Huma,* Miscellaneous Papers pertaining to the American Colonization Society, ACS; *AR,* 25 (Jul. 1849), 218–23; 25 (Oct. 1849), 316; 26 (Apr. 1850), 103–7, 110; 26 (Nov. 1850), 343; 27 (Jan. 1851), 24; 27 (May 1851), 150–56; 27 (Dec. 1851), 376–79; 38 (Apr. 1852), 118–22; 28 (June 1852), 181–84; 29 (Jan. 1853), 23–30; 29 (Mar. 1853), 69–71; 29 (June 1853), 178–81; 29 (Jul. 1853), 220; 29 (Aug. 1853), 252–55. Typical of the Savannah family groups on the *Huma,* illustrating the mix of free and slave African-Americans, are the Roberts family. Isaac Roberts was a slave, bought and manumitted for emigration by his mother. Roberts, his free wife, and their nine children emigrated. He, his wife, and the oldest children could all read and write. Henry Roxborough, a slave married to a free woman, was bought by his aunt to emigrate with his free wife. Both could read.

26. Herndon Appeal, 1854, Miscellaneous Papers pertaining to the American Colonization Society, Library of Congress; Mohr, 17.

27. Whiteford Smith Pocket Diary, Sat., July 21, 1849, Whiteford Smith Papers, Duke University; Robert L. Church and Michael W. Sedlak, *Education in the United States* (New York: Free Press, 1976), 124; Philip Hamer, *The Secession Movement in South Carolina, 1847–1852* (Allentown, Pa., 1918), 36–41; Robert F. Durden, "The Establishment of Calvary Protestant Church for Negroes in Charleston," *South Carolina Historical Magazine,* 65 (Apr. 1964), 72–75; *Public Proceedings Relating to Calvary Church and the Religious Instruction of Slaves* (Charleston, 1850), 6–7.

28. A. G. Hay to J. W. Dulles, March 17, 1856; March 19, 1856. American Sunday School Union Correspondence, Presbyterian Historical Society; Basil Manly, Jr. to Charles Manly, December 1857, Manly Family Papers, Southern Baptist Historical Society; Eugene Portlette Southall, "Attitude of the Methodist Episcopal Church, South, Toward the Negro from 1844 to 1870," *JNH,* 16 (Oct. 1931), 266; Roger H. Crook, "The Ethical Emphasis of the Editors of Baptist Journals Published in the Southeastern Region of the United States up to 1865," (Th.D. diss., Southern Baptist Theological Seminary, 1947), 209.

29. Wade, 171; Mohr, 35–37; David M. Tucker, *Black Pastors and Leaders: Memphis, 1819–1972* (Memphis, 1975), 6; Curry, 193.

30. Petitions on Slavery, Archives of the State of South Carolina, Columbia; Richard Fuller, *Our Duty to the African Race: An Address Delivered at Washington D.C., January 21, 1851* (Baltimore, 1851); Fuller and Wayland, 160; Cuthbert, 163, 201.

31. Robert A. Fair, *Our Slaves Should Have the Bible* (Due West, S.C., 1854). Personal information on Fair from 1860 Census of Abbeville County, South Carolina, as transcribed by Margaret Vaughan McKinney, 1980, 45.

32. Fair, 8–10; 11–12; 24.

33. *DeBow's Review,* 18 (Jan. 1855), 52–53; Fair, 3.

34. *Bible Society Record* (1855), 69–90; Charles Colcock Jones, *Religious Instruction,* 72; Robert Manson Myers, ed., *The Children of Pride: A True Story of Georgia and the Civil War* (New Haven, 1972), 1690.

35. *DeBow's Review,* 25 (Dec. 1857), 561–570; Joseph C. Stiles, *Speech on the Slavery Resolutions* (New York, 1850), 39–42.

36. Stiles to G. Hallock, Washington, D.C., Dec. 24, [1857]; Richmond, Jan. 20, 1858, Huntington Library, San Merino, CA.; *Southern Aid Society: Its Constitution and Address to the Christian Public* (New York, 1854); Green, 163; Victor B. Howard, "The Southern Aid Society and the Slavery Controversy," *Church History,* 41 (June 1972), 211–21.

37. Green, 169, 172; Carleton Mabee, *The American Leonardo: A Life of Samuel F. B. Morse* (New York, 1943), 346–47.

Epilogue

1. Tract Society, 1864, 70.

2. Ira Berlin, ed., *Freedom: A Documentary History of Emancipation, 1861–1867.* Series II: *The Black Military Experience* (Cambridge, 1982), 612, 615.

3. Thomas L. Webber, 138.

4. *American Missionary (Magazine),* V:10 (Oct. 1861), 257; American Bible Society Reports, 1864, 39; Peter Kolchin, *First Freedom: The Responses of Alabama's Blacks to Emancipation and Reconstruction* (Westport, Conn., 1972), 85; Clarence E. Walker, 57; Joe M. Richardson, *Christian Reconstruction: The American Missionary Association and Southern Blacks, 1861–1890* (Athens, Ga., 1986), 13.

5. Rawick, ed., Indiana and Ohio, Suppl., Series I, V, 48; Edmund Drago, *Politicians and Reconstruction in Georgia* (Baton Rouge, 1982), 138, 106; Berlin, *op. cit.,* 640, 686–87, 689, 776–77, 794.

6. Henry L. Swint, ed., *Dear Ones at Home: Letters from Contraband Camps* (Nashville, 1966), 91; Webber, 138; *American Missionary* (Magazine), v:10 (Oct. 1861), 257; Drago, 105.

7. ABS, 1864, 37–39; 1865, 42; Tract Society, 1864, 68–70.

8. James D. Anderson, *The Education of Blacks in the South, 1860–1935* (Chapel Hill, 1988), 15; Ronald E. Butchart, *Northern Schools, Southern Blacks, and Reconstruction: Freedmen's Education, 1862–1875* (Westport, Conn., 1980), 18; Kolchin, 85. As a writer to the Tract Society declared, "even with strenuous efforts put forth for their improvement, the African must still acknowledge the superiority of the Saxon race." *Ibid.,* 42.

9. Leon F. Litwack, *Been in the Storm So Long: the Aftermath of Slavery* (New York, 1979), 501; "Documents: Colloquy with Colored Ministers," *JNH,* 16: 1 (Jan. 1931), 90–94; Butchart, 54; Jacqueline Jones, *Soldiers of Light and Love: Northern Teachers and Georgia Blacks, 1865–1873* (Chapel Hill, 1980), 54.

10. Maria Waterbury, *Seven Years Among the Freedmen* (Chicago, 1891; reprint 1971), 80; Litwack, 453–55; Wesley J. Gaines, *African Methodism in the South* (1890; reprint 1969), 275; William B. Gravely, "The Social, Political, and Religious Significance of the Formation of the Colored Methodist Episcopal Church (1870)", *Methodist History,* V (Oct. 1979), 20.

11. *The American Missionary* (Magazine), V:10 (Oct. 1861), 256; Robert Francis Engs, *Freedom's First Generation: Black Hampton, Virginia, 1861–1890* (Phila., 1979), 13–17; Haviland, 300–301; Drago, 105.

12. Joe M. Richardson, 27, 200, 201; Kolchin, 87–88; Jacqueline Jones, 34; Roberta Alexander, *North Carolina Faces the Freedmen: Race Relations During Presidential Reconstruction, 1865–67* (Durham, N.C., 1985), 84; Harriet Brent Jacobs, *Incidents in the Life of a Slave Girl* (Boston, 1861; reprint), 16.

13. Robert C. Morris, *Reading, Writing, and Reconstruction: The Education of Freedmen in the South, 1861–1870* (Chicago, 1982), 92; Richardson, 200; James D. Anderson, 8; Elizabeth Rauh Bethel, *Promiseland: A Century of Life in a Negro Community* (Philadelphia, 1981), 287–89.

14. Richardson, 245–46; Clarence Walker, 77, 91.

15. "An Address to Christians Throughout the World," *Central Presbyterian,* VIII:17 (Apr. 23, 1863); Southern Baptist Convention, Minutes, 1861, 35; *Pastoral Letter from the Bishops of the Protestant Episcopal Church in the Confederacy* . . . (Augusta, 1862), 10–12; *Southern Presbyterian Review,* 16 (July 1863), 10–20.

16. Bell I. Wiley, *Southern Negroes, 1861–1865* (New Haven, 1938), 168; Paul M. Ford, "Calvin H. Wiley's Views of the Negro," *North Carolina Historical Review,* 16 (Jan. 1964), 13; Clarence L. Mohr, "Slaves and White Churches in Georgia," in Boles, ed., 160–61.

17. Joseph C. Stiles, *The National Controversy* (New York, 1861), 76–77, Adger, 162–63.

18. Cuthbert, 260–65; David Rankin Barbee, "Lincoln, Chase, and the Rev. Dr. Richard Fuller," *Maryland Historical Magazine,* XLVI:2 (June 1951), 117, 120.

19. Cuthbert, 189.

20. Butchart, 189; Bond, 77–81; Clarence Walker, 57.

21. James D. Anderson, 14–18, 282.

BIBLIOGRAPHY

Manuscript and Archival Materials

Duke University, Perkins Library, Durham, N.C.
    Whitefoord Smith papers
    William W. Renwick papers

Georgia Historical Society, Savannah, Ga.
    First Baptist Church of Savannah Records
    Midway Congregational Church Records

Henry E. Huntington Library, San Merino, Cal.
    Joseph C. Stiles Papers

Library of Congress
    Breckinridge Papers
    American Colonization Society papers
    Carter G. Woodson Collection of Negro Papers

Mississippi State Archives, Jackson, Miss.
    Benjamin M. Drake papers

Pennsylvania Historical Society, Philadelphia, Pa.
    Records of Zoar Sabbath School

Presbyterian Historical Society, Philadelphia, Pa.
    American Sunday School Union documents and correspondence

South Carolina Historical Society, Charleston, S.C.
    St. Philip's Church Parish Records

South Carolina Department of Archives and History, Columbia, S.C.

South Caroliniana Library, University of South Carolina, Columbia, S.C.
Francis Asbury Mood papers
Pinckney family papers
Zelotus Lee Holmes papers
John McLees Diary
Pinckney family correspondence

Southern Baptist Theological Seminary, Louisville, Ky.
Charleston Baptist Association Minutes
Basil Manly papers, microfilm
Savannah River Baptist Association Minutes
Sunbury Baptist Association Minutes

Southern Historical Collection, University of North Carolina, Chapel Hill, N.C.
Frances Hanson diary
Ella Gertrude Thomas journal
All Saints Church records
James Hervey Greenlee papers
Courtlandt Van Rensselaer paper
Calvin Henderson Wiley papers

Southern Presbyterian Historical Society, Asheville, N.C.

Tulane University Library, New Orleans, La.
Charles Colcock Jones papers
John McDonogh papers

Virginia Historical Library, Richmond, Va.
First Baptist Church of Richmond Minutes
Friends' Cedar Creek Monthly Meetings, Records

Government Documents

The Code of Alabama. John J. Ormond, Arthur P. Bagby, George Goldthwaite, comp. Montgomery, 1852.

Digest of the Laws of the State of Alabama. C. C. Clay, comp. Tuscaloosa, 1843.

Digest of the Laws of Alabama, 1833. John G. Aikin, comp. Tuscaloosa, 1836.

Compilation of the Laws of the State of Georgia. William C. Dawson, comp. Milledgeville: Grantland & Orme, 1831.

Codification of the Statute Law of Georgia. William A. Hotchkiss, comp. Savannah, 1845.

Digest of the Statute Laws of the State of Georgia. Thomas R. R. Cobb, comp. Athens, 1851.

Civil Code of the State of Louisiana. Annot. Wheelock S. Upton & Needler B. Jennings. New Orleans, 1838.

Civil Code of the State of Louisiana from 1825–1853. Thomas Gibbes Morgan, comp. & ed. New Orleans, 1853.

Acts of the State of Louisiana, 1830.

Louisiana Digest, 1804–1841. Meinrad Grimer. New Orleans, 1841.

General Public Statutory Laws and Public Local Laws of the State of Maryland . . . 1692 to 1839. Clement Dorsey, comp. Baltimore, 1840.

Revised Laws of the State of Maryland. Otho Scott & Hiram M'Collough, comp. Bel Air, Md.: J. Cox, 1859.

The Maryland Code. Otho Scott, et al., comp. Baltimore, 1860.

Code of Mississippi, 1798–1848. A. Hutchinson, comp. Jackson, Miss., 1848.

Laws of Mississippi, 1824–1838. Jackson, 1838.

Index to the Statute Laws of Missouri. James S. Garland, comp. St. Louis: St. Louis Book & News Co., 1868.

Revised Statutes of the State of Missouri, 1845. Evans Casselberry, comp. St. Louis, 1845.

Revised Statutes of the State of North Carolina. Frederick Nash, James Iredell, William H. Battle. Raleigh, 1837.

Acts of the General Assembly of the State of South Carolina, 1830–39, together with Journals of the House and Journals of the Senate. Columbia: A. S. Johnston, 1840.

Supplement to the Revised Code of Virginia, 1819–33. Richmond, 1833.

Digest of the Laws of Virginia, 1841. Joseph Tate, comp. Richmond, 1841.

Code of Virginia. Richmond: W. F. Ritchie, 1849.

Code of Virginia. Richmond: Ritchie, Dunavant, 1860.

Godwin, Morgan. "Schools and Education of the Colored Population in the District of Columbia," *Special Report of the Commissioner of Education on the Improvement of Public Schools in the District of Columbia* (Washington, D.C., 1871; reprint 1969).

McKaye, James. *Mastership and its Fruits: The Emancipated Slave Face to Face with his Old Master. A Supplemental Report to Hon. Edwin M. Stanton, Secretary of War, by James McKaye, Special Commissioner.* New York: Loyal Publ. Society, 1864.

Resnick, Daniel, ed. *Literacy in Historical Perspective.* Washington, D.C.: Library of Congress, 1983.

United States Census Office. Seventh Census, 1850. Washington, D.C.: R. Armstrong, 1853.

United States Census Office. Eighth Census, 1860. Vol. I: Population. Washington, D.C., 1864.

United States Census Office. Compendium of the Ninth Census, 1870. Washington, D.C., 1872.

United States Census Office. Compendium of the Tenth Census, 1880. Washington, D.C., 1883.

Periodicals and Annual Publications

Anglo-African Magazine

African Methodist Episcopal Church Annual Reports

African Repository and Colonization Journal

American Bible Society Annual Reports

Journal of the American Bible Society

American Missionary (Magazine)

American Missionary (Paper)

American Sunday School Union Annual Reports

American Tract Society Annual Reports

Board of Missions of the General Assembly of the Presbyterian Church in the United States of America, Reports

Catholic Historical Society Records

Christian Index

DeBow's Review

Evangelical Quarterly Review

Journal of the Conference of the Methodist Episcopal Church

Journals of the Protestant Episcopal Church in the Confederate States of America

Littell's Living Age

Methodist Magazine and Quarterly Review

Millennial Harbinger

Minutes of the Annual Conferences of the Methodist Episcopal Church

Minutes of the Annual Conferences of the Methodist Episcopal Church, South

Minutes of the General Assembly of the Presbyterian Church in the United States of America

Bibliography

New York Christian Advocate and Journal and Zion's Herald

Presbyterian Magazine

Presbyterian Synod of South Carolina and Georgia, *Annual Sessions Proceedings of the National Convention of the Protestant Episcopal Church*

Protestant Episcopal Diocesan Conventions Reports: Kentucky, Maryland, South Carolina, Tennessee, Texas, Virginia.

Quarterly Review of the Methodist Episcopal Church, South

South Western Baptist

Southern Agriculturalist and Register of Rural Affairs

Southern Baptist Convention Proceedings

Southern Churchman

Southern Cultivator

Southern Presbyterian Review

Southern Quarterly Review

Wesleyan-Methodist Magazine

Articles

"An Address to Christians Throughout the World." *Central Presbyterian* VIII.17 (Apr. 23, 1863): 1.

Andrew, James O. "The Southern Slave Population." *Methodist Magazine and Quarterly Review* 13 (1831): 313–15.

Bailey, David Thomas. "A Divided Prism: Two Sources of Black Testimony on Slavery." *Journal of Southern History* XLVI.3 (Aug. 1980): 381–404.

Barbee, David Rankin. "Lincoln, Chase, and the Rev. Dr. Richard Fuller." *Maryland Historical Magazine* XLVI.2 (June 1951): 115–29.

Bennett, Robert A. "Black Episcopalians." *Historical Magazine of the Protestant Episcopal Church* 43. (Sept. 1974): 231–45.

Birnie, C. W. "Education of the Negro in Charleston, South Carolina, Prior to the Civil War." *Journal of Negro History* XII.1 (Jan. 1927): 13–21.

"Bishop Daniel Alexander Payne's Protestation of American Slavery." *Journal of Negro History* LII.1 (Jan. 1967): 59–64.

Blassingame, John W. "Using the Testimony of Ex-Slaves: Approaches and Problems." *Journal of Southern History* 41 (Nov. 1975): 473–92.

Brooks, Walter H. "The Priority of the Silver Bluff Church and its Promoters." *Journal of Negro History* VII.2 (Apr. 1922): 172–75.

Cade, John B. "Out of the Mouths of Ex-Slaves." *Journal of Negro History* XX.3 (Sept. 1935): 294–337.

Capers, William. "American Methodism." *Wesleyan-Methodist Magazine* 51. (1828): 626–67.

Chartier, Roger. "The Practical Impact of Writing." *A History of Private Life, Vol. III: Passions of the Renaissance.* ed. Chartier; gen. eds. Philippe Aries and Georges Duby; trans. Arthur Goldhammer. Cambridge, Mass.: Harvard University Press, 1989. 111–55.

Clinton, Catherine. "Caught in the Web of the Big House." *The Web of Southern Social Relations: Women, Family, & Education.* eds. Walter J. Fraser Jr., R. Frank Saunders, Jr., and Jon L. Wakelyn. Athens, Ga.: University of Georgia Press, 1985. 14–33.

Cornelius, Janet. "Slave Marriages in a Georgia Congregation." *Class, Conflict, and Consensus: Antebellum Southern Communities.* eds. Orville Vernon Burton and Robert C. McMath, Jr. Westport, Conn.: Greenwood Press, 1982. 128–45.

———. "We Slipped and Learned to Read: Slaves and the Literacy Process, 1830–1865." *Phylon* XLIV:3 (Sept. 1983): 171–86.

Daniel, W. Harrison. "Southern Protestantism and the Negro, 1860–1865." *North Carolina Historical Review* 41 (July 1964): 338–59.

Davis, John W. "George Liele and Andrew Bryan, Pioneer Baptist Preachers." *Journal of Negro History* III.2 (Apr. 1918): 119–27.

Dilliard, Irving. "James Milton Turner: A Little Known Benefactor of his People." *Journal of Negro History* XIX.4 (Oct. 1934): 372–411.

"Documents: Colloquy with Colored Ministers." *Journal of Negro History* XVI.1 (Jan. 1931): 88–98.

Durden, Robert F. "The Establishment of Calvary Protestant Church for Negroes in Charleston." *South Carolina Historical Magazine* 65. (Apr. 1964): 63–84.

Dvorak, Katharine L. "After Apocalypse, Moses." *Masters and Slaves in the House of the Lord: Race and Religion in the American South, 1740–1870.* ed. John B. Boles. Lexington, Ky.: University Press of Kentucky, 1988. 173–91.

Ford, Paul M. "Calvin H. Wiley's Views of the Negro." *North Carolina Historical Review* 16 (Jan. 1964): 1–20.

Foster, Charles I. "Colonization of Free Negroes in Liberia." *Journal of Negro History* XXXVIII.1 (Jan. 1953): 41–66.

Frith, Simon. "Socialization and Rational Schooling: Elementary Education in Leeds before 1870." *Popular Education and Socialization in the Nineteenth Century.* ed. Philip McCann. London: Methuen, 1977. 67–92.

Gallay, Alan. "Planters and Slaves in the Great Awakening." *Masters and Slaves in the House of the Lord: Race and Religion in the American South, 1740–1870.* ed. John B. Boles. Lexington, Ky.: University Press of Kentucky, 1988. 19–36.

Gatell, Frank Otto, ed. "Postmaster Huger and the Incendiary Publications. *South Carolina Historical and Geneological Magazine* LXIV. (Oct. 1963): 193–201.

Goody, Jack and Ian Watt. "The Consequences of Literacy." *Literacy in Traditional Societies.* ed. Goody. Cambridge, England: Cambridge University Press, 1968. 27–68.

Goveiea, Elsa V. "The West Indian Slave Laws of the Eighteenth Century." *Slavery in the New World: A Reader in Comparative History.* eds. Laura Foner and Engene Genovese. Englewood Cliffs, N.J.: Prentice-Hall, 1969. 113–37.

Graff, Harvey. "Literacy Past and Present: Critical Approaches in the Literacy-Society Relationship." *Interchange* 9 (1978): 1–29.

Gravely, William B. "The Social, Political, and Religious Significance of the Formation of the Colored Methodist Episcopal Church (1870)." *Methodist History* V (Oct. 1979): 3–27.

Green, Fletcher M. "Northern Missionary Activities in the South, 1846–1861." *Journal of Southern History* XXI.2 (May 1955): 147–72.

Grimstead, David. "Rioting in its Jacksonian Setting." *American Historical Review* 77 (Apr. 1972): 361–97.

Hall, Robert L. "Black and White Christians in Florida, 1822–1861." *Masters & Slaves in the House of the Lord: Race and Religion in the American South, 1740–1870.* ed. John B. Boles. Lexington, Ky.: University Press of Kentucky, 1988. 81–98.

Hartzell, J. H. "Methodism and the Negro in the United States." *Journal of Negro History* VIII.3 (July 1923): 301–15.

Hayden, J. Carleton. "Conversion and Control: Dilemma of Episcopalians in Providing for the Religious Instruction of Slaves, Charleston, South Carolina, 1845–1860." *Historical Magazine of the Protestant Episcopal Church* 40 (July 1971): 143–71.

Horton, Robin. "African Traditional Thought and Western Science." *Africa* 37.1 (Jan. 1967): 58–65.

Howard, Victor B. "The Southern Aid Society and the Slavery Controversy." *Church History* 41 (June 1972): 208–24.

Hoyt, William Jr. "John McDonogh and Colonization in Liberia." *Journal of Negro History* XXIV.4 (Oct. 1939): 440–53.

Humez, Jean M. "Visionary Experience and Power: The Career of Rebecca Cox Jackson." *Black Apostles at Home and Abroad: Afro-*

Americans and the Christian Mission from the Revolution to Recon-struction. eds. David W. Wills and Richard Newman. Boston: G. K. Hall, 1982. 105–32.

Isaac, Rhys. "Books and the Social Authority of Learning: The Case of Mid-Eighteenth Century Virginia." *Printing and Society in Early America.* eds. William L. Joyce, David D. Hall and Richard D. Brown, et al. Worcester, Mass.: American Antiquarian Society, 1983. 228–49.

Jackson, Luther P. "Religious Development of the Negro in Virginia from 1760 to 1860." *Journal of Negro History* XVI.2 (April 1931): 168–239.

Jernegan, Marcus. "Slavery and Conversion in the American Colonies." *American Historical Review* 21 (Apr. 1916): 508.

Joyner, Charles. "Slave Language and Slave Thought in Antebellum Charleston." *Intellectual Life in Antebellum Charleston.* eds. Michael O'Brien and David Moltke-Hansen. Knoxville, Tenn.: University of Tennessee Press, 1986. 255–78.

Laurens, Edward. "Address before the Agricultural Society of South Carolina, Sept. 18, 1832." *Southern Agriculturalist* V (1832): 534–565.

"Letters Showing the Rise and Progress of the Early Negro Churches in Kingston, Jamaica and Savannah, Georgia." *Journal of Negro History*, I.1 (Jan. 1916): 69–92.

Long, Charles H. "Perspectives for a Study of Afro-American Religions in the United States." *History of Religions* 11.1 (Aug. 1971): 54–66.

Loveland, Anne C. "Evangelism and Immediate Emancipation in American Anti-Slavery Thought." *Journal of Southern History* XXXII (May 1966): 172–88.

Mathews, Donald G. "Charles Colcock Jones and the Southern Evangelical Crusade to Form a Biracial Community." *Journal of Southern History* 41 (Aug. 1975): 299–320.

———. "Religion in the Old South: Speculation on Methodology." *South Atlantic Quarterly* (Winter 1974): 34–52.

McCann, Philip. "Popular Education, Socialization, and Social Control: Spitalfields, 1812–1824." *Popular Education and Socialization in the Nineteenth Century.* ed. McCann. London: Methuen, 1977. 1–40.

McDougle, Ivan. "Slavery in Kentucky." *Journal of Negro History* III.3 (Jul. 1918): 211–328.

McKivigan, John. "The Gospel Will Burst the Bonds of the Slave: The Abolitionists' Bibles for Slaves Campaign." *Negro History Bulletin* 45.3 (1982): 62–68.

Mohr, Clarence L. "Slaves and White Churches in Georgia." *Masters & Slaves in the House of the Lord: Race and Religion in the American*

South, 1740–1870. ed. John B. Boles. Lexington, Ky.: University Press of Kentucky, 1988. 153–72.

Murphy, Miriam T. "Catholic Missionary Work among the Colored People of the U.S., 1766–1866." *Records of the American Catholic Historical Society* 35. (June 1941): 114–25.

O'Neall, John Belton. "Slave Laws of the South." *The Industrial Resources, etc. of the Southern and Western States.* ed. J. D. B. DeBow. II. New Orleans: 1853. 278–90.

Olney, James. " 'I Was Born': Slave Narratives, Their Status as Autobiography and Literature." *The Slave's Narrative.* eds. Charles T. Davis and Henry Louis Gates Jr. New York: Oxford University Press, 1985. 148–74.

Pease, William, and Jane Pease. "Organized Negro Communities: A North American Experiment." *Journal of Negro History* XLVII.1 (Jan. 1962): 19–34.

Perkins, Linda. "Quaker Beneficence and Black Control: The Institute for Colored Youth, 1852–1903." *New Perspectives on Black Educational History.* eds. Vincent P. Franklin and James D. Anderson. Boston: G. K. Hall, 1978. 19–27.

Reinders, Robert C. "The Churches and the Negro in New Orleans, 1850–1860." *Phylon* XXII.3 (Fall 1961): 241–48.

Resnick, Daniel P. and Lauren B. "The Nature of Literacy: An Historical Exploration." *Harvard Educational Review* 47.3 (Aug. 1977): 372–81.

Saenger, Paul. "Physiologie de la lecture et separation des mots." *Annales* 44.4 (Jul.–Aug 1989): 939–52.

———. "Silent Reading: Its Impact on Late Medieval Script and Society." *Viator* 13 (1982): 367–414.

Samuels, S. Jay, and Michael L. Kamil. "Models of the Reading Process." *Handbook of Reading Research.* ed. P. David Pearson. New York: Longman, 1984. 186–208.

Sanderson, Michael. "Literacy and Social Mobility in the Industrial Revolution in England." *Past & Present* 56 (Aug. 1972): 75–104.

Schofield, Roger. "The Measurement of Literacy in Pre-Industrial England." *Literacy in Traditional Societies.* ed. Jack Goody. Cambridge, England: Cambridge University Press, 1968. 311–25.

Schultz, Elizabeth. "To Be Black and Blue: The Blues Genre in Black American Autobiography." *Kansas Quarterly* 7.3 (Summer 1975): 81–98.

Scribner, Sylvia, and Michael Cole. "Literacy Without Schooling: Testing for Intellectual Effects." *Harvard Educational Review* 48.4 (Nov. 1978): 448–61.

Seabrook, Whitemarsh. "Remarks on the General Unsuccessfulness of Sea Island Planters." *Southern Agriculturist* VII.9–12, 177–78.

Smith, Timothy L. "Slavery and Theology: The Emergence of Black Christian Consciousness in Nineteenth Century America." *Church History* 41 (Dec. 1972): 497–512.

Southall, Eugene Portlette. "Attitude of the Methodist Episcopal Church, South, Toward the Negro from 1844 to 1870." *Journal of Negro History* XVI.3 (Oct. 1931): 359–70.

Spufford, Margaret. "First steps in literacy: the reading and writing experiences of the humblest seventeenth-century spiritual autobiographers." *Literacy and Social Development in the West: A Reader.* ed. Harvey Graff. Cambridge, England: Cambridge University Press, 1981. 125–50.

Stone, Lawrence. "Literacy and Education in England, 1640–1900." *Past and Present 42 (Feb. 1969): 69–139.*

Strickland, John Scott. "The Great Revival and Insurrectionary Fears in North Carolina: An Examination of Antebellum Southern Society and Slave Revolt Panics." *Class, Conflict, and Consensus: Antebellum Southern Community Studies.* eds. Orville Vernon Burton and Robert C. McMath Jr. Westport, Conn.: Greenwood Press, 1982.

Swift, David E. "Black Presbyterian Attacks on Racism: Samuel Cornish, Theodore Wright, and their Contemporaries." *Black Apostles at Home and Abroad: Afro-Americans and the Christian Mission from the Revolution to Reconstruction.* eds. David W. Wills and Richard Newman. Boston: G. K. Hall, 1982. 43–84.

Taylor, R. H. "Humanizing the Slave Code." *North Carolina Historical Review* 2 (Apr. 1925): 323–31.

Taylor, William R. "Toward A Definition of Orthodoxy: The Patrician South and the Common Schools." *Harvard Educational Review* 36.4 (Sept. 1966): 412–26.

Vibert, Faith. "The Society for the Propagation of the Gospel in Foreign Parts: Its Work for the Negroes in North America before 1783." *Journal of Negro History* XVIII.2 (April 1933): 171–212.

Webber, Rose-Marie. "Reading." *A Survey of Applied Linguistics.* eds. Ronald Wardhaugh and H. Douglas Brown. Ann Arbor, Mich.: University of Michigan Press, 1976.

Williams, Michael Patrick. "The Black Evangelical Ministry in the Border States: Profiles of Elders John Berry Meachum and Noah Davis." *Black Apostles at Home and Abroad: Afro-Americans and the Christian Mission from Revolution to Reconstruction.* eds. David W. Wills and Richard Newman. Boston: G. K. Hall, 1982. 85–104.

Wolf, Thomas. "Reading Reconsidered." *Harvard Educational Review* 47.3 (Aug. 1977): 405–28.

Wyatt-Brown, Bertram. "The Antimission Movement in the Jacksonian South." *Journal of Southern History* 36. (Nov. 1970): 501–29.

Books

An Account of the Late Intended Insurrection among a Portion of the Blacks in the City. Charleston: A. E. Miller, 1822.

Adams, C. C. and Marshal A. Talley. *Negro Baptist and Foreign Missions.* Philadelphia: National Baptist Convention Foreign Mission Board, 1944.

Adams, Nehemiah. *South-Side View of Slavery.* Boston: T. R. Marvin, 1854.

Adams, Parveen ed. *Language in Thinking.* Harmondsworth, Middlesex, England, 1972.

An Address to the Presbyterians of Kentucky Proposing a Plan for the Instruction and Emancipation of Their Slaves. Cincinnati: Taylor & Tracy, 1835.

Adger, John B. *My Life and Times, 1819–1899.* Richmond, Va.: Presbyterian Committee of Publication, 1899.

Ahlstrom, Sidney. *Religious History of the American People.* New Haven, Conn.: Yale University Press, 1972.

Albert, Octavia V. Rogers. *The House of Bondage or, Charlotte Brooks and Other Slaves.* New York: Hunt & Eaton, 1890; reprint 1972.

Aleckson, Sam. *Before the War, and After the Union: An Autobiography.* Boston: Gold Mind Publishing Co., 1929.

Alexander, Roberta. *North Carolina Faces the Freedmen: Race Relations During Presidential Reconstruction, 1865–67.* Durham, N.C.: Duke University Press, 1985.

Alford, Terry. *Prince Among Slaves.* New York: Harcourt Brace Jovanovich, 1977.

The American Convention of Abolition Societies, vol. I: 1794–1805. New York: Bergman Publishers, Facsimile ed., 1969.

Anderson, James D. *The Education of Blacks in the South, 1860–1935.* Chapel Hill, N.C.: University of North Carolina Press, 1988.

Aptheker, Herbert. *American Negro Slave Revolts.* New York: Columbia University Press, 1943.

———., ed. *A Documentary History of the Negro People in the United States, vols. I & II.* New York: Citadel Press, 1951.

Arnold, William E. *Methodism in Kentucky, vols. I & II*. Louisville, Ky.: Pentecostal Publ. Co., Herald Press, 1936.

Austin, Allen D., ed. *African Muslims in Antebellum America*. New York: Garland Publ., 1984.

Baldwin, Lewis V. *"Invisible" Strands in African Methodism: A History of the African Union Methodist Protestant and Union American Methodist Episcopal Churches, 1805–1980*. Metuchen, N.J.: American Theological Library Assn. and The Scarecrow Press, Inc., 1983.

Barnes, Gilbert. *The Anti-Slavery Impulse, 1830–1844*. New York: D. Appleton, 1933.

Barrett, Leonard E. *Soul Force: African Heritage in Afro-American Religion*. Garden City, N.Y.: Anchor Press, 1974.

Berlin, Ira, ed. *Freedom: A Documentary History of Emancipation, 1861–1867. Series II: The Black Military Experience*. Cambridge, England.: Cambridge University Press, 1982.

————. *Slaves Without Masters: The Free Negro in the Antebellum South*. New York: Pantheon Books, 1974.

Bethel, Elizabeth Rauh. *Promiseland, A Century of Life in a Negro Community*. Philadelphia: Temple University Press, 1981.

Bibb, Henry. *Narrative of the Life and Adventures of Henry Bibb*. New York, 1850; reprint 1969, Miami: Mnemosyne Publ. Co.

Black, Leonard. *Life and Sufferings of Leonard Black*. New Bedford, Mass.: Press of Benjamin Lindsey, 1847.

Blackford, L. Minor. *Mine Eyes Have Seen the Glory: The Story of a Virginia Lady*. Cambridge, Mass.: Harvard University Press, 1954.

Blassingame, John W. *The Slave Community: Plantation Life in the Antebellum South*. New York: Oxford University Press, 1972.

————. *Slave Testimony: Two Centuries of Letters, Speeches, Interviews, and Autobiographies*. Baton Rouge, La.: Louisiana State University Press, 1977.

Boles, John, ed. *Masters and Slaves in the House of the Lord: Race and Religion in the American South, 1740–1870*. Lexington, Ky.: University Press of Kentucky, 1988.

Bond, Horace Mann. *Negro Education in Alabama: A Study in Cotton and Steel*. 1939; reprint 1969, N.Y., Octagon Books.

Boothe, Charles Octavius. *The Cyclopedia of the Colored Baptists of Alabama: Their Leaders and their Work*. Birmingham, Ala.: Alabama Publishing Co., 1895.

Bosman, Willem. *New and Accurate Description of the Coast of Guinea*. London: J. Knapton, 1705.

Bowen, Nataniel. *A Pastoral Letter on the Religious Instruction of the Negroes*. Charleston: A. E. Miller, 1835.

Boylan, Anne M. *Sunday School: The Formation of an American Institution, 1790–1880.* New Haven, Conn.: Yale University Press, 1988.

Brackenridge, R. Douglas. *Voice in the Wilderness: A History of the Cumberland Presbyterian Church in Texas.* San Antonio, Tex.: Trinity University Press, 1969.

Branham, Levi. *My Life and Travels.* Dalton, Ga.: A. J. Showalter Co., 1929.

Bremer, Frederika. *Homes of the New World: Impressions of America. Vols. I & II.* New York: Harper & Row, 1853.

Brown, Hallie Quinn, *Homespun Heroines and Other Women of Distinction.* Xenia, O.: Aldine Publ. Co., 1926.

Brown, Letitia Woods. *Free Negroes in the District of Columbia, 1790–1846.* New York: Oxford University Press, 1972.

Bruce, Henry Clay. *The New Man. Twenty-Nine Years a Slave. Twenty-Nine Years a Free Man.* York, Pa.: P. Anstadt, 1895; reprint 1969, Miami: Mnemosyne Publ. Co.

Burton, Orville Vernon and Robert C. McMath, Jr., eds. *Class, Conflict, and Consensus: Antebellum Southern Community Studies.* Westport, Conn.: Greenwood Press, 1982.

Burton, Orville Vernon. *In My Father's House Are Many Mansions: Family and Community in Edgefield, South Carolina.* Chapel Hill, N.C.: University of North Carolina Press, 1985.

Butchart, Ronald E. *Northern Schools, Southern Blacks, and Reconstruction: Freedmen's Education, 1862–1875.* Westport, Conn.: Greenwood Press, 1980.

Cade, John Brother. *Holsey—The Incomparable.* New York: Pagent Press, 1964.

Cameron, Richard M. *Methodism and Society in Historical Perspective.* New York: Abingdon Press, 1961.

Carter, E. R. *Biographical Sketches of our Pulpit.* 1888; reprint 1969, Chicago: Afro-American Press.

Catterall, Helen. *Judicial Cases Concerning American Slavery and the Negro, vols. I–V.* Washington, D.C.: Carnegie Institution of Washington, 1926–37.

Chartier, Roger, ed., Philippe Aries and George Duby, gen. eds. *A History of Private Life, Vol. III: Passions of the Renaissance.* Cambridge, Mass.: Harvard University Press, 1989.

Chesnut, Mary. *A Diary from Dixie.* Edited by Ben Ames Williams. Boston: Houghton Mifflin, 1949.

Church, Robert L., and Michael W. Sedlak. *Education in the United States: An Interpretive History.* New York: Free Press, 1976.

Cone, James. *A Black Theology of Liberation*. Philadelphia: Lippincott, 1970.

Conway, Moncure D. *Autobiography, Memories, and Experiences of M. D. Conway, vols. I & II*. Boston: Houghton Mifflin, 1904.

Costanzo, Angelo. *Surprizing Narrative: Olaudah Equiano and the Beginnings of Black Autobiography*. New York: Greenwood Press, 1988.

Creel, Margaret Washington. *"A Peculiar People": Slave Religion and Community-Culture Among the Gullahs. The American Social Experience Series, No. 7*. New York: New York University Press, 1988.

Cremin, Lawrence A. *Traditions of American Education*. New York: Basic Books, 1977.

Cressy, David. *Literacy and the Social Order: Reading and Writing in Tudor and Stuart England*. Cambridge, England: Cambridge University Press, 1980.

Culp, Daniel W., ed. *Twentieth Century Negro Literature*. Naperville, Ill.: J. L. Nichols & Co., 1902.

Curry, Leonard P. *The Free Black in Urban America 1800–1850: The Shadow of the Dream*. Chicago: University of Chicago Press, 1981.

Curti, Merle. *Social Ideas of American Educators*. Totowa, N.J.: Littlefield, Adams, 1968.

Curtin, Philip. *Two Jamaicas: The Role of Ideas in a Tropical Colony*. Cambridge, Mass.: Harvard University Press, 1955.

Cuthbert, J. H. *Life of Richard Fuller, D.D.* New York: Sheldon & Co., 1878.

Davidson, Basil. *The African Genius: An Introduction to African Cultural and Social History*. Boston: Little, Brown, 1969.

Davis, Charles T. and Henry Louis Gates Jr. *The Slave's Narrative*. New York: Oxford University Press, 1985.

Davis, David Brion. *The Problem of Slavery in Western Culture*. Ithaca, New York: Cornell University Press, 1966.

——— . *The Problem of Slavery in the Age of Revolution*. Ithaca, New York: Cornell University Press, 1975.

Davis, Noah. *A Narrative of the Life of Rev. Noah Davis, A Colored Man, Written by Himself, at the Age of 54*. Baltimore, Md.: J. F. Weishampel, Jr., 1859.

Douglass, Frederick. *Life and Writings*, ed. Philip Foner, vols. I–IV. New York: International Publishers, 1950–55.

——— . *Life and Times of Frederick Douglass*. Hartford, Conn.: Park Publ. Co., 1881.

——— . *Narrative of the Life of Frederick Douglass*. Boston, 1845, Published at the Anti-Slavery Office, No. 25 Cornhill.

Douglass, Margaret. *The Personal Narrative of Mrs. Margaret Douglass.* Boston: J. P. Jewett & Co., 1854.

Drago, Edmund. *Politicians and Reconstruction in Georgia.* Baton Rouge, La.: Louisiana State University Press, 1982.

Drake, Thomas E. *Quakers and Slavery in America.* New Haven, Conn.: Yale University Press, 1950.

Drew, Benjamin. *A North-side View of Slavery. The Refugee: or the Narratives of Fugitive Slaves in Canada Related by Themselves.* Boston: J. P. Jewett, 1856.

DuBois, William Edward Burghardt. *Black Reconstruction.* New York: Harcourt Brace, 1935; reprint 1963, Millwood, N.Y.: Kraus-Thomson.

Dumond, Dwight L., ed. *Letters of James Gillespie Birney, 1831–1857, vols. I & II.* Gloucester, Mass.: P. Smith, 1966.

Dunham, Charles Forrester. *The Attitude of the Northern Clergy Toward the South, 1860–1865.* Toledo, Ohio.: Gray Co., 1842; reprint 1974, Philadelphia: Porcupine Press.

Eaton, Clement. *The Freedom-of-Thought Struggle in the Old South.* New York: Harper & Row, 1964.

———. *The Growth of Southern Civilization, 1790–1860.* New York: Harper & Row, 1961.

Edwards, James T., ed. *Some Interesting Papers of John McDonogh.* McDonogh, Md.: Boys of the McDonogh School, 1898.

Elder, Orville, and Samuel Hall. *The Life of Samuel Hall, Washington, Iowa: A Slave for Forty-Seven Years.* Washington, Iowa.: Journal Print., 1912.

Ellis, Tracy, ed. *Documents of American Catholic History.* Milwaukee, 1956.

Engs, Robert Francis. *Freedom's First Generation: Black Hampton, Virginia, 1861–1890.* Philadelphia: University of Pennsylvania Press, 1979.

Escott, Paul. *Slavery Remembered: A Record of Twentieth-Century Slave Narratives.* Chapel Hill, N.C.: University of North Carolina Press, 1979.

Fair, Robert A. *Our Slaves Should Have the Bible.* Due West, S.C.: Telescope Press, 1854.

Fields, Mamie Garvin. *Lemon Swamp and Other Places: A Carolina Memoir.* New York: Free Press, 1983.

Fisher, Miles Mark. *Negro Slave Songs in the United States.* Ithaca, N.Y.: Cornell University Press, 1953; reprint 1978, Citadel Press.

Fladeland, Betty. *James Gillespie Birney: Slaveholder to Abolitionist.* Ithaca, N.Y.: Cornell University Press, 1955; reprint 1969.

————. *Men and Brothers: Anglo-American Antislavery Cooperation.* Urbana, Ill.: University of Illinois Press, 1972.

Foner, Laura and Eugene Genovese. *Slavery in the New World: A Reader in Comparative History.* Englewood Cliffs, N.J.: Prentice-Hall, 1969.

Franklin, John Hope. *The Free Negro in North Carolina.* New York: Russell & Russell, 1943.

Franklin, Vincent P. *Black Self-Determination: A Cultural History of the Faith of the Fathers.* Westport, Conn.: Greenwood Press, 1984.

Franklin, Vincent P., and James D. Anderson, eds. *New Perspectives on Black Educational History.* Boston: G. K. Hall, 1978.

Fraser, Walter, Jr., R. Frank Saunders and Jon L. Wakelyn. *The Web of Southern Social Relations: Women, Family & Education.* Athens, Ga.: University of Georgia Press, 1985.

Freehling, William W. *Prelude to Civil War: The Nullification Controversy in South Carolina, 1816–1836.* New York: Harper & Row, 1966.

Freeman, George W. *Rights and Duties of Slaveholders.* Charleston: A. E. Miller, 1837.

Fuller, Richard. *Our Duty to the African Race: An Address Delivered at Washington, D.C., January 21, 1851.* Baltimore, Md.: W. M. Innes, 1851.

————. *Speech of Dr. Fuller at the Anniversary of the American Tract Society.* New York, 1860.

Fuller, Richard, and Francis Wayland. *Domestic Slavery Considered as a Scriptural Institution.* New York: L. Colby, 1845.

Gaines, Wesley J. *African Methodism in the South; or, Twenty-five Years of Freedom.* 1890; reprint 1969, Chicago: Afro-American Press.

Geertz, Clifford. *The Interpretation of Cultures: Selected Essays.* New York: Basic Books, 1973.

Genovese, Eugene D. *Roll, Jordan, Roll: The World The Slaves Made.* New York: Pantheon Books, 1974.

Gillard, John T. *Colored Catholics in the U.S.* Baltimore, Md.: The Josephite Press, 1941.

Goldin, Claudia. *Urban Slavery in the American South, 1820–1860: A Quantitative History.* Chicago: University of Chicago Press, 1976.

Goody, Jack, ed. *Literacy in Traditional Societies.* Cambridge, England: Cambridge University Press, 1968.

Graff, Harvey. *The Literacy Myth: Literacy and Social Structure in the Nineteenth Century City.* New York: Academic Press, 1979.

Graff, Harvey, ed. *Literacy and Social Development in the West: A Reader.* Cambridge, England: Cambridge University Press, 1981.

Green, Elisha. *Life of the Rev. Elisha W. Green*. Maysville, Ky.: Republican Printing Office, 1888.

Gronniosaw, James. *A Narrative of the Most Remarkable Particulars in the Life of James Albert Ukawsaw Gronniosaw*. Bath, England: W. Shirley, 1770.

Guilday, Peter. *The Life and Times of John England, First Bishop of Charleston, 1786–1842, vols. I & II*. New York: The America Press, 1927.

Hamer, Philip. *The Secession Movement in South Carolina, 1847–1852*. Allentown, Pa.: H. R. Haas & Co., 1918.

Hammon, Jupiter. *Address to the Negroes in the State of New York*. New York: Carroll & Patterson, 1787.

Harding, Vincent. *There Is a River: the Black Struggle for Freedom in America*. New York: Harcourt Brace, 1981.

Harrison, William P., ed. *The Gospel among the Slaves*. Nashville, Tenn.: Publishing House of the M.E. Church, South, 1893; reprint 1973, New York: AMS.

Haviland, Laura. *A Woman's Life-Work. Labors and Experiences*. Chicago: C. V. Waite, 1887.

Heard, William H. *From Slavery to the Bishopric in the A.M.E. Church*. 1924; reprint 1969, New York: Arno Press.

Henry, Howell M. *The Police Control of the Slave in South Carolina*. Emory, Va., 1914.

Herskovitz, Melville. *The Myth of the Negro Past*. New York: Beacon Press, 1941.

Hicks, William. *History of Louisiana Negro Baptists from 1804 to 1914*. Nashville, Tenn.: National Baptist Publishing Board, 1918.

Holsey, Lucius. *Autobiography, Sermons, Addresses, and Essays*. Atlanta, Ga.: Franklin Printing and Publ. Co., 1898.

Howe, George. *History of the Presbyterian Church in South Carolina, vols. I & II*. Columbia, S.C.: Duffie & Chapman, 1870.

Hughes, Louis. *Thirty Years a Slave, From Bondage to Freedom: Autobiography*. Milwaukee, 1897; reprint 1969, New York: Negro Universities Press.

Hurd, John Codman. *The Law of Freedom and Bondage in the United States*. Boston: Little, Brown, 1858–62.

Jacobs, Harriet Brent. *Incidents in the Life of a Slave Girl, Written by Herself*. Boston: Lydia Maria Child, ed. & publ., 1861; 1987 ed. Cambridge, Mass.: Harvard University Press, ed. Jean Fagan Yellin.

Jenkins, William S. *Pro-Slavery Thought in the Old South*. Chapel Hill, N.C.: University of North Carolina Press, 1935.

Johns, John. *A Memoir of the Right Reverend William Meade.* Baltimore, Md.: Innes & Co., 1869.

Johnson, Clifton. *God Struck Me Dead: Religious Conversion Experiences and Autobiographies of Ex-Slaves.* Philadelphia, 1945.

Johnson, Thomas L. *Twenty-Eight Years a Slave or, the Story of My Life in Three Continents.* Bournemouth, England: W. Mate & Sons, 1909 (7th ed.).

Jones, Charles Colcock. *Religious Instruction of the Negroes.* Savannah, Ga.: Thomas Purse, 1842; reprint 1968, Negro Universities Press.

———. A Catechism of Scriptural Doctrine and Practice. Phila.: Presby. Board of Publ., 1852. 3rd ed.

Jones, Charles Colcock, and Josiah Law. *Annual Reports of the Association for the Religious Instruction of the Negroes, 1–13.* Savannah, Ga., 1833–48.

Jones, Howard. *Mutiny on the Amistad: The Saga of a Slave Revolt and its Impact on American Abolition, Law, and Diplomacy.* New York: Oxford University Press, 1987.

Jones, Jacqueline. *Soldiers of Light and Love: Northern Teachers and Georgia Blacks, 1865–1873.* Chapel Hill, N.C.: University of North Carolina Press, 1980.

Jones, John G. *Methodism in the Mississippi Conference, vols. I & II.* Nashville: Southern Methodist Publ. House, 1908.

Jones, Thomas H. *The Experience of Thomas Jones, Who Was a Slave for Forty-Three Years.* Boston, 1862.

Jordan, Winthrop. *White Over Black: American Attitudes toward the Negro, 1550–1812.* Chapel Hill, N.C.: University of North Carolina Press, 1968.

Joyce, William L., David D. Hall and Richard D. Brown, et al. *Printing and Society in Early America.* Worcester, Mass.: American Antiquarian Society, 1983.

Kennedy, William Bean. *The Shaping of Protestant Education . . . 1789–1860.* New York: Association Press, 1966.

King, Joe M. *A History of South Carolina Baptists.* Columbia, S.C.: Genl. Board of the S.C. Baptist Convention, 1964.

Kingsley, Zephaniah. *A Treatise on . . . Slavery . . . by an inhabitant of Florida.* 2nd ed.; 1829.

Klein, Herbert S. *Slavery in the Americas.* Chicago: University of Chicago Press, 1967.

Klingberg, Frank J. *Anglican Humanitarianism in Colonial New York.* Philadelphia: Church Historical Society, 1940.

Koger, Larry. *Black Slaveowners: Free Black Slave Masters in South Carolina, 1790–1860.* Jefferson, N.C.: McFarland & Co., 1985.

Kolchin, Peter. *First Freedom: the Responses of Alabama's Blacks to Emancipation and Reconstruction.* Westport, Conn.: Greenwood Press, 1972.

Kuykendall, John. *Southern Enterprize.* Westport, Conn.: Greenwood Press, 1982.

Lane, Isaac. *The Autobiography of Bishop Isaac Lane.* Nashville, Tenn.: Publ. House of the M.E. Church, South, 1916.

Laqueur, Thomas. *Religion and Respectability: Sunday Schools and Working Class Culture, 1780–1850.* New Haven, Conn.: Yale University Press, 1976.

Lerner, Gerda. *The Grimke Sisters from South Carolina.* New York: Houghton Mifflin, 1967.

Levine, Lawrence W. *Black Culture and Black Consciousness: Afro-American Folk Thought from Slavery to Freedom.* Oxford: Oxford University Press, 1977.

Lewis, George. *Impressions of American and the American Churches.* Edinburgh: W. P. Kennedy, 1845.

Litwack, Leon. *Been in the Storm So Long: The Aftermath of Slavery.* New York: Vintage Books, 1980.

———. *North of Slavery.* Chicago: University of Chicago Press, 1961.

Lockridge, Kenneth. *Literacy in Colonial New England: An Enquiry into the Social Context of Literacy in the Early Modern West.* New York: W. W. Norton, 1974.

Loveland, Anne C. *Southern Evangelicals and the Social Order, 1800–1860.* Baton Rouge, La.: Louisiana State University Press, 1980.

Mabee, Carlton. *The American Leonardo: The Life of Samuel F. B. Morse.* New York: A. A. Knopf, 1943.

Majors, Monroe A. *Noted Negro Women: Their Triumphs and Activities.* 1893; reprint 1971, Freeport, N.Y.: Books for Libraries Press.

Manly, Louisa. *The Manly Family.* Greenville, S.C.: Furman University Press, 1930.

Manross, William. *The Episcopal Church in the U.S., 1800–1840: A Study in Church Life.* New York: Columbia University Press, 1938.

Marrs, Elijah P. *Life and History of the Rev. Elijah P. Marrs.* Louisville, Ky.: Bradley & Gilbert, 1885; reprint 1969, Miami: Mnemosyne Publ. Co.

Mathews, Donald G. *Religion in the Old South.* Chicago: University of Chicago Press, 1977.

———. *Slavery and Methodism: A Chapter in American Morality, 1780–1845.* Princeton, N.J.: Princeton University Press, 1965.

Mathews, Mitford M. *Teaching to Read Historically Considered.* Chicago: University of Chicago Press, 1966.

McCann, Philip, ed. *Popular Education and Socialization in the Nineteenth Century.* London: Methuen, 1977.

McCloy, Shelby T. *The Negro in the French West Indies.* Lexington, Ky.: University of Kentucky Press, 1966.

McColley, Robert. *Slavery in Jeffersonian Virginia.* Urbana, Ill.: University of Illinois Press, 1964.

McCulloch, Samuel Clyde, ed. *British Humanitarianism: Essays in Honor of Frank Klingberg.* Philadelphia: Church Historical Society, 1950.

McDonnold, Benjamin W. *History of the Cumberland Presbyterian Church.* Nashville, Tenn.: Board of Publ. of the Cumberland Presbyterian Church, 1893.

McFarlin, Anjennette Sophie. *Black Congressional Reconstruction Orators and their Orations.* Metuchen, N.J.: Scarecrow Press, 1976.

McFerrin, John B. *History of Methodism in Tennessee, vols. I–III.* Nashville, Tn., 1873.

McKaye, James. *Mastership and its Fruits: The Emancipated Slave Face to Face with His Old Master. A Supplemental Report to Hon. Edwin M. Stanton, Sec. of War, by James McKaye, Special Commissioner.* New York: Loyal Publication Society, 1864.

McLeish, John. *Evangelical Religion and Popular Education: A Modern Interpretation.* London: Methuen, 1969.

McTyeire, Holland, et al. *Duties of Masters of Servants: Three Premium Essays.* Charleston, S.C.: Southern Baptist Publ. Society, 1851.

Meade, William, ed. *Sermons Addressed to Masters and Servants, and Published in the Year 1743 by the Rev. Thomas Bacon. Now Republished with Other tracts and Dialogues.* Winchester, Va.: John Heiskell, 1813 (?).

Miller, Floyd J. *The Search for a Black Nationality: Black Emigration and Colonization, 1787–1863.* Urbana, Ill.: University of Illinois Press, 1975.

Miller, Randall. *Dear Master: Letters of a Slave Family.* Ithaca, N.Y.: Cornell University Press, 1978.

Mitchell, Henry H. *Black Belief: Folk Beliefs of Blacks in America and West Africa.* New York: Harper & Row, 1975.

Mohr, Clarence L. *On the Threshold of Freedom: Masters and Slaves in Civil War Georgia.* Athens, Ga.: University of Georgia Press, 1986.

Morris, Robert C. *Reading, Writing, and Reconstruction: The Education of Freedmen in the South, 1861–1870.* Chicago: University of Chicago Press, 1982.

Mullin, Gerald. *Flight and Rebellion: Slave Resistance in Eighteenth Century Virginia.* New York: Oxford University Press, 1972.

Murray, Andrew. *Presbyterians and the Negro—A History.* Philadelphia: Presbyterian Historical Society, 1966.

Murray, Pauli. *Proud Shoes: The Story of an American Family.* New York: Harper & Row, 1956.

Myers, Robert Manson. *The Children of Pride: A True Story of Georgia and the Civil War.* New Haven, Conn.: Yale University Press, 1972.

Nichols, Charles H. *Many Thousand Gone: The Ex-Slaves' Account of Their Bondage and Freedom.* Leiden: Brill, 1963.

O'Brien, Michael, and David Moltke-Hansen, eds. *Intellectual Life in Antebellum Charleston.* Knoxville, Tenn.: University of Tennessee Press, 1986.

Pascoe, Charles F. *Two Hundred Years of the S.P.G.: An Historical Account of the Society for the Propagation of the Gospel in Foreign Parts, 1701–1900.* London, 1901.

Pastoral Letter from the Bishops of the Protestant Episcopal Church in the Confederate States of America. Augusta, Ga.: Chronicle & Sentinel, 1862.

Patton, William. *A Sermon with the Constitution of the African Benevolent Society.* Newport, R.I., 1808.

Payne, Daniel. *History of the African Methodist Episcopal Church.* Nashville, Tenn.: Publishing House of the A.M.E. Sunday School Union, 1891; reprint 1968, New York: Johnson Reprint Corp.

———. *Recollections of Seventy Years.* Nashville, Tenn., 1888; reprint 1968, New York: Arno Press.

Pearson, P. David, ed. *Handbook of Reading Research.* New York and London: Longman, 1984.

Pease, Jane H., and William H. Pease. *They Who Would be Free: Blacks' Search for Freedom, 1830–1861.* New York: Atheneum, 1974.

Pegues, Albert W. *Our Baptist Ministers and Schools.* Springfield, Mass.: Willey & Co., 1892.

Pelt, Owen D., Ralph Lee Smith. *The Story of the National Baptists.* New York: Vantage Press, 1960.

Perdue, Charles L., Jr., Thomas E. Barden and Robert K. Phillips, eds. *Weevils in the Wheat: Interviews with Virginia Ex-Slaves.* Charlottesville, Va.: University Press of Virginia, 1975.

Perry, William Stevens. *Historical Collections Relating to the American Colonial Church, vols. I–V.* Hartford, Conn., 1870–78.

Phillips, Ulrich Bonnell. *American Negro Slavery.* New York: D. Appleton & Co., 1918.

Pike, Gustavus D. *The Jubilee Singers and their Campaign for Twenty Thousand Dollars.* Boston: Lee & Shepard, 1873.

Pinckney, Charles Cotesworth. *An Address Delivered in Charleston before the Agricultural Society of South Carolina.* Charleston, S.C.: A. E. Miller, 1829.

Plumer, William, ed. *Thoughts on the Religious Instruction of the Negroes of this Country.* Savannah, Ga.: E. J. Purse, 1848.

Ponton, Mungo Melanchthon. *Life and Times of Henry M. Turner.* Atlanta, Ga., 1917; reprint 1970, New York, Negro Universities Press.

Posey, Walter B. *Frontier Mission: A History of Religion West of the Southern Appalachians to 1861.* Lexington, Ky.: University of Kentucky Press, 1966.

Proceedings of the Meeting in Charleston, S.C., May 13–15, 1845 on the Religious Instruction of the Negroes. Charleston: B. Jenkins, 1845.

Public Proceedings Relating to Calvary Church and the Religious Instruction of Slaves. Charleston, S.C.: Miller & Browne, 1850.

Raboteau, Albert J. *Slave Religion: The "Invisible Institution" in the Antebellum South.* Oxford: Oxford University Press, 1978.

Randolph, Peter. *From Slave Cabin to the Pulpit.* Boston: J. H. Earle, 1893.

———. Sketches of Slave Life; or, Illustrations of the 'peculiar institution.' Boston: Published for the author, 1855, 2nd ed.

Ravenel, Harriott Horry. *Eliza Pinckney.* New York: C. Scribner, 1896.

Rawick, George, ed. *The American Slave: A Composite Autobiography.* Westport, Conn.: Greenwood Press, 1972, 1977, 1980. 19 vols; Suppl., Series 1, 12 vols.; Suppl., Series 2, 10 vols.

Report of the Proceeding of the Formation of the African Education Society, Washington, Dec. 28, 1829. Washington, D.C.: Rothwell & Ustick, 1830.

Resnick, Daniel P., ed. *Literacy in Historical Perspective.* Washington, D.C.: Library of Congress, 1983.

Richardson, Harry V. *Dark Salvation: The Story of Methodism as it Developed among Blacks in America.* Garden City, N.Y.: Anchor Press, 1976.

Richardson, Joe M. *Christian Reconstruction: The American Missionary Association and Southern Blacks, 1861–1890.* Athens, Ga.: University of Georgia Press, 1986.

Robinson, H. Alan. *Reading and Writing Instruction in the United States: Historical Trends.* Urbana, Ill.: University of Illinois Press, 1977.

Rogers, George C., Jr. *Charleston in the Age of the Pinckneys.* Norman, Okla.: University of Oklahoma Press, 1969.

Rose, Willie Lee. *Rehearsal for Reconstruction: The Port Royal Experiment.* Indianapolis: Bobbs-Merrill, 1964.

Russell, John Henderson. *The Free Negro in Virginia, 1619–1865.* Baltimore, Md.: Johns Hopkins Press, 1913.

Ryland, Robert. *A Scripture Catechism for the Instruction of Children and Servants.* Richmond: Harold & Murray, 1848.

Savage, W. Sherman. *The Controversy over the Distribution of Abolition Literature, 1830–1860. New York, 1938; reprint 1968.*

Schor, Joel. *Henry Highland Garnet.* Westport, Conn.: Greenwood Press, 1977.

Seabrook, Whitemarsh. *Essay on the Management of Slaves.* Charleston: A. E. Miller, 1834.

Simmons, William J. *Men of Mark: Eminent, Progressive, and Rising.* Cleveland, O., 1887; reprint 1968, New York: Arno Press.

Simms, James D. *The First Colored Baptist Church in North America.* Philadelphia, 1888; reprint 1969, New York: Negro Universities Press.

Slaughter, Philip. *The Virginian History of African Colonization.* Richmond, 1855; reprint 1970, Freeport, N.Y.: Books for Libraries Press.

Smedes, Susan Dabney. *Memorials of a Southern Planter.* Baltimore, Md.: Cushings & Bailey, 1888; 3rd ed.

Smith, Charles Spencer. *A History of the African Methodist Episcopal Church, vol. II.* Philadelphia: Book Concern of the A.M.E. Church, 1922; reprint 1968, New York: Johnson Reprint Corp.

Smith, H. Sheldon. *In His Image, But . . . Racism in Southern Religion, 1780–1910.* Durham, N.C.: Duke University Press, 1972.

Smith, Hugh Banton. *American Reading Instruction.* Newark, N.J., 1965.

Smith, Timothy L. *Revivalism and Social Reform in Mid-Nineteenth Century America.* New York: Abingdon Press, 1957.

Sobel, Mechal. *Trabelin' On: The Slave Journey to an Afro-Baptist Faith.* Westport, Conn.: Greenwood Press, 1979.

———. *The World They Made Together: Black and White Values in Eighteenth-Century Virginia.* Princeton, N.J.: Princeton University Press, 1987.

Soltow, Lee Edward Stevens. *The Rise of Literacy and the Common School in the United States: A Socioeconomic Analysis to 1870.* Chicago: University of Chicago Press, 1981.

Southern Aid Society: Its Constitution and Address to the Christian Public. New York: Day book female type-setting establishment, 1854.

The Southern Enterprize. Philadelphia: American Sunday School Union, 1833.

Starling, Marion Wilson. *The Slave Narrative: Its Place in American History.* Boston: G. K. Hall, 1981.

Starobin, Robert, ed. *Blacks in Bondage: Letters of American Slaves.* New York: New Viewpoints, 1974.

———. *Denmark Vesey: The Slave Conspiracy of 1822.* Englewood Cliffs, N.J.: Prentice-Hall, 1970.

Staudenraus, Philip J. *The African Colonization Movement, 1816–1865.* New York: Columbia University Press, 1961.

Sterkx, Henry E. *The Free Negro in Ante-Bellum Louisiana.* Rutherford, N.J.: Fairleigh Dickinson University Press, 1972.

Sterling, Dorothy, ed. *Speak Out in Thundertones: Letters and Other Writings by Black Northerners, 1787–1865.* Garden City, New York: Doubleday, 1973.

Stiles, Joseph C. *Modern Reform Examined, or the Union of North and South on the Subject of Slavery.* 1853; reprint 1969, New York: Arno Press.

———. *Speech on the Slavery Resolutions.* New York, 1850.

Still, William. *The Underground Rail Road.* Philadelphia, Pa.: Porter & Coates, 1872.

Stroud, George M. *A Sketch of the Laws Relating to Slavery in the Several States of the United States of America.* Philadelphia: Longstreth, 1856; 2nd ed.

Swint, Henry L., ed. *Dear Ones at Home: Letters from Contraband Camps.* Nashville, Tenn.: Vanderbilt University Press, 1966.

Sydnor, Charles S. *The Development of Southern Sectionalism, 1819–1828: Vol. 5, A History of the South.* Baton Rouge, La.: Louisiana University Press, 1948.

Taylor, Susie King. *Reminiscences of My Life in Camp.* Boston, 1902; reprint 1968, New York: Arno Press.

Thompson, Ernest Trice. *Presbyterians in the South, vols. I–III.* Richmond, Va.: John Knox Press, 1963.

Thompson, Henry Paget. *Into All Lands: The History of the Society for the Propagation of the Gospel into Foreign Parts, 1701–1950.* London: Society for the Propagation of Christian Knowledge (S.P.C.K.), 1951.

Thornwell, James Henley. *Report on Slavery.* Charleston, S.C.: Presbyterian Synod of S.C. and Ga., 1851.

———. *A Sermon Preached at the Dedication of a Church Erected in Charleston, S.C., for the Colored Population.* Charleston, 1850.

Tragle, Henry Irving, ed. *The Southampton Slave Revolt of 1831: A Compilation of Source Material.* Amherst, Mass.: University of Massachusetts Press, 1971.

Bibliography

Trapier, Paul. *The Church Catechism Made Plain*. New York: Protestant Episcopal Sunday School Union, 1855.

Tucker, David M. *Black Pastors and Leaders: Memphis, 1819–1972*. Memphis, Tenn.: Memphis State University Press, 1975.

Turner, Mary. *Slaves and Missionaries: The Disintegration of Jamaican Slave Society, 1787–1834*. Urbana, Ill.: University of Illinois Press, 1982.

Tyack, David B., comp. *Turning Points in American Educational History*. Waltham, Mass.: Blaisdell Publ. Co., 1967.

Tyms, James D. *The Rise of Religious Education among Negro Baptists: A Historical Case Study*. New York: Exposition Press, 1965.

Van Debrug, William L. *The Slave Drivers: Black Agricultural Labor Supervisors in the Antebellum South*. Westport, Conn.: Greenwood Press, 1979.

Wade, Richard C. *Slavery in the Cities: The South, 1820–1860*. New York: Oxford University Press, 1964.

Walker, Clarence E. *A Rock in a Weary Land: The African Methodist Episcopal Church During the Civil War and Reconstruction*. Baton Rouge, La.: Louisiana State University Press, 1982.

Walker, David. *Walker's Appeal in Four Articles*. Boston, 1830; reprint 1969, New York: Arno Press.

Wardhaugh, Ronald, and H. Douglas Brown, eds. *A Survey of Applied Linguistics*. Ann Arbor: University of Michigan Press, 1976.

Warren, Max. *Social History and Christian Mission*. London: S. C. M. Press, 1967.

Waterbury, Maria. *Seven Years Among the Freedmen*. Chicago, 1890; reprint 1971, Freeport, N.Y., Books for Libraries Press.

Wayman, Alexander. *Cyclopedia of African Methodism*. Baltimore, Md.: Methodist Episcopal Book Depository, 1882.

Weatherford, Willis Duke. *American Churches and the Negro*. Boston: Christopher Publ. House, 1957.

Webber, Thomas L. *Deep Like the Rivers: Education in the Slave Quarter Community, 1831–1865*. New York: Norton, 1978.

Webster, Noah. *The Elementary Spelling Book*. Cincinnati, 1848.

Wikmaranayake, Maria. *A World in Shadow: The Free Black in Antebellum South Carolina*. Columbia, S.C.: University of South Carolina Press, 1973.

Wiley, Bell I., ed. *Slaves No More: Letters from Liberia, 1833–1869*. Lexington, Ky.: The University Press of Kentucky, 1980.

———. *Southern Negroes, 1861–1865*. New Haven, Conn.: Yale University Press, 1938.

Wills, David W., eds. and Richard Newman. *Black Apostles at Home and Abroad: Afro-Americans and the Christian Mission from the Revolution to Reconstruction.* Boston: G. K. Hall, 1982.

Wilmore, Gayraud S. *Black Religion and Black Radicalism: An Interpretation of the Religious History of Afro-American People.* Garden City, N.Y.: Doubleday, 1972.

Winkler, E. T. *Notes and Questions for the Instruction of Colored People.* Charleston, S.C.: Southern Baptist Publication Society, 1857.

Wood, Peter H. *Black Majority: Negroes in Colonial South Carolina from 1670 through the Stono Rebellion.* New York: Knopf, 1974.

Woodson, Carter G. *Education of the Negro Prior to 1861.* Washington, D.C., 1915; reprint 1968, New York: Arno Press.

————. *History of the Negro Church.* Washington, D.C.: Association Publ., 1921.

————., ed. *The Mind of the Negro as Reflected in Letters Written During the Crisis 1800–1860.* Washington, D.C.: Assn. for the Study of Negro Life & History, 1926.

Wright, Richard Robert, Jr., ed. *Encyclopedia of the African Methodist Episcopal Church.* Philadelphia: A. M. E. Book Concern, 1916; 2nd ed.

Wyatt-Brown, Bertram. *Lewis Tappan and the Evangelical War Against Slavery.* Cleveland, O.: Press of Case Western Reserve University, 1969.

Zahniser, Marvin R. *Charles Cotesworth Pinckney.* Chapel Hill, N.C.: U. of North Carolina Press, 1967.

Dissertations

Cornelius, Janet Duitsman. *"God's Schoolmasters": Southern Evangelists to the Slaves, 1830–1860.* Urbana, Ill.: University of Illinois at Urbana-Champaign, 1977.

Crook, Roger H. *The Ethical Emphasis of the Editors of Baptist Journals Published in the Southeastern Region of the United States up to 1865.* Louisville: Southern Baptist Theological Seminary, 1947.

Harris, J. William. *A Slaveholding Republic: Augusta's Hinterlands Before the Civil War.* Baltimore: Johns Hopkins University, 1981.

Hughes, John E. *A History of the Southern Baptist Convention's Ministry to the Negro: 1845–1904.* Louisville: Southern Baptist Theological Seminary, 1971.

Kuykendall, John Wells. *Southern Enterprize: The Work of National Evangelical Societies in the Antebellum South.* Princeton, N.J.: Princeton University, 1975.

Bibliography

Reilly, Duncan Alexander. *William Capers: An Evaluation of His Life and Thought.* Atlanta: Emory University, 1972.

Reilly, Timothy. *Religious Leaders and Social Criticism in New Orleans, 1800–1861.* Columbia, Mo.: University of Missouri, 1972.

Sernett, Milton Charles. *Black Religion and American Evangelicalism: White Protestants, Plantation Missions, and the Independent Negro Church, 1790–1860.* University of Delaware, 1972.

Winsell, Keith. *Black Identity: The Southern Negro, 1830–1845.* Los Angeles: U. C. L. A., 1971.

Index

Abolition. *See* antislavery movements

ACS. *See* American Colonization Society

"Address to Christians Throughout the World" (1863), 147

Adger, John B., Presbyterian preacher and missionary used catechism for slaves to teach Armenians to read, 47; protested South Carolina literacy law, 54; described blacks as "the poor," 113; ordered reading material for slave mission school, 116; "school of slavery", 116, 148

African Benevolent Society, Newport, 25–26

African Civilization Society, 134

African Education Society, 121–22

African Methodist Episcopal Church (A.M.E. church): in Charleston, 29, 38; closed by whites in Charleston, 30; educational developments, 83, 123; gains in membership, 94; closed in New Orleans, 101; missions to freed slaves, 143, 145; literacy requirements for preachers, 147. *See also* Payne, Daniel; Heard, William; Gaines, Wesley; Turner, Henry M.

African Mission School Society, 121

African Repository, promoted black education in U.S., 120–21; approval and publicity for efforts of black educators, 122; publicized success of schooling for slaves, 122; linked emancipation to literacy, 122; proposed slave school for manumission and emigration, 123

African Union Society, Newport and Providence, 25

African-American emigrants to Liberia: reasons for free black emigration and colonization, 119, 134; emigrants' desire for literacy, 119; slave petitions for help in purchasing freedom for emigration, 119; letters from literate former slaves in Liberia, 118–20, 135; plans to "civilize" Africans through literacy, 120–24. *See also* American Colonization Society; African Civilization Society; National Emigration Convention

African-American religion: as creative community-building, 85; as resistance to white oppression, 85–86; based on African belief systems and white theology and ritual, 92

African-American religious leaders under slavery: spiritual and utilitarian benefits of literacy to, 87, 90, 92; described as supporting slavery in sermons, 86; preaching